Also by Mark Baker

Nam
Cops
Women

Simon & Schuster

New York   London   Toronto

Sydney   Tokyo   Singapore

Mark Baker

What men *really* think

About women, love, sex, themselves

SIMON & SCHUSTER
Simon & Schuster Building
Rockefeller Center
1230 Avenue of the Americas
New York, New York 10020

Manufactured in the United States of America

10   9   8   7   6   5   4   3   2   1

Library of Congress Cataloging-in-Publication Data
What men really think: about women, love, sex, themselves/
* [compiled by] Mark Baker.*
*   p.   cm.*
*   1. Men—United States—Interviews.   2. Men—United States—*
Attitudes.
HQ1090.3.W59   1992
305.31—dc20   91-33071   CIP
ISBN 0-671-70255-6

A slightly different version of "Abortion" appeared in Esquire *magazine.*

"Sixteen Tons" (Merle Travis) © 1974 Unichappell Music Inc. & Elvis
Presley Music. All rights on behalf of Elvis Presley Music administered
by Unichappell Music Inc. All rights reserved. Used by permission.

Acknowledgments

My thanks to the men who told me the stories of their lives. They had the strength to be honest with me and with themselves. Gentlemen, I hope each of you finds I've done justice not only to your words, but also to the voice and intellect behind the words.

Bob Bender is a good editor, a bit of an anomaly in today's publishing world. The old-fashioned craftsmanship and expert eye and ear he applies to my work make it better every time. Thanks, Bob, for all your help. I'd like to thank Charlie Hayward and Bill Grose for standing behind my books. They've been nothing but fair and generous with me, even when a book didn't sell too well.

Esther Newberg has made it possible for me to make a living in this business for over ten years now. She fights for my rights and tells me when she thinks I'm wrong. I will continue to kiss her in public whether she likes it or not.

Bob and Gloria Baker brought me up with love and respect, and that has a lot to do with the kind of person I try to be and the ideals I have for manhood. I always try to make them proud of me.

Frank Fortunato deserves special mention here. He was the first to see the pages of the manuscript, some of which the reader won't be seeing thanks to his sound judgment.

Many of the remaining pages strike a note of revelation because of his insight and ability to tease out the truth. Thanks, Frank. You're a true friend.

The following people have given me access to their friends and relatives for the interviews in this book, a place to stay on my journeys back and forth across the country, moral support and encouragement, and usually all three: Joan O'Sullivan, Helen Pantzis, Peggy Grossman and Joe Woodard, Bryan and Judy Collins, John and Cindy Davis, Marty Perlman, George Moon, Peter and Cathy O'Sullivan, Tim and Nancy Conaway, Loretta Nash, Michael Melia, Johanna Li, Brit Hansen, Sloan Harris, Gypsy da Silva, Christopher Shea, Margaret Johnson and Ray Ottenburg, Lisa Grunwald, Michael Solomon, Richard and Maryann Nilsen, Bob Leuci.

Veronica stands by me through good and bad times. We've had more than our share of both. She knows me like no one else on the planet, and loves me anyway. It may sound like an old country and western song, but nothing brings out the best in a man like the love of a good woman. Everything will be okay, as long as we're together.

—M.B.

This book is dedicated to Sean and Noah.

Contents

Introduction

This book is about how men think and what men believe. These pages are filled with the words of men talking about themselves and those closest to them, distilled from interviews with one hundred individuals. The youngest was 22, the oldest 90. Most of them were between the ages of 30 and 50.

They come from fifteen states all over the continent and from all walks of life. There is a world-renowned psychiatric medical researcher, as well as a taxi driver who lives in a broken-down van that won't start. There's a carpenter, a screenwriter, a secretary, an advertising executive, a cop, a sculptor, a dentist, a union official, a lawyer, a printer, a couple of bartenders, various building contractors, a TV producer, a laborer, a gynecologist, a few schoolteachers from elementary school to high school to college, two actors, an insurance underwriter, a pilot, a forklift driver, a priest, and on and on.

But I wasn't really interested in their jobs, their public life and public face. American men live undercover lives, because the culture has taught them to hide their pain, rein in their emotions, and stick to a rigidly logical analysis of life. His business associates, his fishing buddies, even his wife aren't sure what a man is really thinking or actually feeling. I wanted men to talk about women and how they relate to them, about love and sex and children. I asked them to tell me about their fears and their dreams.

I guaranteed these men anonymity so they could loosen their armor a little, drop the macho act, and ramble on about themselves. A few of them just couldn't do it. They couldn't release their grip and relax. We never got past the introductions, and I did more talking than they did. Some men wanted to talk about their feelings but were so out of practice in this pursuit that they couldn't come up with the vocabulary of emotion. What was surprising, though, was that so many of them could talk, really talk, about what was important to them. The biggest lie in the generally accepted male stereotype is that men all have a Gary Cooper "Yep–Nope" cowboy taciturnity.

When men talk to each other, they warm up with banter and bravado. They take the measure of the other man by trying to entertain him. This is bar talk, full of the weather and sports and business, jokes and exaggeration and lies.

If they like each other and are not in direct competition for a woman, a job, or the attention of an audience of other men, they will move on to buddy talk—what men say to each other in serious conversation when women aren't around. I first heard this kind of conversation as a boy sitting under the kitchen table while my father reminisced with his friends above my head about Iwo Jima and Guam during World War II. This is a combination of war stories and woman troubles, gossip, grousing, and philosophical argument. Men engage in buddy talk driving in a car on a regular commute or between innings at the ballpark when they send their kids off to buy hot dogs. A good friend of mine and I have this kind of discussion when we step outside after dinner in the summer to smoke cheap cigars by the glowing embers of the barbecue grill. Some men are lucky enough to have this kind of conversation with their wives from time to time. This book is filled with buddy talk.

There is also something more rare in these pages—man talk, a term I am using to cover what men will admit about themselves and their feelings, in absolute confidence, only to a trusted male friend or to a total stranger or to a mistress. Man talk is the unadorned personal secret of who a man thinks he is. It is rarely heroic or noble. In fact, sometimes it's not even true, except in its emotion.

The emotions men seem to return to most often these days are anger, resentment, and regret. There is an underlying sense of dissatisfaction with their lives that colors this book throughout. That's something most people wouldn't expect. After all, men are the ones in power in our society, the ones in charge, the ones who made the rules. The assumption is—particularly among women—that men live zestful, unencumbered lives full of choices, that they can do what they want to do, the way that they want, when they want to do it.

Men deny that supposition with startling bluntness. Although they often lack eloquence, there is a raw power in the accumulation of personal conviction. Given the chance to speak their minds with impunity, they flaunt taboo, cut against the grain of media hype about "Today's Liberated Man," and rail against the confines of our culture.

There are two reasons for the rancor expressed in these pages. First, men are not supposed to complain. It is considered wimpish, unmanly. Men don't whine. Their accepted role is to fix things, to right wrongs. So given the chance to get things off their chests, some men just indulged in some guilt-free grumbling.

The second reason is the obvious one: Many men *are* unhappy. If they've modeled their lives on the traditional male role, they feel they've painted themselves into a corner. Much of their performance is considered old-fashioned, ineffective or—at worst—illegal. Gender roles are changing in America. It is a volatile, chaotic time. But men are ill-prepared to step off into the unknown. It's just not clear to them yet what other choices they have, much less which of those choices they should take. For all the cultural emphasis on the adventure-loving spirit of men, the majority of men don't deal well with uncertainty. Ask any woman who has been in a car with a male driver who loses his way. When men get lost, they get embarrassed, sullen, and very quiet. I got them to talk.

Although I make no claim that this book is the truth about every man in America, I do believe *What Men* Really *Think* is an honest book. It's a no-frills approach—no pat answers, no grand concept, no mythopoetic explication or heavy-duty psychological scrutiny. There are no references between these covers to Peter Pan, the Pied Piper, or Oedipus. I don't suggest how men should behave, nor have I tried to write a book about what men could become.

Many women may walk away from this book with only their worst suspicions about men confirmed. But that would be a shame. There's no angling for sex or peacock feather spreading going on here. Very few of these men are trying to impress anyone. This reasonably unobstructed view of what men are all about is an opportunity for some women to finally find a key to understanding the men in their lives.

Men who read this book will, I suspect, feel like they're looking directly at themselves in a mirror for the first time in a long, long while—warts and all. Men excel at self-delusion, so this may be a novel experience for many of them. I've pulled no punches to make them look better or worse than they are. What I hope I have accomplished is to state plainly the obvious about American men. That's something that hasn't happened very often.

One: **Women**

"Women, can't live with them, can't live without them."
"Women, can't live with them."
"Women, can't live with them, can't shoot them."

The wolves are as skittish as rabbits these days. Fifteen years ago, this joke would have been followed by uninhibited belly laughs. Now, it is a giggled aside. The jokester cuts his eyes from side to side, searching for complicity in his audience, and then he offers a furtive, if sardonic, disclaimer. "Nah, no-no-no, that's not the way I feel about 'em. I like women. I really do. I *love* 'em, know what I mean?"

The male chauvinist pig did not become extinct in 1975. Faced with intense media pressure, egalitarian judicial review, and just a tiny twinge of guilt, the pig evolved into the male chauvinist chameleon. Like his earlier incarnation, the chameleon holds the conviction that women are inferior to men in general, but he knows how to blend in convincingly with his cultural surroundings. At cocktail parties, he backs out of conversations with women about gender and equality, instead of saying something inflammatory enough to get a drink dumped down his pants. In dulcet tones of reason, he tells the female job applicant that she just doesn't fit the aggressive company profile, when what he's

thinking is that a man in his position really should have a prettier, less ambitious secretary than this girl. He plies the pick-up
scene cloaked in his stealthy "I'm a sensitive listener"
demeanor, instead of pushing the hard sell come-on of sex,
drugs, and rock 'n' roll.

To be honest and fair, the vast majority of men belong to this
breed at some time or other. In his heart of hearts, almost every
man holds that women are physically weaker than he is, less
intelligent than he is, somewhat alien to logic, and emotionally
unpredictable. All men do not feel this way all the time about all
women. But it's there, even in those doing their best to purge
their thoughts and behavior of sexism. More often than not,
when you scratch a male feminist, you'll find a male chauvinist
chameleon.

Men have been conspicuously silent on the subject of women
for many years now. When most of what they thought and said
suddenly became inappropriate, men just shut up. It was the
easy way out. And after all, females are "the target sex," so there
isn't much profit in insulting them to their faces. When I offered
men the opportunity to speak their minds with impunity on what
they really thought about women, they were never at a loss for
words. Men have found it galling to have to hold their tongues,
after generations of believing that they were in charge, so their
rage and belittling comments were predictable. What was less
expected were men's recognition of their immense underlying
need for women also reflected in this anger, and the unadulter-
ated admiration men expressed for women.

Men are angry with women, but not with specific women. The
object of their anger is a mostly imaginary society of females
known in common male parlance as the Women's Liberation
Movement, as though it had a board of directors and a permanent mission at the United Nations. Men need a worthy opponent, a real enemy to complain about. Complaining about
individual women is construed as mere whining. Furthermore,

just because they've clammed up about women for years doesn't mean their brains have stopped working. They see our culture changing all around them.

Their anger falls into at least three distinct variations. The vengeful are men outraged that the slaves have dared to shake off their shackles. They want to find the ringleaders of the libbers, as they call them, and string them up. Then they will turn back the clock to a simpler time. But to these men, women seem to stand united, like the Hollywood version of Roman slaves in revolt, each one shouting, "No, I am Spartacus." All these men can see is the rapid erosion of their personal power. They use the word "emasculated," even though the very mention of it sends shivers down their collective spine. Yet, there is wavering even among the hardliners. For instance, a 32-year-old construction laborer said, "I hate to see women working, because for every one of them collecting a paycheck a man is out of a job!" Then he thought for five seconds about his wife, who brought in half their income and who had been a single mother before they were married, and his ex-wife, to whom he had only recently begun paying child support after several years of delinquency, and added, "But, I guess with all the divorce and everything going on these days, they got to eat, too, so a lot of them has *got* to go to work."

The great pool of middle-of-the-road, middle-American men are confused and resentful at being held responsible for the invention of a system they only inherited. One of their redeeming qualities is a general sense of fair play, and they're crying foul. They claim the rules for being a man have been changed repeatedly in the middle of the game and growl, "Women don't know *what* they want." They feel they have been excluded from any meaningful dialogue, because they have been unable to successfully discard thousands of years of acculturation and an eon of genetic programming overnight. As a 40-year-old, politically liberal college professor said, "I find it frustrating to be expected to change momentarily. Women want us to change very quickly, when I don't think it's so clear how we're going to change or what it is we *have* to change."

The male sympathizers with women's struggle for independence and equality are disoriented. Many of these men are jealous of women's sense of heightened consciousness and community. They are lumped with "the enemy," no matter how hard they try to help, stiff-armed by the rhetoric of feminism. A young veterinarian told about his sense of rejection. "A couple of years ago, I wanted to march in the pro-abortion rally in Washington, D.C., so I went to a planning meeting publicized at the college. When I walked into that room full of women, they all turned and looked at me at once, and it soon became very clear that I was not wanted or welcome there. It didn't change my convictions about women's right to control their bodies, but it made me mad. I wanted to help."

There is gloomy disappointment for this faction as they watch women absorb and express more and more of men's worst attributes, instead of fulfilling their potential to change the tone and direction of our society the way they said they would. A landscape architect approaching his fiftieth birthday put it this way, "Somewhere along the line, the Women's Movement lost its vision of itself as promoting the equality of human beings, and framed itself against the bulwark of male prerogative. They've gone after the power and authority that is characterized as part of the so-called World of Men. The grand casualty in their logic is that the role that men play is seen as being virile, positive, and whole, when in fact men are sterilized as humans in fulfilling the height of authority and power. To be concentrated enough to get to that top male place in corporate America, for instance, really erases the rest of your life. Women have become male eunuchs, as much of a eunuch as is the man."

Men fear women. For all their posturing superiority, men recognize that they don't know much about women. They suspect

that women know much more about men. Just below the conscious level is the realization that men depend almost entirely
on women for a definition of themselves. What good is it to be
the apex of creation without an audience to applaud you? How
can a man be protector and breadwinner, if women get equal
pay for equal work? The more autonomous women become, the
more scary it is for men. Like children afraid of monsters in the
dark, men fear their own obsolescence, much as women might
if suddenly men could reproduce. "There's an old saying that
God gave us two ears and one mouth, so that we'd listen twice
as much as we talked," a 41-year-old long-distance trucker told
me. "Men are always shooting their mouths off. Nine times out
of ten, if you let a woman talk, she'll make an ass out of herself
just as easy as a man can, and there ain't a whole lot of difference between the two. Most of the time, we just never give them
the opportunity to make assholes out of themselves. Or if they
do, we tend to put some other reason on it, other than they're
plain human beings who are just as much jokes as we are. It
appears that we have allowed ourselves to be duped. We are
more than willing to say that they have something that we want
more than we have what they want."

Men admire women. Men like the way women look and the way
they feel to the touch. Men like the smell of women, natural and
cosmetic, and the pitch and timbre of their voices. This sensual
pleasure men take in women is not exclusively sexual. It is an
appreciation of their otherness, their non-maleness.

Similarly, what men denigrate as women's emotional weak-
ness is sometimes secretly envied by men whose uncried tears
are slowly transformed into ulcers and heart attacks. What is
discounted as the illogical, irrelevant prattling of the weaker sex
at times flings some refreshing color and insight on the black-
or-white arithmetic of male accounting. A 38-year-old housing
contractor, recently divorced and the father of two small children, said, "Daily life, nowadays, women aren't brave in a phys-

ically manifest way. They are not out there chucking sticks of dynamite around. But they're more emotionally brave than men. They're more likely to confront the emotional sides of issues, instead of the theoretical sides."

The company of women is the one place other than in solitude where a man can escape to solace. The domineering male culture that some women find abhorrently oppressive can be an equally brutal world for men. It was a man talking about his fellow men when he coined the expression, "dog eat dog." A 46-year-old dealer in rare books and sports memorabilia who has never married and claims to be retired from the pursuit of women said, "They've got something you want more than anything—they've got that love that we need so much—but you don't know how to get it out of them. You better be afraid of women, because you can be hurt by women. They are the only ones who can hurt you."

Ask *any* American male over the age of 21 what he thinks of women, and nine times out of ten the first words out of his mouth will be, "Women: can't live with them, can't live without them."

I've never met a woman who is as smart as me. Isn't that awful? But I don't think I have. I've met men, and I've read stuff by men that I knew were way ahead of me, but I've never met a woman who made me feel that way. I can't remember talking to a woman or reading anything by a woman that left me aghast or agog or that I just didn't know what they were talking about. Men have the potential to be smarter than women.

Now, I know that statement is totally sexist. I also know that it's not true. It's just what I think. You asked me what I feel. It's totally unfounded. There's no reason I can't live by it.

I've always had the notion that women understand us better than we understand them. That's the problem.

I race motorcycles, not as much as I used to because I got too much iron in my body, my bones don't bend as well as they did in my youth. But when I first started racing, it took me a long time to figure out that the best place to be is in second place. If you're in second place, you know what's going on. If you're in first place, you only think you know what's going on.

Our society is set up so that in the human race the men are in first place, and the women are in second place. The men *think* they know what's going on. The women *know* what's going on.

Traditionally, men have been concerned with trying to get things done and figure things out. The women just sit back there and watch what happens. They've watched us stab ourselves in the back. They've watched us lie and cheat and steal our way through everything and anything. It's part of the nature of the conquest. They know more about us, because they've always been beat up by us. We know less about them, because we never thought they were important enough to know anything about, to find out what makes a woman feel the way a woman does.

But in our society, the way it is perceived is that we don't pursue women. Women pursue us. The woman "catches" the man. The one doing the hunting has the edge. We don't know when we're being hunted. We don't know when we are about to be overtaken and lose the race. Our problem is that we always thought that we were racing against men.

Most of that has been our own fault, because there has been this tradition that a man always takes care of a woman, we put them up on a pedestal and honor women. First off, if we keep them on the pedestal all the time, when they got to shit, they got to shit on us, because they can't get down off the Goddamn pedestal. There's a whole lot of truth to that and it puts things all back into perspective, doesn't it? They're just like you and me.

I like the way they make themselves into some image or idea of what they should look like and what attitude they should present. They have such a wide variety of costumes, paints, gems, and things to hang on themselves. That's all considered natural and wonderful. It's very creative, really, to be able to paint yourself and clothe yourself to be a certain kind of person today, to present a certain kind of image tomorrow. I love and admire that in women, because it says life can be different and adventurous and theatrical every day. For guys, that's not true.

Guys, they wear jeans or they wear business suits. That's it. You're either an efficient, capable businessman, or you're a cowboy. Women get to be sexy and casual and elegant and handsome and smart and silly, this wide range of personae they can successfully present to the world.

Women complain that there are people they are not allowed to be, which is what men are. But the difference between men and women is that men only have a couple of things they can be, and maybe women can be those. But it's the *only* ones men can be.

If women ruled the world, it would be a better place. It wouldn't be as well organized, but the kinder, gentler stuff that President Bush is talking about would be a reality, because they're all mothers.

Deep down inside, they are all mothers, even the ones who haven't had kids. I've never found a woman who wasn't a mother. Even a lesbian who is built like a pyramid and hates men has a lot of mother in her.

I don't see how you could go wrong having your mother rule the world. Because she's your mother, everything will be fine in the end. It'll be okay.

Women wouldn't go to war. I can't imagine two women staring at each other over a table and saying, "No. We're going to stop talking and go to war!" I *can* imagine them scratching each other's eyes out. But not making their sons go to war because they were afraid to scratch each other's eyes out. They would come up with some sort of system where they would do the scratching thing and keep it on a personal level.

You see, women are braver than men. A woman would sit there and scratch eyes out with some other woman before she would send her son off to do it. Men send their sons out all the time to fight war, every generation, with regularity. Women would take it on themselves, whatever it had to be.

I like women more than men, because they come from their hearts. Men hardly ever do that. That's one of the things about men that's disappointing. It's really hard to ever see men coming from their hearts.

It's a hell of a thing to admit that women are a hell of a lot stronger than we are emotionally. It scares the piss out of us.

My wife's mother, Janine, had a stroke last month. She's been living with her boyfriend, Harley, for the last several years. Harley has been driving me and my wife crazy, because he's so shaky. "Is there any hope for her?" he keeps saying.

We were down at the hospital two weeks ago, and I got ahold of him, and I said, "Harley, you got to cut this shit out. You're making everything look like it's a fucking disaster."

When I got a real close look at him, I realized that he was scared out of his fucking mind. He was scared like a little kid. I thought to myself, "Jesus Christ, this better not be me. It better not happen to me. I don't want to be a basket case."

Then I started to realize over the next few days how dependent I am on my wife. Our roles are very different. I mean, she earns five times as much money as I do. She's got all kinds of advanced degrees, a brilliant woman. She could organize ants. She's just that way, and a truly beautiful person. Probably the only woman that I've ever totally trusted, and there's nothing more to say about that.

I realized how much I depend on her. I know she sort of depends on me, too, but sometimes I'm a lazy bastard. I don't do what I'm supposed to do. It's the male disease. It's fucking awful, but she knows that.

I saw the fear in Harley's eyes, and I thought, "Fuck, what if my wife ends up like Janine? Worst of all, what if I end up like Harley?"

A really good friend of mine is working her way up in a big company. She's had a rough time doing it. Every once in a while she'll call, upset and crying about something her boss has done to her. I can't understand that. I say, "Why the fuck are you crying about this? Why the hell don't you get pissed off and tell the son-of-a-bitch where to go? Why do you go into his office and cry for? Jesus, you're playing right into his hands."

I know the guy she's talking about, and he's an asshole from the word go. It's one thing to be an abused assistant vice president. It's another thing to be a female abused assistant vice president. You're right down there at the bottom of the barrel, especially if you go in there and whimper at him. "Go tell him to fuck off. For one thing, it'll shock the shit out of him. If nothing else, you've got the element of surprise on your side. He won't know what the hell to do."

Why do women do that? Why is it more likely for a woman to break down emotionally in that type of situation than a man? I didn't say all women do. Say that to a woman, and she'll fucking fly in your face. But a lot of women do break down. A lot of men do, too. The problem is that men who do that aren't in positions where it makes much difference. They haven't moved into those managerial positions. Women move into those jobs, break down in the heat of a battle or under stress, and it's because they're a woman. Men break down in the same situations and they're just wimps. They can't handle the job. Period. Get somebody else.

I feel a little pissed off these days. I've done my bit in support of feminism, and now they're not living up to their end of it. Oh, no, they're not. It's a very weird thing.

I really believe in the equality thing. But I still get a lot of shit for being a male chauvinist pig when I'm really just reflecting a lot of my own acculturation, which I'm working against as hard as I possibly can. But I still can't be right. I feel like I'm getting a bad rap for something I don't have that much control over. I'm doing my best.

And women aren't coming up with any solutions either. They either become just like men and are heavy-duty, so you just want to smack them for being like men—at least do the same things to them that you would do to a man who tried to pull that shit. Or they want the equality without the responsibility.

There's a lot of women who were never really part of the Women's Liberation Movement, they're not even really women's libbers. They're in a much better place than their mothers were, but it's nothing that they've done. They've just been themselves, which is okay, but they've fallen into this blaming of men for all their problems.

There's all these greeting cards out now that put men

down. Sometimes they're very humorous. Sometimes it's done in very cutting ways, ways that would get them sued, fined and driven out of business if they said the same things about women.

My wife will just say something offhand, some reference to men, when she's talking to her women friends, and I know if she thought about it, she wouldn't mean what she's saying. They all do it now. It's as bad as when we were calling all women chicks and talking about laying So-and-so. They do it without even thinking. We did it without even thinking.

Most of the time, I don't pay any attention to it. But every once in a while, it really pisses me off, and I have to call her on it. "Do you really believe that *all* men are slobby, unfeeling, self-absorbed assholes?" I can't just sit there and let it roll off my back, because it's plain horseshit. It's offensive to me. If anybody in our relationship is a slob, it's her, for one thing. And if I made a similar sweeping generalization about women, she'd kill me.

What always pissed me off about my wife was that she didn't live her values, really. She thought that women ought to be out working and have equal rights to work and to do all the things that have been traditionally reserved for men. She also believed the labor should be shared between the couple. But as it turned out, it didn't work that way at all.

She didn't work, she just stayed home most of the time. I did more than half of the housework. It didn't come out to be equal, not in the least. Part of her frustration for a long time was the fact that she thought that she ought to be working to live out her values, but was just a little too scared of the world to go out there and do it. She was frustrated, and she had a lot of angry feelings toward men in general.

It took me a long time to figure out that I was the person who she chose to put those feelings on. I got in the way of her anger towards men. I wasn't blunting her ambitions. I wasn't smothering her or holding her back. Her predominant emotion in the marriage and in life was fear and anger. It dawned on me that she was taking a lot of anger that she had for her father or her brother out on me. I was the one who got stuck in the middle and was the conduit. At the time, I was just bewildered at the magnitude of the anger and said, "Hell, why are you doing this to me? I haven't done anything to deserve this. Go yell at your dad. Don't be yelling at me."

Willow tried developing a career initially and did some reasonably good things which didn't bring her a whole lot of feeling of personal success. Then at mid-marriage, she got turned on by the Women's Movement, became not only a feminist, but became a separatist. It is indeed tough to be a separatist and be married at the same time. It was not only separatist in the classic feminist perspective, but separatist in the holistic, individual sense.

"I have got to be totally separate from you in order to feel whole, yet I'm going to stay in this marriage. I not only don't need you and don't want you, but I'm going to keep you around at the same time to prove to you that I don't need you and don't want you."

That just didn't work too well, although I somehow had enough collective male guilt to say, "Well, okay." I was really hurting and it was difficult, but I couldn't bring my-self to say, "Hey, what you have to go through and what you need to separate from isn't necessarily me. You need to define yourself. I admit that you may have a lot of male shit in your baggage that you have to get rid of, but I don't necessarily have to be part of the process or the garbage that you kick out."

However, I was convinced that I was a part of it, that I needed to assume the collective male obligation for being a jerk. At least I always cooperated enough to stay in the same house. I definitely cooperated enough to say, "Okay, I see the point of doing things fifty-fifty, and we'll do it fifty-fifty." We managed to pull off the pragmatics, but we could never pull off how to stay intimate, or how to be intimate and yet separate.

Women have been talking intensely and deeply now for at least twenty years about men and about being women. They are very articulate on the subject of the rela-tionship between the sexes. It is a problem when you get into a situation with a group dynamic with women and have arguments. They're there. They're right up there. They can push the button and run the rap.

Guys haven't done that, and they don't like to get in-volved in that argument anymore. For one thing, you figure you're going to get shouted down. Men do feel that women gang up on them.

So men, in general, tend to shut up and not to engage in

dialogue about sexism and the problems between men and women. Any men who are engaging in that kind of dialogue are already converted. They are male feminists, talking to women about the difficulties of being women. Obviously, that has limited usefulness for men or women.

The only hope is that women will accept men a little bit more and not be so angry about things. Women are really angry, I find. You can't make a mistake with them. It's hard not to make a mistake inadvertently. You can say something to a woman nowadays that she feels is sexist or chauvinistic, and it can really cut you dead. There's none of this backpedaling, "Oh, well, hey, I'm sorry. I made a little faux pas. Let me start again." Then come back and start at the beginning, or continue where you are and say, "Yeah, I have to raise my consciousness about that." There is no accepted, polite phrase to make it better. You will be cut out of the mainstream after that, and considered one of the filthy herd again.

In the '60s, we needed our consciousness raised about racism. I remember a black man who I was working with who said to me once, "Everybody is a racist. Everybody has racist feelings. Don't tell me that you never, ever in your life had the word 'nigger' in your head, and I won't tell you that I never thought of you as a honky motherfucker."

What is important is, when you notice your racism flaring up that you deal with it, that you try to understand why you're being racist, that you step back from it, stop doing it, and you call the person next to you on the same kind of behavior. It's not racist to be angry and afraid of people who are from another race. We're all angry and afraid about each other. What's racist is to indulge the fear and hatred and not deal with it.

Women have to understand this about sexism also. A man can reveal some sexist attitudes, and rather than being clubbed to the earth or sent back into the herd of pigs, you can still talk to him. You can still understand, and you can go on. But because women are very angry, the tendency is to cut you off, cut you out. That's unfortunate.

This is my theory about organizational or ideologically motivated women, or the Women's Movement, or Women's Liberation, if you prefer. I've always seen Carry Nation as a pivotal historical character in the discussion of this phenomenon, because she was unusual for a demagogue. She had a sense of humor, and certainly had more balls than anybody else who lived in Kansas in the 1880s, which is saying something.

What most people don't realize is that at that time, there were two wings of what was then the Female Suffrage Movement. There was one wing led by the sane, responsible and hatchet-faced Susan B. Anthony gang. They believed in expressing their political discontent by variations in their underwear—the Bloomer Girls.

Then there was the other wing, the Prohibitionist wing, who flocked to the standard of Carry Nation. Basically what they thought is, "If we can get these bastards out of the gin mill and home with their paychecks intact, then the millennium will be at hand."

Their method of achieving this was to come roaring into the saloons with edged weapons, smash up any kind of bottled goods or kegs or candid and stimulating artwork that might have been on the wall, and scare the shit out of people. Some men were psychically scarred forever by these attacks and many of them had their Sunday afternoon drinking destroyed.

The pertinent fact of the matter is, because it was much

more entertaining persecuting a bunch of poor, fucking refuge-seeking rummies than it was agitating for the vote, women got the vote about forty years after they should have gotten it or could have gotten the vote, largely because of this experiment with Prohibition.

The tendency of women in any organized force is to derail themselves on tangential emotional issues, which is certainly not unknown in human relationships, and is very clearly demonstrated in the history of the Women's Movement. Prohibition is the first time that happened in gaudy terms. The second time that happened was in the middle to late 1970s when the Women's Movement imploded, along with the rest of the Democratic Party, because of their suicidal infatuation with the buffooneries of the ball-cutting lesbian militants. Again, it was more entertaining to persecute people than it was to organize, or to attain any meaningful political objectives.

My experience with women in corporations is that most of them are very butch. Now, whether they really are or not, I don't know. I always get the feeling that they're only acting that way. But they will be the most intractable people in the room, the hardest liners.

Also, they are usually nasty. I've had a couple of women bosses. I have found that the bosses of mine that are women have picked up all the worst things of male bosses. Being women does not mean that they will be more sensitive toward oppressing you with their own personal shit. That's always the worst thing about a boss. You're trying to do your job, whatever it is, and the boss is saying, as women always complain that bosses say, "Go out and get a Mother's Day card for me and send it to my mother. This is a bad lunch you picked up for me. Go make coffee. Go do this. Go do that." You're doing a lot of things to help make your boss feel grand. I thought that having a female boss would be great. I won't have to put up with all that macho garbage.

Not so. The women bosses I have had all have done that abusively to the people who were working for them. "Call my dentist. Call my hairdresser. Where's the car? Get me a cup of coffee."

The first time, I thought, "Well, it's an aberration." But I've had three female bosses at this point, and the story is always the same.

When these women look at the system and look at the men around them, maybe they are convinced that if they don't do those things and have the accoutrements of power, they won't be well respected. Or, on the other hand, perhaps they feel, "Hey, the guys are getting this. Why shouldn't I get this?"

Women have not feminized the evils of the inhuman business world. They've plunged in and stand there shoulder to shoulder doing the same shit to people who work for them as men are and adopting the values of business. I wish I could say something different, but that has been my own experience.

It may be that the women who enter those institutions are not really feminists, except in the sense that they want to be independent. They just want the same supposed opportunities that men have. So they're going to get ulcers now. They're going to have their children hate them also, and not be around to raise the families. I don't think that's working out quite as we hoped it would, that women would bring a new view, a new attitude to the world of business.

They seem to me to be doing the same thing everybody else is doing.

The assumption is, being a man and being aggressive is okay. Being a woman and being aggressive is *not* okay. That's not the *fact* in any business I've ever seen. *Anybody* who's too aggressive is slammed down, unless they own the company, or they're the son of the owner of the company. It has nothing to do with who has the right to be aggressive. If you've got the money and the power, you can act any way you want. Everybody else plays a game which is very different than that. I feel sorry for women who think that the way to succeed is by being hyper-aggressive, because it ain't true. If a man was hyper-aggressive, he would have the same problems in the same position. Everybody would hate him, too. They would, and they do.

I was harassed sexually on the job. In this particular case it was a very important buyer, and I was the account executive. It started out with, "I have two tickets to the theater. Why don't you go with me?"

"Fine," I would say, because when somebody from your number one account calls, you don't say no. You don't really have a reason to say no. On top of that, I wanted to go see what she was going to see. She had tickets to

everything, because she was so important that everybody was wooing her. I was trying to woo her, too, because I was trying to get her to buy our product. But by no
means did I ever make any sort of emotional or sexual
connection.

If anything, I was more like Mr. Hayseed, in terms of
what's going on. I was a gung-ho, fucking just out of the
cornfield kind of character. "Do-dah, do-dah. I want to be
a success." It was terribly important to me, and I had a
wife and an apartment, and a chance at this big job. I
thought everything I did was so important. "Oh, my God. If
I lose the business, I'm out of a job."

She was a three-hundred-pound woman who was kind
of grisly, to tell you the truth, and a bit out of control. I
played into it, because I was interested in keeping the
business for the company and all that bullshit. But I was
also incredibly naive.

Then one time she invited me back to her apartment
after we had been to a screening of a new movie. I felt the
pressure. I felt this woman wanting me to go to bed with
her, and I didn't want to, because she weighed three
hundred pounds. She was a good buyer, she had a nice
personality outside of this little weight thing, but when she
reached over on the couch and grabbed me and smooched
me and all that crap, no, I didn't like it. I didn't think it was
a good thing. And on top of that I had to go home that
night and worry about what's going to happen tomorrow.
Is she going to cause me trouble? Is she going to cut my
orders in half? Is she going to get me fired? People do goofy
things like that.

It's been happening to women for ages. But it happens
to men, too. You don't hear about it very often. I wouldn't
tell this to anybody. I wouldn't. I can hear the reaction now:
"You? Mr. Top Dog in your company, you got taken by a

woman?" You don't think people talk like that? Bullshit, they sure as hell do.

$\mathbf{T}$here is something that definitely happens with women's cycles. I know that this is a real sensitive area. But, good grief! There are hormonal changes that occur for twenty-five to thirty percent of a woman's monthly life. There's a lot of time when they are not as stable, they're a little more irrational and a little harder to deal with.

With a staff of forty-eight women, there's no way I know what's going to happen next. You can't find out where they are in their cycle. That's hard enough with one woman. You try to remember, "Why am I getting hit across the face with this stuff? Oh, God, here it comes again." I'd have to have pre-employment physicals and then put all that data into the computer to keep track of them all.

"Excuse me, but how regular are you? Twenty-eight days? And what happens to you?"

Honest to God, I've got to put it down on my calendar about my girlfriend. I'm aware of her cycle, because pretty regularly—like every time—she is very affected by it, and I can predict her behavior. That's a little scary to me.

As a man, I would like more definitive information about that. It may be out there someplace, although you can't talk about it. You can't use it as an excuse for the way people behave. It's not recognized as a factor. *Nobody* wants to talk about it these days. You certainly wouldn't ever want to talk about it as the employer, as the manager or boss. It's so taboo. You can really be accused of being a male chauvinist pig around all that. But it's definitely there. There's no way of avoiding it. It seems to me that ignoring women's menstrual cycles and ignorance about them just adds to the misunderstandings between the sexes.

I figure it's like a toothache. When a toothache hurts you—God!—you don't know what to do. You confused. You don't know which way to turn. So by them having off-brand pains from cramps and menstruation, plus nothing to do but flirt and sit around, I think they would *have* to be confused.

It's like night and day. The relationship will be great. Then about five days or four days or three days before they're about to get their period, all of a sudden, the relationship is shit, and they're mad as shit. You just can't do anything right, and she can't see what she ever liked about you.

If you're with a woman for a long period of time, it gets bizarre, because you know when her period is coming. Even if you lost track of what day of the month it is, or even if she's one of the irregular cycle ones, you know it's coming.

"Oh, jeez, hon, is it almost time for your period?"

"Yeah. So? What about it?"

I have a theory. With the one week of pre-menstrual

cycle, plus the one week of menstrual cycle, and the one week of post-menstrual cycle, that means there is only one week of every month when women are what they would term their normal selves. I see that as a perversion of the usual meaning of the word *normal.* In my accounting, it is actually the other three weeks that they are their normal selves. There's one week when they act like wonderful little angels. You can have sex with them, have fun with them, talk over the larger questions of life with them and have a great time. But the other three weeks, they're "abnormal"? No. The evil twin is their normal selves.

They don't want to admit that, especially the feminists. It does get in the way of all the debunking stuff they have to do. You know, the "Would you want a woman to be president?" stuff.

"Gee, I'm on the rag. Where's that red button?"

Brrrrgroom!

They hate for you to say that. The fact is, it's the truth. Jesus Christ, it's so true. It can be just as true of men, and women don't hesitate to point out that men would blow up the world at the drop of a hat because a prehistoric surge of testosterone flipped them over into misplaced mating season overdrive. They kind of like comparing us to animals, but they just don't want to acknowledge the physical side of themselves.

I'm beginning to meet women who think of themselves as intellectuals. I'm not being derogatory, that's just the way they think. They have a different aspect about them than the run-of-the-mill woman who is not intellectual, or who may be intellectual but does not define herself that way.

They call themselves "Thinking Types." In the process of pursuing higher education, they've taken these personality tests where you answer a couple of hundred questions and rate your extroversion versus introversion, your thinking versus feeling, whether you're judgmental versus accepting. It is graded differently for women and men, because women are often more feeling than thinking, so they throw in a few extra feeling points for men and a few extra thinking points for women right off the bat.

Most of these women fall into the thinking category. They have more male psychological characteristics. They don't have hair on their bodies, they're just all "thinkers." They're the most screwed up, see. At least, they're the ones who have the most potential for being screwed up, because they're the ones that are the furthest away from their mammalian nature.

The main reason the human race is in any trouble whatsoever is that we don't take care of and understand our mammalian nature. We are first and foremost mammals. There are things about femininity and masculinity that go along with that. We're not paying any attention to those things.

These women are starting to think about their mammalian nature without knowing it. They're finally thinking there may be some kind of conflict here about not having babies, or having babies and a job at the same time.

To me, it's the most natural thing in the world. Women have a certain amount of chemistry in them that is encouraging them to be mothers and to do that whole thing. When you start screwing around with your chemistry, you're probably going to have a lot of bad reactions to it. We do this to ourselves more and more. Not only are we mammals, but before that we were reptiles, and we have parts of that left in our brains. The way we see goes way back in our genetic codes and disposition, for instance. We have the same kind of eyes as an octopus has.

There's too much humanization in society and culture. The main difference between men and women is real obvious: women have to take care of the kids. I mean that on a very instinctual, mammalian level. What would it be like if all of a sudden men had the genetic and the biological predisposition and the social responsibility that they *had* to take care of kids, their kids, even friends' kids, any kids that came along. All of a sudden, men felt real responsible for them and had to take care of them, which is exactly what happens to women, from what I can tell. They can't help it.

What if, all of a sudden, women had no particular thing to do—which is what men have to do, no particular thing. You don't see families very often where the women does nothing and the man takes care of the kids and has a job. But you see lots of families where the man does nothing except score crack cocaine that day, and the woman has the job or stands in line at the Welfare *and* takes care of the kids. That's instinctual, hormonal and biological that this woman feels this need to keep it all together. The man doesn't feel that way. He's happy to go along for the ride.

If just that one thing were reversed, that one instinct—who knows how many gallons of chemistry pour into that over a lifetime—give men the mothering instinct, and it would just change everything completely around. That's why I feel the baby thing is the big difference between men and women. That's the reason that men are men and women are women. You can change everything else and you really haven't changed anything. Put dresses on men and have women whistle at them. Or give women the penises, but leave everything else the same, still it doesn't really change anything. What really changes things is when women have to raise babies, because they *have* to, they just internally have to. There's no other way for them to be.

Why now, when women have more freedom and more money and more latitude than they have ever had, why aren't they happy? They don't seem to be happy. The reason they are not happy is that there is a psychic tremor in the mass female unconscious brought about by technology. If you believe what Darwin said, that females are programmed to mate with the strongest of the species, thus to insure a heartier strain of offspring, then in the last fifty years of this new age of technology, we have a problem. How do we define strength? Plainly, you can no longer define strength in terms of physicality, because we men have invented a series of machines that can do anything we can do and do it faster, longer and better. It's no coincidence that the novel *Frankenstein* was written by one of your early Suffragettes, Mary Wollstonecraft Shelley. She saw that we would build a monster that would eventually turn and strangle us, and then piss on our prone forms.

When you consider the whole fucking span of human history, what is the function of a man? Oh, the man goes out, he kills the meat, he drags it back to the cave, he fights with the other men who can't find any meat and want to take ours. Then he goes out, and he spends his superior physicality, his strength on farms and down fucking mine shafts and in the sweat boxes of factories. That was the commodity we men had to sell.

No longer. The feminists are saying, "A woman can do any job a man can do." Granted—*if* she has access to the fucking technology that makes that possible. If she has a pastel-colored backhoe with daisies stuck on it, she can dig any ditch a man can dig. Certainly, no question about it.

But, on some psychic level, women are reacting to this ongoing disempowerment of men, this insidious loss of strength on the part of men that technology has brought about. We are not the men our ancestors were.

The feminist movement is not necessarily a rational quest for equality with men when the target gender is steadily losing force and influence. Historically, once you attain freedom, you get an unoccluded view of your own limitations. That's a bummer. That's some of what they're feeling right now from the freedom they have gained. With sexual equality comes the realization that both genders are more or less equally fucked.

In our society there is an ongoing conscious and semi-conscious attempt to blur the distinctions between the genders, to masculinize women and to feminize men, that is not indicative of sexual preoccupations on the part of the people who are doing it. I don't think they even realize they are doing it, but it is to a purpose.

It is that we have effected our own evolutionary throttle. We are evolving ourselves into a new kind of administrative mode in which gender doesn't matter. It doesn't matter in terms of male physical strength. And on the women's side, too, it doesn't matter in terms of what were once their obstetrical limitations, because those limitations no longer exist. They now have control over their own reproductive lives and pipes. Nothing Jesse Helms or any other third-rate rodeo clown has to say about that is going to mean a thing. So on their part, women are being injected into the workplace in record numbers.

The goal of this ongoing campaign to blur the distinction between the genders is to come up with a unisex, inter-changeable, malleable, obedient, pliable society of techno-serfs who will serve the machine. The men will not have the necessary testosterone to overthrow the machine, to rebel and fight as we have always done in the past. The women, with their new, mandatory liberation, East German style, will have no other options then but to put on their Gamma Delta Drone Worker Jumpsuit and Serve The Machine!

I wonder what it would be like, if we were able to live without cultural and social pressures. What would we be if we each had our terrible burden laid down? Both men and women feel oppressed by their lives, and they take it out on each other. Both sexes have plenty of bones to pick.

I don't have a feminist analysis of the world. If I get in these kinds of conversations and there is a woman in the room, I'm always accused of not really understanding a woman's situation, not understanding the true oppression of women. I suppose it's true that I don't *really* understand the true oppression of women, not being one. But although women think I'm crazy when I say it, in some ways if we had to go around again, I'd try it as a woman.

I understand women's complaints about stunting ambi-tions and the inability to live your life in all its varied pos-sibilities. But women don't understand that men's options aren't as many or as broad as they think. Maybe they are in terms of what kind of careers we can have, but they aren't in about what kind of emotions we can feel. They aren't about what kind of people we can be. Our options aren't wide about the kinds and varieties of relationships we can have with other humans. We don't have a lot of relationships with children. We don't have a lot of relationships with men who aren't business associates. We usually don't have relationships with women as friends.

Our relationships are simple. They don't vary too much. We're lucky if we have more than two friends. Women, it seems to me, have lots of friends. They seem to me to be able to fit many more kinds of relationships into their lives than men can fit into their lives.

Even in the oppression of the home and how stultifying and spirit-killing it can be—and it can be and often is—at least it's direct and meaningful. You are helping someone grow. You are helping keep someone alive. You're not pushing paper across a desk to collect a dollar.

So I would be willing next time to try it the other way. I'd probably be an ardent, screaming feminist. But I'm not sure I wouldn't rather be a dissatisfied woman than a dissatisfied man.

Boy, you can't help but get pissed off at women. Jesus Christ! They're a different breed. I just don't believe anybody who says, "I love women. I love everything about them." It's like saying, "I love snakes."

But thank God they're different. The mystery of heterosexual relationships is none of us want somebody exactly like ourselves. When I really dislike somebody, it usually turns out that he's just like me. That's why I have an incredible attraction to women. They'd *better* be different. What'd I want a 350-pound woman who can beat me at boxing, outfish me, and drive faster than I can?

Two: **Men**

Sixteen tons and what do you get?
Another day older and deeper in debt.
St. Peter don't you call me, 'cause I can't go.
I owe my soul to the company store.

I went skiing for a week in the winter of 1991 with five other men
—a man who fixes up properties and rents the apartments, a
bartender, a roofing contractor, a commercial builder, and a
stockbroker. We were all about the same age, late thirties to
early forties, but from a wide variety of backgrounds and life-
styles. Five of us were married, and the other guy has been living
with the same women for so many years he might as well be
married. We all knew that one man, but the rest of us knew each
other only vaguely or not at all. We shared a small, three-bed-
room condo. Within twenty-four hours, we were a group. By the
end of the week, we were a small tribe that cooked and ate and
drank together. And trusted one another. It was a phenomenon
I have not experienced very often. This was also the first vacation I've taken without my wife and children in almost twelve
years of marriage.

That week was one of the most relaxing weeks I've had in many
years, which is saying a lot considering the Gulf War began the

second day of our trip. I looked back afterwards and tried to figure out what had made it so pleasurable.

After our initial introductions, there was virtually no shop talk. The work world disappeared almost entirely, except of course for the stockbroker, who felt it necessary to stay in touch with his office and clients. But at least the captains of industry have the decency to open the stock market *after* the lifts start operating, so we were all out of the condo by the time he got on the phone. It didn't matter how much money you made last year if you were whipping up *huevos rancheros* for six ravenous men, or if you went tumbling head over ski poles when you tried to get off the lift chair at the top of the slope. The absence of talk about work didn't mean we filled the void instead with meaningful, angst-ridden male-bonding dialogue. The conversation was dominated by weather conditions, trail grooming, and the inadvisability of wearing Lycra and Spandex snowsuits if you are an overweight woman.

Perhaps the subject that those of us with children returned to most often was our wish to have our kids share this experience someday—but not this time. Although we burned up the phone lines a little while every evening calling home to make contact with family and hearth, we were really on leave from that responsibility as well. The only duty to be fulfilled was a personal one—get down off the mountain in one piece by the end of each day.

What made it all so relaxing was that we had successfully escaped from the main definitions of our male lives into a bracingly beautiful piece of outdoors where time could be frittered away in totally physical activity. I'll never forget skiing one afternoon in a snowstorm. Visibility was suddenly restricted to about twenty-five feet. Skis disappeared. Another member of our little tribe and I seemed to be flying down the mountain, or rather floating in falling snow and gray cloud, disconnected from the Earth and everything else except the wind in our faces. Later, someone admonished us about the danger of what we had done, but at the time there was only elation. I was free—brain, body, and conscience—from my work and the main reason for my work, my family.

That may sound terrible, especially to many women, but that's because they do not understand what men are really all about or the pressurized interior existence men accept as normal life. I am not a very representative example of the majority of men in America. I'm one of the truly lucky men in the world, because I have a stable and happy marriage, which is still interesting after over a decade, and because I'm basically my own boss and actually enjoy my work. I've never considered my life a burden. But when I briefly set aside these two interconnected obligations, I was amazed at their psychic weight.

Men are defined by what we do. Ask a man who he is, and he'll tell you what he does for a living. I used these five men's occupations to describe them in the first paragraph and I doubt that anyone, male or female, found that odd. A man's social and educational status, his personal intelligence, even his character are read by the world in the one or two words it takes to name his job.

A few men bulge out of the strictures of their lives with obsessive energy, single-minded striving, and overweening ambition. A carpenter I interviewed put it this way: "The thing I really like about men is that they have built empires, even personal empires and companies. Guys have all this wild initiative and salesmanship. It's kind of cool, the 'let's-build-the-Pyramids' kind of thing. There might be fewer toxic waste dumps and Styrofoam cups if women ran things, but there would probably be fewer pyramids and Empire State Buildings, too."

As admirable and masterful as it may be, empire building was never the occupation of the common man. Very few people even have gratifying work, much less a feeling of accomplishment. As a teacher who would like to be a full-time screenwriter expressed it, "The ideal is to do something that you like, but you can't do that. When the feminist movement for liberation first started, they talked about how the men get to go to work and women are trapped in the house. It's always seemed to me that raising children has got to be much more fulfilling than what the vast majority of men do on a daily basis between nine and five: pushing paper, making money in some abstract way, doing something that doesn't affect anyone in a positive and direct manner. The only thing you say to yourself is, 'At least, I'm bringing this home for the family.'

"Then you come home to the family, and you're miserable from sitting forty hours a week doing bullshit. It's not a good way to live.

"It's also one of the reasons why money has become the end in itself of the work you're doing. If the only thing the money means is, 'It supports my family, it helps me take care of my wife and children,' the way you have to define yourself as a man is how much of that money you can bring home. Having to earn money is a very uncomfortable thing for men. I know plenty of men enjoy it, plenty of men get obsessed by it. But it's a soul-destroying thing."

The big describer of men in America today is not swaggering machismo or sexual prowess or the heroic ability to beat all comers on the racquetball court. Everything is secondary to money and our ability to provide for those whom we think expect it from us. The scythe that has cut down so many men in the last ten years from Wall Street to the assembly line in Detroit is unemployment. Men are busy living up to expectations of success, whether real or imagined, and in our society that adds up to cold, hard cash. Too often, financial success is the extent of the role we play. We are brought up admiring intrepid explorers, brave and selfless warriors, a gentle God/man bleeding to death for our sins, but we end up living for a paycheck.

If a man manages to make more than enough money to survive, there's nothing to do with it but to buy things, things he hopes will define who he is. As a 50-year-old union official sees it, "The bad joke on women is that they gather possessions. 'My wife is out shopping. I'm finished.' I don't think it's a funny joke. It's a cover-up for the fact that men are more acquisitive than women ever are. What's more boring in the world than to drive to Philadelphia with a guy who just got a new house. You hear about every fucking room and how he's going to fill them. We blame it on the Yuppies, but that's bullshit. We had it in the '50s and '60s, too. The house in the suburbs, the Saab. That's identification. Men have to do that."

Materialism is empty and transitory, yet judging the meaning of one's life by an internal gauge that is calibrated only to one's own aspirations and values is almost an anti-social act when the society is so concentrated on work, conformity, and the dollar. The proliferation of the new men's movement can be traced to the fact that many men are feeling adrift in life, hollow at the core. For all the magazine stories and TV news coverage of various emerging philosophical directions and self-help groups, the majority of men perceive the attempt to redefine men as falling into two main groups, the touchy-feely group and the gorilla consciousness group. Neither angle satisfies many men.

The consciousness raising/sensitivity training school of thought meets the most cultural opposition among men. It goes against the grain of everything they've been taught since the first time they skinned their knees falling off a bicycle. Here's the manly code succinctly summarized by a heavy equipment operator who teaches high school mechanics shop:

"Most of us grew up in that time period where men don't cry and men don't talk about their problems, they just work them out. They grin and bear it. They deal with it and go on to fight for whatever they have to fight for, as long as it's macho enough to be worth fighting for: Truth, Justice, and the American Way—and don't say nothing rotten about my mom."

The reactionaries who would have us return to a glorification of masculinity underestimate men's self-knowledge. An architect, who has fled to a farm in the mountains to escape what he calls "the medieval society of the pandering client relationship" that was his profession, had this to say: "The men's movements that I've been reading about are mostly this resurrection of Primal Man, going around grunting and whooping and hollering. Okay, fine, make all the noise you want, but don't give me that shit. Good old *Brutality Rex*. Fuck that. It misses the mark. Talk about it, cry, feel, but to be a mere and utter mortal, you don't have to huff and puff about, pounding on bongo drums. Don't confuse manhood with being a brutal primate. The men's movement seems to be back to the cigar-and-martini man, instead of onward and upward with what we've learned. That's retrograde. Sort of a Victorian image, longed for.

"It's ridiculous horseshit to claim there is some kind of universal male mystique anyway. There are as many male mystiques as there are men. In fact, there are almost as many male mystiques as there are women. For every woman's image of a man, hopefully, there is some male who will fit that view."

Women—and men—assume that since males are the dominant sex in our culture, all men must have full control over their lives. In fact, that is not the case. "If we're really in charge, how come we got such a lousy job description?" asked a 35-year-old public relations man from the West Coast. "It's amazing to me how narrow the definition of what it is to be a man is as opposed to the females' definition, especially these days when things are opening up for women in our society. What at one time was totally unacceptable for women is now just different or even courageous behavior. Whereas for men, as soon as you step out of those very narrow lines, the core of your masculinity is called into question. It's not just that you are different, you're not even a man. You step out of that macho thing, you're lost, and you become a menace to other men and masculinity."

Unmanly as it may seem, men live in fear for much of their lives: fear of inadvertently stepping out of those narrow bound-aries and losing part of their manhood, fear of other men, fear of women, fear of not being successful, fear of being afraid. Fear is something all men hold in common, along with its corol-lary, stress—and all the physical harm that stress brings. A man keeps his fear inside himself until it kills him.

The hardest period in my life was when I went unem-ployed for a year and a half. When people said, "What're you doing?" and they didn't know me, I'd say, "I'm a con-sultant."

Besides being very broke, it was a real crisis, public and personal. I wasn't myself. I wasn't participating. I won't deny the importance of the public world. I was supposed to get a fucking job. I had to make some money.

There was this one day, I was walking along going to pick up a check that I knew wasn't going to be there. I just came in second again in some job application process, and I stopped in the middle of Broad Street, and I just stood there. Feet wouldn't move.

I don't know how long I was there. Anywhere from sixty seconds to two hours. I was so personally threatened, I couldn't move. I'd been in a lot of trouble and a lot of scrapes, but nothing as serious as that had ever happened to me. I've never had a tragic life. It's not a tragedy when your electricity gets turned off. Being unemployed was the worst thing that ever happened to me, because what it said was, "They won't let you play. They just won't let you play."

In my generation of men, you are who you are with. What

you do is a major factor. What you do is a man's main definition. It isn't the task. As often as not, it's the title. That's why banks that never paid that well always had so many assistant vice presidents, it was something to give the employees. Okay, a guy says, "I work *for* . . . ," then he's not as important as the guy who says, "I am *with* . . ." CEO's are more important than small entrepreneurs. Men who had a college education are more important than men who did not. It doesn't make any difference how much fucking money the neighbor made who was a plumber and pulled down three dollars an hour more than the assistant vice president in some financial firm, because that other guy's got a college ring on. The bigger the ring, the shittier the college. The more you just got by, the more you wear it.

Try to go to a party or a bar and spend time talking with a guy you don't know without asking him what he does. Even if you get away with that, you're still trying to figure it out in your head, because the public function is important to the character. You want to know where they are in the male status realm. It has meaning.

At 40, you're supposed to have made it, you know where you're going to go and the sky's the limit. Or you get a stable position in the upper-middle status. That means you're deemed harmless, so you can stay there, and you know you're going to be there—*forever.* You're not a player, but they'll keep you. You can do what you want, because it has to get done. Hopefully you'll get early retirement.

For a guy turning 50, it's not just, "I can't play three-on-three basketball anymore," or "That woman really is too young for me. She told me." It's also, "Where the fuck am I? Have I done anything? Those expectations, where are they?"

Men who retire, they die two months later, because somebody took their public world away. There's no expectation to fulfill. The real problem for men in giving up work is giving up the progressive series of expectations as each year goes on. If you take that away, that's the major describer of men's lives. There's nowhere to go without it.

Men in that sense are frightfully in need. Needy. I hate that word. It's such a negative, selfish word. Needy. But men are needy for participation in the world that has some recognition. Suddenly, you wake up one morning, and when someone asks, "What do you do?"

"I used to . . ."

I was raised as a prince. My father is a plumber, and my mother is the daughter of an itinerant photo engraver. But I was raised as King Arthur in terms of their expectations of me. That's what I was fed. A lot was expected of me. I don't think it made any difference that I was the oldest kid. People loved me. I'm very ingratiating. I can be sort of friendly. I'm a lot of fun. Those are survival traits. I used to be a lot better looking when I had hair.

I was the hope of my family, the one who was going to get them up. Their idea of moving over into the mainstream was for me to go to college and be a teacher. I thought that was such a weak idea, you know? I just couldn't buy it. If all this adds up to being a teacher, what's it all about?

I wasn't raised to be Donald Trump. When you have an Irish Catholic mother with a great imagination—in her mind I don't know what she sees when she looks at me— she's always wanted her sons to be something great. But, because of the situation that she came from, she never had any idea what real success was like. It wasn't like Mrs. Vanderbilt raising her children to take over the family fortune. There was nowhere to go. Once she let you go, it was just a springboard into nothing. She was raising you for a very amorphous idea in her mind. She sure wasn't raising me to be a plumber.

All this attention that I got, all this dealing with adults, doing the right thing, and being the good guy breeds these little rebellions that you go through—the little things that you hold back from the expectations of the people who have total power over you. Obviously, it's like the slave mentality. All of a sudden, you're 18 and free, and you go, "Fuck this! I'll just kill myself. It'll only take me two or three years and I'll be dead before I'm 21. The Prince is dead, long live the Prince."

I basically went on a system of self-destruction for the next six years. Flunked out of college the first year. Ended up in the hospital when I was 20 years old with kidney failure from drinking. Got blood poisoning. Got scars all over my shoulders from where my blood infection broke out. It took me a long time to recover.

I was not a happy person for a number of years. I'm not sure why. It can't really be accounted for from anything I can think of.

I'm a perplexed individual on some levels, because I don't understand success. I don't know how they get there. I've never been able to figure it out. I can't do it. You ask me something, I can do it. I can fix things for you. Maybe I'm just a fucking mechanic, but I'm a mental mechanic.

I'd been a musician, performing since I was 15, and I loved writing the songs. On the other hand, I had no clear idea of what I was going to do with music. There were no models. I had no idea that there were people around who did things just from ideas, who had no jobs like teachers or plumbers. I had to develop the entire thing for myself. It took me a long time. I was a mess. A fucking mess for years. I'm surprised I survived it sometimes. Even now I still haven't figured out how to make music work.

Maybe I was born unhappy. Nah! People have a certain situation at a certain moment they're born to confront. You either get there or you don't. It's some literary thing like from Faulkner or Hemingway. Predestination.

Nature builds you, and you're a machine with a certain propensity for things, like action. You go through your daily life and deal with the people that you know and make your daily bread. But, there is another mechanism that's involved in a human being. All of a sudden people happen. The top rips off your airplane, and you're flying 360 miles an hour. You crawl up on a seat and hold on to somebody for four hours, so they don't get sucked out of the plane. That's extraordinary and can't be explained by any measure of who you were up until that time. It doesn't matter who your mom and dad were or what happened when you were a baby. The guy who sees the plane crash into the Potomac and he jumps off the bridge and saves sixteen people and a couple of kids, he might be a little guy who never ran a hundred yards in his life.

It's the little farm boy who kills the giant dragon. When you read Louis L'Amour, Max Brand, and Zane Grey, it's the myth of the Old West. It's the myth of America. The guy who never did particularly much, but he rises to the occasion to find out that he's just, cellularly speaking, triumphant.

The thing is, I don't think you know who you are until you're tested. Part of that test is an ongoing thing, the spirit to prevail, my spirit against your spirit, the ability to absorb punishment.

But the important part is the Big Test. If you're unfortunate, you wait for the Big Test, and it never comes. Then you've wasted a lot of time. If you're smart, while you're waiting, you go along and enjoy yourself, be kind to people, try not to take up too much room.

I've only figured that out recently. I begin to see these things in a little different light, because I have a little boy. He looks at you and you are God. I find it very endearing. You don't really have to do very much to be a good guy with him. You just got to pay attention and help him out. Feels pretty good a lot of the time. Much more good than bad.

I don't know what it would have been like if I'd had my first kid at 21 when I was still a totally self-destructive person. I wonder about that sometimes. I still don't think that I'm extremely healthy. If I was healthy I'd be more successful in external terms, and that becomes more important as my kid grows up. I'm responsible for much more than when it was just me. If I'd overdosed then, it would just be me laying there in the gutter with a blue face. Not anymore.

Just the other day, I thought, "Maybe, it'd be better in the long run, since my wife's mom has some money, if I just walked out and like left a note on the table saying, "Goodbye for now. I'll get in touch with you when I make good."

Don't you think of that every once in a while? I mean, they're not going to starve. I can make as much money anywhere as I'm making here. Then again, I thought, "Well, jeez, they're going to miss me. I know they are. And I'd sure miss them." You get used to them after a while.

It's very banal, but recently I received tenure at the university I'm employed at. It was a very elevated feeling I got from that. But it wasn't about professional achievement. What occurred to me was that my main gate as a man had in some way been taken care of, and I'd done that at a rather young age. It was a great relief that if I did not walk into class dead drunk or with my dick hanging out, I now had a salary that was going to be there. There'd be a pension at the end of it. My kids could go to the college. This weight of responsibility of being a man was lifted from me in a way that I hadn't expected. But it was what tenure was about. I was relaxed to a level that I hadn't felt since I was married, seventeen years ago. It's helped me.

Men feel that the choices they make in life are obligations to support other people. Most men aren't in a situation where tenure or royalties or some stock annuity will eliminate that burden. Men and women underestimate the pressure of that enormously. I don't think women understand the depth with which men feel that, the pain of that responsibility and the burden.

My father-in-law, now grandfather of my two children, was tremendously uptight as a father. He had three girls and a boy. They remember him as difficult, temperamental, flying into rages, impossibly inflexible, a horrible man to get along with. He is, of course, the model grandfather. The children adore him. Now as elder statesman for the family, he is soft with all the children, giving, generous with his own children.

Part of the reason is, he made it. He accomplished the thing he had to do, which he wasn't sure he could do, and all men worry about.

"Am I bright enough?"

"Am I tough enough?"

"Can I provide what is really necessary for me to provide?"

He'd done it. Two of his daughters are married. The other one is a graduate student on the way to an academic career. His son is a professional and he's working out fine.

My father-in-law is in semi-retirement. He had an insurance business that now has had enough clients, long enough, that it is like an annuity. He's a different man than the other man, without all that pressure on him. He's more liberal. He's more understanding. He's more tender. He doesn't fly into rages. He's got compassion.

But before, the pressure that he felt inside himself was so intense, it was easy to get him angry. He can't explain that. First of all, he's not very introspective, so he doesn't think about it. But second of all, even if he understood it, he's of a generation that could not have explained that to somebody, could not have turned around when he was younger and said, "You don't understand, I sweat all day. I'm worried all day about every client I get, and every dollar I make. When I come home and things aren't easy here, I *flip out.* I'm busting my hump over there, because I'm trying to raise my family. I come home and there's no place for me to rest. So I'm angry all the time." He didn't understand that and his children didn't understand that, so for twenty years in the house they were screaming at each other.

There's a lot of men like that. Under our system, very few people get to make choices about how they make their living that is in some way gratifying for themselves.

I can't bear people who complain a lot. I know that it's important not to suggest solutions to people, just to witness their complaints and be sympathetic. Still it gets me on edge, because it's my duty to solve it, be daddy and solve it. It always makes me nervous, and there's a certain limit I have to the amount of complaint I can hear.

Okay, eighty percent of the time, you have kind of an equal partnership with your mate. But when the chips are down, then that old thing comes up and we're responsible. That may not be totally logical, but I feel like *I'm responsible*, because *I'm the man*. When Wanda gets sick, I feel that *I'm responsible*. When her cousin wanted to borrow the fucking car, I felt like *I'm responsible*. If that dipshit goes out and wrecks the fucking car, Wanda can't get to work. *I'm responsible*. Plus I'd be responsible for the dipshit, too. Even when the dog is sick, I feel *I'm responsible*.

I'm still responsible for myself, and I've always been completely comfortable with that. But when I say I'm responsible for myself, there is a wide latitude of what can happen to me and I'll still be okay. There is not that latitude with the things and the people that are connected with me. I can't allow them to get fucked up while *I'm responsible*.

I grew up with the man as the provider. The man was probably slightly more intelligent. The woman was more feeling and probably a drain financially. That's an unfortunate thing that is really deep in my brain. That is how I approach the marriage I'm in now, and that's how I feel it is. That's reality now. I wish it wasn't really.

If there was one thing I could let go of a little bit, it might be that financial thing. I don't even know why it's such a big deal to me. But I went into this marriage thinking, "Well, it's going to be a financial burden," and it has been.

The wedding itself and the honeymoon and rings. I know where I was a year and a half ago financially, and I know where I am today. I'm probably about six or seven thousand dollars lower than where I was. I'm not hurting, but if I let my wife go, she would just keep spending and spending.

Men are raised to sacrifice. Women think that men are out for themselves, want what they want and are only interested in getting it. In fact, men are supposed to give things up all the time. They're supposed to subvert their own desires to make a home. It's very true about fatherhood that you are supposed to give to your children. There's a lot in men that's built toward giving themselves up and giving it away, whatever it is. Women not only don't appreciate that, they don't believe it. They think you're only saying that to justify your nasty tendencies.

As you get older, one of the things that happens is that you give up your big ideas. More and more of the things you thought were going to make you so central and important to the world you give up to just *be* in the world.

Most men are not built to think that what they're doing is more important than their relationships with other people. But women think that. They think that men who work sixty hours a week are doing that totally for self-aggrandizement, to stay away from home, and to stay out of the messiness of their relationships with their children and their link to wife and self. That's a very narrow view of the facts.

It's true that men are often emotionally crippled. It's easier for them to provide the main demand personally by acquiring money and doing work, than it is to be there emotionally. But they haven't been taught how to be there emotionally. We really don't know how.

One of the things that always used to bore the shit out of me in business was being with men. There was this formulaic discussion of baseball, which I have absolutely no connection to. Always sports or drinking or making money. I don't mean to be a goodie-goodie, but I just couldn't get behind that. It was always so limited and boring. But men didn't want to discuss feelings. If you started to discuss any of that stuff, it was like you were gay.

Is that the protective cover which young males were given in medieval times, because they were supposed to go off to war, and they weren't supposed to have any feelings? Is that why we're trained the way we are, to be brave little soldiers? All my body pain is *here,* at my heart. I'm supposed to be a brave little soldier. I'm not supposed to know fear.

A lot of women don't understand that men have dreams. They understand that men have dreams of wealth. We go to Wharton and decide that we're going to have a lot of money. But I wonder if women understand that men have dreams that are as ineluctable as anything they may have. I'm not assuming that women don't have them. I'm just saying that men have dreams.

The same guy who went to Wharton and ended up at

Merrill Lynch, the same guy who may be kind of nasty on the freeway, down inside may have dreams about what he wishes he was, or what he wishes he will be someday. I don't mean dreams about owning things or fucking women. I mean dreams so personal that he's afraid people would laugh at him for having them, impractical, crazy, very impossible dreams.

I've never heard women talking about their dreams. Maybe it's because they've been busy addressing very serious problems like date rape and not being paid what they should be paid—name it, there's a hundred things on the agenda. But at the same time as they work toward fulfilling their potential or whatever it is they are pursuing, I get the notion that women don't think men have dreams. I *know* that we do. I know I do.

I was with three men down at a nearby tavern. We had some business to cover. We're not really friends. We're even difficult colleagues, so we had to sit at lunch to settle some stuff, in public and not with your back to the door. Average age—45. It was me—Irish—a Jewish guy, a Greek guy and a guy who said it didn't matter, who's probably Eastern European of some kind. I can't figure it out yet, probably he's Albanian.

Anyway, the lunch ended, and it went well, so we kind of relaxed and started talking. We found out that the four of us grew up within miles of each other. Working-class neighborhoods. So we knew the same ice cream parlors— so you know the times have changed—and we knew the same schoolyard, and when we had a little bit of money, where the fancy restaurant was.

One guy had a daughter who has headaches, talked about her. Another guy has grown kids, and the other guy, believe it or not, has got little kids that he does Boy Scouts with. I got four grown kids *and* a new baby. It was kind of a soft moment.

I've known these guys for half a decade, been at meetings with them, argued with them, gossiped about them. Was going to get them and they're going to get me. I'm a pain in the ass. I got a big ego and I work for the boss. And there is this soft moment, almost a location in space, where we should be very similar, coming out of the same class, lived in an ethnic neighborhood, all had the same experiences at a fairly innocent time—date rape was a French kiss.

What I found interesting was, that last conversation of softness was politically more productive than what we thought was a productive lunch where we solved a lot of problems. Probably the only breakthrough was the soft half-hour talking about our kids, and more importantly where we came from.

There is with men a very definite striving to maintain original loyalties and meaningful friendships. That's why we have cronyism throughout any of the systems that are open: politics, unions, schooling. We don't have the same cronyism in banks. The bottom line is too important, and you can't afford it.

One of the great crimes committed on men in their lives is when an old friend turns on them, or that they stop playing sports and there's no more locker room thing. Men still gather, and the more they can gather with people who have a self-conscious response to where they come from, the more comfortable they are. Men need the notion of neighborhood even though it's not there anymore, because they've moved to the suburbs. They need the tribal connections.

The best way to maintain security is to have moorings, and men do that very deliberately, self-consciously. I'm an absolute player in—what is it the sociologists call it?—male bonding. I've changed my life a number of times in the thirty-five years of my fifty years I could do that, and still maintained the connections, the system of friendships —not the same guys, but the system of it. The same class, the same ethnicity, the same upbringing, where you don't have to say something to make it understood.

Couple times a week on the way home from work, I like to stop off at the bar for a few beers. I sit there at the bar, have a few beers, eat a hard-boiled egg, maybe play a little shuffleboard. I know those boys since high school. One of them's a drunk, all of them's a little fucked up one way or another. But I've knowed them a long time and I like talking to them. Every fall we go hunting together.

The old lady, she don't like it.

Men and women get together because it's a biological unit. It's the old idea. Men are born and they are half a soul. Only by being together with a woman can they become whole. That's true. I do believe in that.

On the other hand, it's much more important on the most basic level in being a male to know what your territory is. Nowadays, since there is no territory to protect like grazing land or nomadic spice routes, because it's not six miles to the next human, we tend to form relationships because we feel that's a territory. "Here's somebody I can trust. Here's somebody that I don't have to worry about." It's almost a tribal thing, salving some sort of want that you have for a little space, to fill just a little space of your own.

Machismo is a surface thing, false bravado, to push down and keep away those things we're afraid of: fear of making mistakes and fear itself.

So much of men's lives are spent posturing, trying to get people to think well of us, or be afraid of us, or like us. So much of that is completely wasted energy. It's just keeping in place a facade that people can already see through. Plus it squelches the real stuff. What you're pushing out to the world is this false front, this mask you've got to keep from cracking. Where's the real you?

What's most insidious about macho behavior is it hides a legitimate homophilia. A lot of male behavior is to impress other males and has nothing to do with impressing women. It is a very bizarre, back-handed, out-of-touch series of signals men are putting out to reassure each other. It is not in competition for the women. It has nothing to do with any kind of biological bullshit. It is self-infatuated and agonizing competition that does no real human good. In fact, it causes a great deal of anxiety. But to acknowledge that we are huffing and puffing and strutting in front of each other is then to say that we are much more involved male to male than is allowed. If you really look at it, it's a form of hurting yourself while being overly involved with maleness.

It's not open to discussion. It is taboo. The only place it's talked about is if you ask a bunch of women. They'll tell you what a bunch of crap it is. They don't care two piss holes in the snow about macho.

I'm envious of men who can physically touch another man without worrying about what it looks like to other people or to the men they are touching. It always takes me a while when I know a man who's a hugger, who puts his hand around my shoulder, to sort of warm up to it, get used to it and say it's okay. Once I loosen up, then I like it. When I do it to other men that I like who are uptight about it in the same way I am, I'm always disappointed. I'm uncomfortable, because they're uncomfortable with it, and I want them to like it. I want to walk up and put my arm around a guy's shoulder and find it is okay.

Usually you put your arm around a guy's shoulder, and you feel him stiffen up. He's kind of waiting for you to get your arm off his shoulder, so the conversation can really continue. Most of what's going on when you have your arm around another man's shoulder is, "What does he mean? What is he doing? How do I get away from this without offending this guy?"

I envy that in women, their physical ease with one another, because touching is obviously very important, since language is so insufficient to express how you really feel. It can be so useless where a hug or a kiss would mean so much. We all have known those moments.

A man's big gesture is, he puts his hand on your shoulder and squeezes it for a second, and then passes. That's it. That's all you get. When you get it, you know it was important. That it was a big thing.

Watching baseball or football, when women see all these guys slapping each other's ass and hugging and jumping up and down, they always think it looks silly. But women do it all the time. Every time women meet who know each other, they kiss, they hug, they put their hands on each other's knees and thighs and backs and rub each other, massage one another. But when male athletes do it on TV, women think it's hilarious.

"Look at those guys. God, a bunch of homos."

Maybe women are threatened by it. If heterosexual men can find some physical comfort from one another, that's scary for them, right? "They won't try to get it from us. Uh-oh."

Men are a very limited and maladaptive gender. There are two strategies that we follow, a sexual strategy and a survival strategy.

Why do we have such big balls? We have such big balls because we compete by creating masses of sperm and by promiscuous depositing of the sperm everywhere we possibly can. That's the chimpanzee sexual strategy.

The gorilla strategy is to have small balls, big muscles. Big arms keep all the other males away from the harem. According to anthropologists, men got the big shoulders and arm muscles, not to fight each other, but rather to go out and hunt big animals—that is our survival strategy.

In men's lives today, body size and physical ability are decreasingly important. I'm not convinced that a man can fly an airliner any better than a woman can.

Is there anything that males do that is in any way important or necessary that couldn't be done by another gender? Anything at all? We don't bear children. We're just sort of sperm refrigerators or cookers—we keep the sperm at a precise temperature. In the winter, the balls get up close to the body, and in the summer they come down.

But aside from the progenitive act, really, when you think about survival, is there anything that we're doing that's not destructive? Our survival strategy—go out and kill the big animal—has proven too wasteful. Are women responsible for the overheating of the ozone layer, agricultural over-exploitation, and so much overpopulation that there may not be a future? Is it the fact that women fear their only existence is to be fertile and productive, or do we have these testosterone conquests to make?

Male function to me seems to be pathetically theatrical, invented. Whenever I see these conferences of idiots sitting around a table, I think, "Who's cooking the food? Who's cleaning the rooms? What are all these guys in there *doing?*"

In every other species in which the male doesn't have a fundamental gender responsibility for the nurturance of the young, they are the decorated gender, the ornamental gender. In our species, for some reason, women are the decorated ones *and* the burden bearers, and we are both drab and dangerous. Now what kind of survival or anthropological or evolutionary meaning does that have? It's nuts. I don't get it. How do you come to feel that you are useful as a man in the world today, other than ceremonially?

Men are habitual. Men's habits become very important to them. They tend to do the same thing over and over again in the same way.

Men like to come home and have a beer and do the thing they do after dinner, watch TV, have another beer, go to sleep, wake up at the same time the next morning. If they can, they get on the same train. I know lots of guys who say, "I get on the 7:17. I'm at my stop by 8:25. I'm in the office eleven minutes to nine, hang up my coat, and take a cup of coffee to my desk, where I look at yesterday's reports." Men think that way and they like to be that way.

Women aren't that way. It's partly because if on a daily basis you are dealing with the vicissitudes of children and the changes they are going through and running a house, everything is different every day. But for most men, it's not a new set of problems. It's the same task facing them every day. Whatever business, whatever the job is, it's the same job. Women's jobs—the job in the home at least—vary more and they are more flexible.

Which is fine. But what we're told and we see in the movies and on television is men acting in the opposite way: men are supposed to be adventurous. Men are supposed to want to go out and do new and different things. Find the headwaters of the Missouri River, or even, "Let's go here tonight, honey."

"No," she says. "I'd rather not."

In real life, it's the woman who wants to make a change and the man doesn't. It's the woman who wants the guy to retire and go someplace else to live, wants to take a different vacation this year, wants to go someplace we haven't been before. Wants to try a different restaurant, wants to go to a different club. No, the guy wants to go out and have the same steak that he had last Friday and the Friday before that. Baked potato, Thousand Island dressing. Men want everything to be the same all the time.

I always had this one image of myself, rightly or wrongly. Now I walk past the mirror, take a look and say, "That's not the right guy. I don't know that guy. Just keep going."

I know this is not healthy, but I know it is true. I don't believe that life is worth living unless there is the opportunity of getting interest from a woman or being able to find a woman that you care about.

There are men who believe that life really isn't worth living when there isn't a sense of pleasure in life anymore. We can't just be observers of life, pacifists in the whole action of life. When that time comes, an awful lot of us just feel, "What's the point?"

For me, the driving point of succeeding and earning a living and being able to live okay is that there will be a woman in my life sometime. I have this image of this woman that I've never met. She's multifaceted, so I've met a piece of her in one woman and a piece of her in another, but I've never met that whole woman. That woman is out there for me somewhere, so I'm going to keep looking. But if it gets to the point where I suddenly meet her and I'm not going to be able to convince her to come with me because I've lost it all, that's the most depressing thing in the world.

When you're in your thirties or even your forties, it's easy. You change careers, find a new lover, move to a different city. But as you get older that changes. You begin to realize you don't have the time to do everything you wanted to do. You begin to feel stuck with whatever you've gotten yourself into. The light at the end of the tunnel may be a nuclear meltdown, the heavenly host decked out in glory, or you, yourself, with a flashlight coming from the other direction.

I've had a couple of serious angina attacks, so I know what a heart attack feels like. At least, I thought I did. Then I talked to this guy who's had two serious heart attacks, and he never felt a thing. He broke out in a sweat, had an upset stomach. He said, "I don't feel well."

They took him to the hospital. The next thing he knows, they're clapping these big electric shock things on his chest.

Everywhere I go, I run into homeless people, all across the country. Many of them are winos or people who just got booted from various sanitariums. But there is also a large number of people out there who just got a real long run of bad luck.

There was this guy out West. I took his picture. He had been an accountant. Now he makes little wire toys at a country market. He overextended himself, lost his money, and then his wife left him. The kids cut him loose. He just couldn't stand it anymore. He had a nervous breakdown.

He's extremely well-read, better read than I am, because he reads all the time. He spends his days sitting and making these little wire toys. At night, he sleeps wherever he can find a place. He has no money. But you don't get the slurred speech and dull-witted conversation. What I got was real talk.

"How can you still be a clear-thinking person," I asked him, "and allow yourself to live like this?"

"I don't know how to do it any other way now," he said. "I don't know what to do. I can't get an apartment. I don't have the money. I can't do anything."

"How long do you expect this to last?"

"Until I kill myself."

Why couldn't that happen to me? The nervous breakdown would be the easy part.

Three: **Sex**

If women seem possessed by the chemistry of their reproductive systems, men are driven by their hormones, just as a nail is driven into a board. When I worked as an editor at *Hustler* magazine, I was not so impressed by the sexual content of the material we published as by the response from our audience. That was more truly indicative of male sexuality. Men see sex everywhere in a startling array of objects not normally associated with sex by women. At *Hustler* we received a remarkable number of fruits and vegetables marred by some protuberance or cleavage and accompanied by a letter that invariably read, "Boy, I'll bet you guys will like this. Doesn't this carrot (grape, apple, eggplant, Bell pepper) look just like a cock and balls (tits, vagina, buttocks, etc.)?" When the magazine began featuring readers' erotic photographs of their girlfriends and spouses, we were deluged with Polaroids.

Most touching were the sincere, if torrid, love letters written by readers to the models whose naked bodies filled the pages of the magazine. On rare occasions, a lovestruck man would appear in the reception area of the editorial offices, in Columbus, Ohio, to plaintively ask after the health and whereabouts of Tina from the April issue or Lola from October. Sometimes these guys would show up with flowers. They always begged the receptionist for a phone number or pressed a love note on her intended for their fantasy lovers. Confronted by someone who has fallen in lusty love with a printed piece of paper, one is forced to consider that there is some truth in the old expression that men will follow their dicks into a meat grinder.

For some men the surge of testosterone at puberty seems as natural as sap rising in a tree in the spring. As a 38-year-old publishing executive told me, "The whole thing with women is getting into their pants. I saw early on it wasn't romance. It was, Get into their pants.

"A lot of guys in high school were into sports and cars. I played sports and I liked cars, but I wasn't after the short-term reward these things had in and of themselves. I was motivated by the fact that if you played football, a lot of girls thought you were 'tuff.' Eventually, if you had a car, you could take these girls out where you do things to them. I just knew it felt *good*. Like a full belly feels good. So I sowed a lot of wild oats in my early years and had that out of my system by the time I got my wife pregnant. We were both 16."

This story was told with seriousness, but no small amount of irony at how it ended. Most men recall their early sexual lives as a combination of an almost total absence of reliable, realistic information about sex and of physical frustration. They grew up with the overblown fantasies of James Bond and *Playboy* centerfolds in a society that they thought resembled the colonial New England of Hester Prynne and her big scarlet "A."

When a young man has his first sex, it is as likely to be an embarrassing, unsettling, and unsatisfactory experience as it is to be pleasurable and fulfilling. It rarely meets exaggerated expectations.

A college professor, 40, who has been married for seventeen years talked about the fear and self-doubts of his early sexual life: "The big myth is that as a youth the man goes out and gets fucked as soon as possible, and it goes great. Then he begins a life of errant fucking. The truth is that sexual education as a boy is bad. No one tells you it might not work out, that there are things in your head and in your life that might make you afraid of sex to the extent where you're impotent, or that you might have a premature ejaculation, or that you just might be so frozen you can't do it well. *Nobody* tells you that.

"When I first began to have sex, and it didn't work out for me, I was in a panic. I thought there was something really wrong with me. Maybe I'm a homosexual. Maybe my life is headed for terrible disaster. And I had no one I felt I could talk to. You can't talk to other males about it. They're going to think you're a fag and that's going to make it more difficult. We are fixed on our genitals and so vulnerable in our sexual identities. Sex is confusing and scary to most of us."

The great majority of the men interviewed for this book reached puberty before the so-called sexual revolution. Their throbbing hormonal engines, more often than not, raced head-on into the brick wall of virginity and chastity imposed by a Puritanical society. A 45-year-old book dealer who has slept with hundreds of women and has pursued sex obsessively through much of his adult life expressed it this way, "I've always thought that if I was getting hand jobs even or had a girlfriend and was playing with her pussy when I was 14, that I wouldn't have been on such a sex rampage *for the rest of my life!* But you can't answer that 'What if?' I might even be dead today, if I'd gotten that early satisfaction. I might have managed to get myself killed by being even more into sex."

The conflict between so much sexual yearning and so little consummation for young men contributes to the heightened significance they put on "scoring." Considering the emphasis on male sexual performance in American culture, it's no wonder some men are launched on a lifelong pursuit of sexual conquest. Women are the prey and personal sexual gratification is the prize. Eventually, many of them complain about the emptiness of the carnal act and the loneliness of their lives. A 48-year-old crime novelist who was offhandedly unfaithful to his wife for the first twenty years of their marriage said, "I realized, 'Oh, yeah, there's plenty of fine women. But to fuck at your best takes forty-five minutes.' So now what happens? You spent all that money for dinner or whatever you had to do, now what do you got? You got a relationship? When you finish, you realize, 'Well, well, she wasn't anything spectacular.' Sex is great for what it is, but it's just fucking. And when it's over, it's over. For most of us, if you discount all the fooling around beforehand, it takes about five minutes. You're sitting there the morning after, and nothing is as revealing as that early morning light. It's like that with everything. You think something is better and it's not."

Men are convinced that women are not as interested in having sex as they are. Most men believe that men's and women's biological imperatives are, at the very least, at cross purposes. A building contractor, 40, presently back in college earning a master's degree in elementary education so that he can teach children with special needs, explains it this way, "The way for men to get their genes into the gene pool is to go out and fuck every woman they can get their hands on, immediately—next! The way for women to successfully pass on theirs is to find some guy to take care of them while they're having the baby. We haven't built our society around the nature of male sexuality. We've mistakenly decided to have this marriage thing, just because the Hebrews got a misprint on one of their tablets. God couldn't be that stupid to make men and women the way they are and then to say, 'And I want them to get married and stay married forever.' "

Men who are married and chaste have one thing in common: They all complain that they don't get enough sex. The real problem seems to be a simple one of communication. It boils down to a difference in the definition of intimacy between the sexes. Women look for intimacy in meaningful conversation and the exchange of problems, ideas, and feelings. "Sex is the traditional way of being intimate for men," explains a 36-year-old printing plant supervisor. "Hey, this conversation is pretty neat. I feel very comfortable. *Let's go to bed!* We'll talk some more later. I promise."

Even those men in stable, satisfying relationships with women complain of sexual ennui and of how they long for variety. They tend to explain this longing as a unique male physical need, altogether unknown to women and foreign to female natures. If they are rudely awakened from this self-delusion by a wife's affair or a girlfriend's infidelity, men are intensely jealous creatures. One of the greatest conflicts in men's sexual lives is their craving for freedom and promiscuity and their demand that women remain unfailingly faithful.

Men like animal imagery to describe their behavior, so they would like to see themselves in a perfect world as majestic stags defending their harems of gentle does against horned interlopers. In the reality of modern life, men are more like the chimpanzee in the zoo, stripped of his natural surroundings and troop of companions, masturbating through the bars. As a 40-year-old catering manager describes his drive to sexual expression in contrast to his perception of women's sexuality, "I can't imagine ever getting to the point where I don't masturbate. If I live to be 80, I may not masturbate as often, but I'll still do it every once in a while just to make sure it still works. Can you imagine ever not masturbating at least once in a while? Women would never sit around discussing whether or not they would be masturbating at 80. Most of them seem to be happy that it's not working anymore at a certain age."

A close friend of mine who knew I was working on this book sent me something he found on a New York subway train that he thought might be pertinent.

The Plain Facts

Scientists have determined that the average time of intercourse is four minutes. The average number of strokes per minute is nine, making the average intercourse consist of 36 strokes. Since the average length is six inches, the average girl receives 216 inches, or 18 feet per intercourse. The average girl does it about 3 times per week, 50 weeks out of the year, and 150 times 18 makes 2700 feet, or just a little over one-half mile. So girls, if you're not getting your one-half mile, why not let the man who gave this to you to read help you catch up?

Sexually yours,

And there follows the name John, his telephone number, and a post office box address in Brooklyn. It's an old joke, and it was obvious from the photocopy that it had been lifted from a magazine or a risqué postcard bought for a buck in a novelty shop. When I asked my friend what was so extraordinary about this version, he replied, "You don't understand. This was just one of fifty or a hundred copies littered all through this one subway car. Who knows how many there were all through the train, or how many trains this guy rides every night spreading the word? Is he a mathematical genius using his home computer to figure the odds on getting laid from this, or just another desperate slob resorting to a personal media blitz? I mean, that's driven."

But don't laugh too long at John. There's a little bit of him in all men.

My buddy from downstairs, Ricky, and I were 9 or 10, and we'd taken a whiz in the park. These two girls walked past and said, "Whoa, I saw you! I saw you!"

"What'd you see? What'd you see?" We're dying to find out what they saw. If anything, we wanted them to see.

That's the thing, "Yeah, look at mine, look at mine. Let me see yours." Because we don't know what it looks like. Although Ricky had already like glimpsed his little sister's. But because Ricky was Catholic, this was a big ominous thing. You couldn't just take a peek at it to see what it looked like. He would only get glimpses of it. And he wouldn't tell you what it looked like, because it was his sister, and it was against the rules.

But, I mean, fuck, if he was a buddy, he could have told me at least was it in the front, was it in the back, was it directly under, to the side? Because my mother had already given me this story about how babies come from women's . . . well, she said "bottom" actually, which I equated with the idea that they kind of like shit them out, basically. The only thing I knew for sure was that they didn't have a penis, or whatever it was that I called mine at the time. Maybe I called it my dick. I probably called it my pee-pee.

So I got this bogus stuff from Ma. Rick wasn't telling me anything. So here we are in the park, and we found out the name of one of these little girls is Linda, and she's going to show us hers, if we show her ours. Linda's friend is already *on her way home.* She's not getting in on this. The other guys who are with us are like, "No-no-no-no-no. I think we're leaving, too."

"Okay," Ricky says, "let's take a walk with Linda into the woods." So we take a walk with Linda into the woods—for a long time I used to remember her last name, too, but I can't anymore. Linda is this 9- or 10-year-old girl who apparently is pretty experienced here. She's telling us how she's done it before with her friend, this kid who lives in her house.

Okay. Ricky is like hip, because Ricky's already had these real lessons about sex from our friend Julius, a teenaged kid upstairs in the building. So like Ricky knows what's supposed to happen. He is asking the questions here. "So, which one of us do you want to do it to you?"

Linda picks me. I'm thinking, "Don't you have to do other things first, like live to be 21?" Plus I had no idea where the fucking thing was. I did not know where it was, and I wasn't about to go fumbling around. Okay?

She takes down her pants—I think she wore pedal pushers—and I'm looking for it. I don't see a thing. When I looked down at her, there was nothing there, but like stomach that kind of went on forever. I'm thinking, "My mom told me it was at the bottom some place, or at the back, so that must be where it be."

I have a conference with Ricky and he says, "Okay, I'll do it first." Goes back to Linda and says, "I have to do it first." I don't know what kind of excuse we made up for me, but I was standing there, and I was going to watch.

I'm making sure nobody's coming. She lays down, Ricky gets on top of her. Before he does, I'm looking there and I see this little, teeny little crack down there. I'm saying, "Wow! That can't be it." So Ricky is on top, and I guess he gets it inside there. I don't know, because I'm not that close. I'm just kind of standing there peeking over. He's moving around there. Then they get up and we move to a different location. Ricky gets on top again, and he's moving around there, and she lets him do it again. The question, which is really great, that Ricky asks her is, "How long is it before you let somebody kiss you?"

"Usually, I have to know them for a while first."

Nobody knew what the fuck we were doing. We were kids. Poking around in there? For what? Ricky was almost 11. He was worried, because at 12 you could ejaculate, right? If he did that, he could make her pregnant, and that would really be like a mortal, mortal sin. He'd have to live in hellfire forever. So he got really worried about that, which was why, after he confessed it the following week, he was almost ready for sainthood, man. The next time I saw Ricky, he was in his Boy Scout uniform and going to meetings. The priest had given him the talk, and he was a changed man after that.

I didn't do anything. I was too fucking afraid. My thing was you had to kiss first, you had to grope around a little bit first, you didn't just like do it. Plus I was extremely embarrassed. I'm not even sure if I showed her mine. I probably did, but I don't remember, so maybe I just never did. I was following Ricky around trying to collect some data. "Okay, now I can find out exactly what's going on here." But I could never seem to gather *enough* information to make sure I could do okay on my own, or that it would be okay.

I had no idea what it felt like. At 10 or 11, maybe I had masturbated myself into black-out condition in my bathroom. My father beating on the door, "What are you doing in there, Martin! What are you doing in there?"

"Noth—ing. Uhn-na-uhn-na-uhn-na!" Meanwhile, I'm flogging my poor wanger to death—what a life!—and waiting for something to come out. Because that was the magic stuff, that stuff that came out. *Something* is supposed to come out.

"What is it?"

"I don't know."

Oh, God. I think I worked on that for a while before I got it to come out. "Hey, I can do that!" I felt a lot more confident. If I met Linda like a year later, I might have taken her up on the whole experience. But that's like the story of men's lives with women: "If only I'd met her a year later." I was choking the chicken for all it was worth there, man. I was really trying to get that out of there. But, no, I never scored with Linda.

We walked out of the park, and my mom sees us coming up the street. She's already looking for us, calling us for like an hour. Not that we were late. It was like five o'clock in the afternoon, and we were supposed to be in at 4:30. But she sees us leave the park with a girl. The girl goes one way, we go the other way. In my mind it's like, "What could possibly go wrong? How could we possibly even be suspected of wrongdoing?" But my mother knew we were up to no good. It must be on your face when you're a kid if you're really doing something wrong, because she was just so inquisitive about what were you doing and who was the girl.

We never saw Linda again. Looked for her. I looked for her everywhere, because I was dead set on doing it next time I saw her. If I had that opportunity again, I would never pass it up. I cursed myself for years after for not doing it, because then it would have been just *over.* It would have been great. I would have had so much up on everybody, had I done that. And she was cute. She was a cute little gal. I often wonder what happened to her.

Guys would fight if you told them the facts of life. "No, my parents didn't do that. They ate special food. That's how they got pregnant."

"No way. They fucked."

"You say my mother did what?" You took your life in your hands in my neighborhood talking about where babies came from.

Me and Harry had gotten all our information from this teenage guy, Richard, who was 16. He lived upstairs. Richard would tell Harry and me everything. Richard had a sister who was our age. So it was always like, "Here's what a blow job is. Here's what straight fucking is. But if I ever catch you with my sister, I'll fucking kill you. If you *ever* do this to my sister, I'll fucking *kill you.*"

Me, I kind of liked his sister, but I'd never even go near her, because God forbid Richard even *thought* I was doing anything with his sister. Forget about it. He'd fucking kill me.

So I'm finding out all this stuff from Richard, but I still don't get it. I'm just sort of along for the ride, because he talks mostly to Harry who was a couple of years older than me. Every time they talk, they'll talk a certain amount of time in front of me, then all of a sudden they'll stop talking to me.

One day I'm looking for Harry. The house has a basement, coal bins, everybody would throw all the extra shit that wouldn't fit into their apartment down there in a little area. I open a door down there and here's Harry with this monster dick in his mouth. He's giving Richard a blow job.

Let me tell you something, it was one of the scariest experiences in my life. In retrospect, hey, mine's an okay size, but in those days, when you're a 10-year-old and you see one of those things in another kid's mouth, it's like *whoa!* Forget about it, man. It was huge and there was Harry, "Shut the door! Shut the door!"

He's having a great time. It seems, in exchange for all Richard's knowledge, Harry's been practicing on him. After that, baby, there was this whole invisible thing. Nobody's talking about this, because everybody knew everybody. It wasn't strange people or strangers, it was Richard's family and Harry's family—we lived in the same building. It wasn't the place to be doing that kind of stuff, and nobody wanted to get caught by anybody else there.

No, no, no. This was too far out for me. So I swore I would never tell. And that was it, you know. It was hidden, man. I never told a soul.

I never even realized I was being sexually abused, or the kind of danger the whole neighborhood was in, until a few years ago when I remembered the guy and said to myself, "Oh, yeah. So that's what was going on."

I was in fifth grade. About a half mile down from our house there was this strip mall with a barbershop in it. In the summer, all the mothers would send us down there on our bikes to get our burr haircuts. A burr haircut on an 11-year-old should take about three minutes. You'd be in this guy's chair for an hour. He never talked to me, never exposed himself. But he would take your hands and move them to the outside of the arm rests, so that while he was cutting your hair he could rub his crotch up against the outside of your hand.

Jesus, it was creepy. You'd move your hands away and clasp them together in between your knobby little knees. He'd pull them back up there and position them again where he wanted them. I didn't really know what was going on. I just knew something was wrong, because it made the gorge rise in my throat.

But I was still at that age where you don't question adults' actions. I never told anybody. I didn't know what to tell. I just avoided haircuts like the plague. Looking back, I'm lucky it didn't get worse.

I was traumatized going to junior high school, because I was going to have to wear a jock strap in gym. If I didn't need one before, why did I suddenly need one in junior high school? If I didn't need one, what was wrong with me? Were my genitals *that* small, that I don't need a jock? Was that it?

I was 14 or 15, and I was standing on the corner with my friends. This older guy comes by. He says, "Okay, everybody line up." We all lined up. Some people knew what he was going to do, but this was my first experience, so I didn't know. He came around and put his middle finger under everybody's nose and he said, "Okay, everybody take a whiff."

"What's that? What's that?"

"That's Mary Louise So-and-so."

I thought, "Jeez, I know her."

"That's what she smells like. *That's* pussy. That's what it's all about, guys."

After he left, that's all anybody could talk about. "I'd never wash my hand for a week." And all this other stuff.

So your introduction to sex was this really boorish, tough sort of thing. But at the same time there were expectations: What is it you're going to do? When is it going to happen to you? When are you really going to be able to do that?

I didn't know any girls that smelled. I can remember touching a few, but they never had any smell. This one girl smelled very strong. In fact, a few guys said, "He probably just stuck that finger up his ass while he was dreaming her up."

I can remember being 13, making out with this girl and feeling her shoulder, and people thinking that I was feeling her breast and telling me, "Oh, wow! Oh, wow!" To this day, I could swear that I didn't have my hand on her breast. I was just like kissing her and running my hand in circles over her shoulder. My sex life was much more imagined by people than it actually was. People imagined me to have a great sex life. And still do to this day.

A hole did appear between the boys' locker room and the girls' locker room. It was a secret. Me and about six other guys knew about it. It was behind the equipment room. We'd go in and get to look.

But more than looking was listening. I was shocked to find out how blue women can be. They would talk about guys in a much more vulgar way than even guys talk about women. About guys, about their buns, about their dicks, their skinny ones and their fat ones. Was it a long one or a short one? Talking in very graphic terms. I looked at women differently after that. I'd walk down the street and see some woman walking along, looking as though sex were the furthest thing from her mind, and I'd think to myself, "Oh, no. I know what you're thinking about."

You get a hard-on in class and you think about Sister Mary Concepta so your cock would go down, so you wouldn't have to walk down the school hallway like that. You got a triphammer libido when you're that age. Cindy Quince, for instance, flashes her legs, and she would give you a hard-on that would last for forty minutes. You'd have to think of the ugliest, meanest nun, and what she might look like naked. That's the kind of horny I'm talking about. All guys are like that. You're not getting laid. You're too shy, and too afraid of girls anyway.

I liked reading a lot. Anything that was banned or had to do with dirty books I liked, too. There was this store that would sell you tits and ass magazines. It was normal to jerk off to dirty magazines. You couldn't get near the real thing, but at least it was energy expressed toward the target sex.

Then the next step, you go into New York on the bus. The kid I did this with came from a very well-to-do family, and he was a juvenile delinquent. At fourteen and fifteen, he and I would go into Times Square to buy rock 'n' roll records from Slim's Subway Record Store and switchblade knives from whoever would sell them to us. Then we'd have to steal nudist magazines. They wouldn't sell them to us, because they knew we were under age. We knew they wouldn't sell them, so we just stole them.

When we got home with this literature, we never sold it. We'd just keep it, until our mothers found it, or we lent it to someone and never got it back. So I always had that prurient interest in girls that was only satisfied by this stuff.

Henry Miller had a big effect on me when I was in eleventh grade. I bought *Tropic of Cancer* when it came out for the prurient stuff. It wasn't all that prurient, but his message was one of hope to guilt-ridden Catholics. Catholics are just a ball of guilt. You're into all this sexual stuff, but you feel terribly guilty about it, because they tell you that you have to be. You're sort of devout, so you're taking their shit for the real thing. Henry Miller was saying, "So fuck the Catholic Church, and fuck what people think. Just go out and do what you really feel like doing, what you have to do."

He wasn't that good a writer—a terrible chatterbox—but he had this message of hope, of free-spiritedness, for lack of a better expression. "Here's how you should look at life: I don't have a penny, I'm the poorest guy alive. I chase pussy all day. I revel in the ideas of the great writers of all time. I'm a complete bum and failure in the eyes of society, but look at how happy I am." These were great ideas to me in eleventh and twelfth grades, and they cured me of Catholicism.

I remember going to New York and sitting with a hard-on watching the movie, *Isle of Levant*, in the World Theater on 49th Street. It was a nudist camp movie. There was a court decision that they would let this stuff run only if it was socially redeeming nudist camp stuff.

It was the corniest thing. It was two French girls dubbed in English. One is a nudist, and she's going to take the friend to a nudist outfit. This was the generic, all-purpose plot for all the nudist films. It was always an attractive female who was being introduced to nudism, not some four-hundred-pound guy with a thyroid problem. Totally propagandistic.

The Isle of Levant wasn't that bad. At least it was made in Europe so there was less impetus or pressure to justify the film's existence to the censors.

What happened is that you had to follow these girls to the Riviera and all these Mediterranean vacation spots, watching them in bikinis, waiting for them to get to the Isle of Levant, where they will walk around with just a G-string on. You sat through the movie on tenterhooks, and maybe the last half hour of the film, they finally got there and the other one got talked into going topless. And you got to see these girls bouncing around with their tits and their asses in the inevitable volleyball game, shot from behind at an angle where you couldn't see the pubes on the other side of the net. Or people batting beach balls back and forth. Or people parading around with towels held in front of their genitals to greet each other. Or sitting coyly so the genitals were hidden. Maybe once a film the camera would stray, and you'd get just the slightest glimpse of pubic hair.

It certainly made me want to go and check out what was going on in a nudist camp. It certainly looked better to me than joining the local golf club. It's got to be easier to get laid if you start out meeting a gal who had her clothes off. That was one level that you'd already passed through. This was adventure.

By this time, I'm a high school graduate, working for the Ford plant, going to college at night. I bought a Sunbeam Alpine. I had no other ambition.

I saw this ad for a nudist camp, Sunset in the Pines, and I called up. I was supposed to go with this friend of mine, another hornstick who hadn't gotten laid all through high school either or not enough certainly. We were going to start a new sophisticated life.

Drove out there in my brand-new car. I was grilled by the owner's wife about why I was interested in nudism. "Well, it's a healthy, outdoor way of life." I tried to remember all the lines that they spouted in the movies I'd seen in Times Square touting the nudist lifestyle. I'm sweating under this grilling.

"You're probably curious, too," she says, "about nudism."

"Yeah, yeah, yeah,"

Came to find out later she and her husband were a real profligate pair of swingers. We came to hate them. But the place was a wonderland of ideas. Half the people were New Yorkers. I had no exposure to sophisticated people. Most of them weren't swingers or sex fiends. They were horny young people like myself, but college educated, intelligent, bright, crazy people. There was also this older coterie, like the Lutheran minister who came up with his wife on a motorcycle.

At night, there really wasn't much hanky-panky there. The place was physically beautiful, just a canopy of stars. You go from cabin to cabin and drink wine and smoke pot. Or you'd hang out and sing folk songs while people played guitars. The usual corny shit, but it was sort of a college thing that I never had. Plus everyone had a girl. Everyone was getting laid. This was a whole new world.

I found Karen Porter. Now Karen Porter was half Jewish and half Baptist. Her mother was this big, roly-poly Jewish liberal from Brooklyn and her father was a chiropractor from Alabama. Karen was 19, she had a perfect body, she was only once removed from being a virgin, and her parents brought her to a nudist camp. She had the firmest tits. You could have held up the Acropolis with those tits, and she was blond, about five-six.

She had all the young studs in there chasing her around the place, but she chose me, because I had a nice car and I was reading Ralph Ellison's *Invisible Man.*

All week, I'd look forward to going there and spend the weekend sleeping in a dormitory with twenty other guys, wheezing and coughing and farting, and seeing Karen Porter and being introduced to all these new ideas, these adult ideas. This was what was hip and what was liberal and what was in. My adult life began with going up to Sunset in the Pines in the summer of '65. The die was cast and the whole thing was on wheels. I was this hip, cool guy now, a New York sophisticate, who just happened to live in New Jersey and work at the Ford factory.

I know it's hard to believe, but I didn't know shit about sex until after I got to college. I'd had wet dreams which just seemed mysterious and made me feel guilty. I'd do my best to hide the evidence. I hadn't masturbated. My father had never given me "the talk." My mother had given me a book to read at one time, but it was like by Ann Landers, skirted all the nitty-gritty and just confused me more. I was almost 18 years old and had no real idea where babies came from. I had no knowledge of what went on below the waist between men and women. The closest I'd come to erotica was the descriptions of Polynesian women with naked breasts in a Reader's Digest abridged edition of *Mutiny on the Bounty,* which somehow had been allowed in the house. We're talking ignorant and dumb, here.

I got to my freshman year in college and the first few weeks was fraternity rush. Only one fraternity was mildly interested in me and not very much, but I got invited to the dinner for candidates at the end of the week. It was going fine, the basic rubber chicken fare, when suddenly they started making a big to-do. Shouting, shoving the tables and chairs back in this show of chaos, setting up a movie projector and screen. They turned out the lights and started showing 8mm porno loops, the old black-and-white stuff where the guys keep their socks on. This was supposed to be a wondrous treat for the new boys.

It was too much for me. I watched for a few minutes, kind of shocked and stunned, and then I couldn't hold back the tears. I didn't know what to do. I pushed my way out of there, trying to hide my sobs, and ran back to the dormitory.

I always thought that women didn't want sex as much as men or boys, since I, myself, was afraid of sex. Women knew more about sex than I did, I'm sure of it. They were clear about what they wanted and didn't want. They talked more about it with somebody. Men don't really talk about it, particularly adolescents. But you've got to pretend that you know all about it. I didn't know anything. It just seemed frightening.

Now, I look back and say, "Oh, that's why we were out in the woods. Yes, it was her idea, wasn't it?" But I didn't do anything.

I was in college, and I didn't have enough money to go home over spring break. My roommate was a rich kid from New York. He said, "Since you're not going home, I'm going to stay with you." What we did was draw a circle on the map of how far we could go in a weekend, and we threw darts. Wherever the dart landed was where we were going to go. He had a new car and we drove out in this '58 Chevy. We stayed in a hotel in this little town and we were going sightseeing.

We asked the hotel clerk in our cool way, "Are there any whorehouses around here?"

"Sure, there's a whorehouse," and he gave us the address. "But you can't just drive out there. You got to go by cab." He had some deal worked out with the cabdriver outside. He drives you there. Then he sits outside and waits for you and charges you while you're in there.

My roommate said, "Don't worry about it. I'll pay for everything. Don't worry about how much this costs."

I went in and there was this girl, about my age, gorgeous. Blond, blue-eyed, round and beautiful. The madam says to me, "You can have straight, half and half, around the world, all sorts of stuff."

"What's around the world?"

"You'll see. You want around the world?"

"I want around the world." She takes me and this beautiful girl to a room, opens the door and tells her, "Around the world."

"Good," the girl says. She was sitting there in this little nightie. "Okay, get undressed."

"Do we have to keep all these lights on?" I asked her and I turned one off.

"You can't do that," she turns the light back on. "She doesn't want us to put all the lights out."

I get undressed and I'm laying there. She starts kissing my feet. I said, "What's going on here?"

"Don't you know what around the world is? I'm going to do this all over you."

Well, I started giggling. I put my hands over my mouth. Then I put the pillow over my face. I couldn't stop laughing. It was ticklish in the most weirdest way I ever felt. She's kissing my legs now. Then she starts laughing. The next thing we know, we're wrestling like we're adolescents. I go running around the room, and I'm wrestling with her all over the place. She was just like rough-housing with me.

Finally, I like pinned her, and she said, "You know, you've only got about five minutes left. If you're going to do something, you'd better do it."

"I don't know," I said. "What can I do?"

"Don't worry about it," she says. "Just lie still."

That was my first real blow job. I put the pillow over my face again and let out this incredible scream, "Whoa! What is that?!?"

She loved it. She got up, she had tears in her eyes from laughing so hard. She said, "You come back any time you like."

I explored this life with such a vehemence that I wouldn't allow for any sort of wavering or woman who might come into my life, because I really felt this was what I wanted. Contrary to myth, you're a young boy going out, you're going to be raped or attacked by every male— wrong. Nobody looked at me.

On a Saturday night alone, I didn't know how to go about

being gay. I sort of knew where to go. There's a sleazy bar I knew of that basically catered to a low-life element and transvestites. So I just walked in and walked out. I don't know what gave me the idea, but I thought if I just sat on a car in the neighborhood, I might get picked up or meet somebody. I said, "That's what I'm going to do."

I really wasn't looked at very much. I was gawky. I was older than my face, but then, actually my face was already old. I was riddled with problems and sadness. I wasn't fresh. I was like "the serious poet." Finally, this guy came up to me and he said, "It's you."

"What are you talking about?"

"You're trying to steal my lover."

"I don't know what you're talking about."

"I know it was you!" He had a knife, and the knife was right in my stomach. Here I was sitting on a car, trying to meet somebody, and there's this knife. This wasn't what I had in mind, this raving maniac who was convinced that I stole his lover. He would not for the life of him—or me— believe me. He prodded me with the knife and said, "Start walking."

He was going to take me up into an apartment building. I knew if I went up there, I could forget it. I'm pretty feisty and a fairly good runner. I just dodged across traffic. Cars were coming, but I didn't give a shit. I just ran in front of them. He ran after me. I ran down in the subway. He ran down in the subway, "You mother fucker, you stole my lover!" I got in that train bound for home, and I didn't want to see that place again.

You have this fantasy that you meet beautiful, young men, and they all want to be with you, but it's not that way. Life doesn't work out that way.

In 1965 one night, I was being cruised by this guy. I looked back, but I sort of looked like yes and no. Finally, we talked. He was good-looking. I made an appointment with him for two nights later.

We went up to his apartment and it was purely sex. I was frozen. I couldn't do anything, He jerked me off. It had to take thirty minutes. I was sweating bullets, until I finally came. It was hard work, and it was not very pleasurable. I didn't know what the hell was going on. I thought, "Gee, I don't like this at all." I didn't take to it like a duck to water.

"Maybe I'm wrong," I thought. "Maybe I'm not gay." I didn't do anything for a year. I just went back into the closet. It wasn't women, and it wasn't men. I didn't know what it was. It was that I just had a hard time giving or accepting love of any sort. I was not carefree and happy. I was still traumatized by my life so far.

Then I decided that I was going to go full force at it, and I did. It was hard work to release myself sexually. It was not easy. I did not go to a bar and get picked up just because I was 20 years old. I did not go home with a lot of Romeos.

I would do anything, and I would receive anything, just for pleasure, and just to try to give someone else pleasure. I wonder how often that's a common theme in all of us, that we try so much. I was feeling so inadequate it was my decision to make sure that the other person would benefit from this experience.

But along the way I began to learn what I did like and what I didn't like. I began to be less hard on myself if, for example, I couldn't get an erection, which happens. Particularly with gay sex, the whole fabric and character of it is anonymous. You don't court. I can see somebody and say, "Hey, I like you." We can get into bed and I might not know what to do, because it's often not based on anything but a first impression.

Gay men have a tough time, because there is no set formula. You know certain things you are going to do in bed with a woman by nature of biology. You have a certain role. You don't always have to play it that way, there are other things. But with gay men, you don't know who's the dominant, who's not. Who's going to fuck who? Some men don't like to fuck at all. Some men are not into it or can't do it. These are the issues that present the problems to me. How do you know what to do? Every man is different, and you are different with every man. There are no pre-scribed rules about what you should do. You may want to fuck someone, and you may be the one who gets fucked. This was what I was learning.

In one way, it was far nicer before Stonewall and Gay Liberation than it was afterwards, because there was a lot more romanticism. You'd get out on the dance floor and start dancing to Dionne Warwick and really start to com-municate on that dance floor. This was when there was no such thing as the Mine Shaft and fist fucking and that really anonymous, impersonal sex carried to an extreme. It was a cult that you were in, a sort of secret club.

This friend and I would always go out and flirt with women. He was so good-looking that women would just be dying to get into his pants, but he would almost never do anything about it. He was always one woman at a time. He'd go out and flirt like crazy, and just drive them nuts, but he wouldn't follow through. Which would drive me nuts, because quite often we'd be after the same woman. She'd be interested in him. I would know with my whole being that he wasn't going to do anything about it. But he would screw it up for me, because at the end of the night, she's not going to say, "Oh, shoot, he won't go home with me. Well, how about you?" It never happens that way. Pissed me off. We had a couple of blow-outs about that.

"Listen," I said, "if you can tell I'm kind of hot after a woman, and you know you don't want to do anything at the end of a night, then stay out of my face. Don't pay attention to her. Don't come on to her, like you always do. Find someone else. There's millions of them out there who want you."

The whole ego thing is the crucial factor in getting women. More important than looks or anything else is how you feel about yourself. It's a reason why, when you're involved with somebody, it seems like there's more women interested in you than when you're not. You're not out there looking. You feel good about yourself, and it's easier for you to put out the vibes. If you're in a relationship, they're all over the place. Once you end that relationship, there's not a woman to be found. You have to go out and beat them over the head with a bat.

You go three or four weeks—or a couple of months— without getting laid, and the frustration builds up. That's a killer. The longer it's been, the lower the self-esteem, the more frustrated you get, and the crazier you become. It's a real cyclical thing. The crazier you become, the less attractive you get.

My friend Jeff is a prime example. Jeff goes months without getting laid. So he walks up to a woman, and the first thing he says to her is, "You want a jump?" One in fifty women may really be turned on by that, and say, "Yeah!" But the other forty-nine are going to say, "Fuck you, asshole." Whereas, if you're not to that extreme point, you can be a little bit cooler or more suave. Then you're going to have a much better chance.

I honestly believe that women like sex. They maintain that they like it *as much as* men. Maybe they do, and maybe they don't. I don't believe that. They handle it so differently that it's hard to believe them. Honestly, there are so many women I see that I'd like to have sex with, kind of just for the aesthetics. When I was growing up, definitely scoring was big, the conquest was the big deal. I don't feel that way anymore. I'm way beyond keeping score at this point. There's just so many women that I see that I'd like to explore. It's just so great to explore a new woman. Not just attractive women. All different types of women, sometimes it's a very perverse attraction.

I don't know if women are into exploring men. For quite a few women, it has to be deeper—there has to be something going on, like a prospective relationship. They'll have periods when they will just go out and fuck somebody. They'll be horny, they'll see a hot-looking guy in a bar, and they'll nail him, take him home for a night or two. Then that's it. Men are like that quite a bit of the time—like always. Women are like that just sporadically—like maybe once in each lifetime. So if you're lucky to be out in the right bar and you get that woman when it's happening, when the lightning strikes, it's great. Never happened to me.

It would be interesting to be an object of sexual desire like women are. Women are imprisoned by that. They don't like it. But I'm never admired. Nobody ever says, "Wow, look at his body! Boy, he's cute. I'd like to get my hands on him. Yoo-hoo, pal, buddy, want to go on a date with me?" No one of the opposite sex has ever said this to me, and I think it would be interesting to try it. It would be interesting to be desired in the way women are desired by men. Even when women do desire men that way, they don't let them know, so guys are always coming to women for sex and hoping it works out.

Laying in bed, you put your hand on your wife's back, and she doesn't move.

"Oh, well," you say to yourself, "that's good."

Then down. She still doesn't move.

"Hey, maybe this is going to work out."

The woman is in the position of, "He wants me. It feels good that he wants me. Desired . . . ahhh."

All of a sudden, all the things we'd been doing all along were sexist and bad. The fact that every time you look at a woman you're undressing her with your eyes— that's chauvinistic and bad. It's damn natural to me. With any decent looking woman, lots of times my first thought is, "Jeez, I wonder what she looks like naked?" My next thought is, "I wonder what she's like in bed?"

I get a lot of enjoyment out of looking at them and fantasizing about them. I don't feel like I'm really degrading them. Maybe a little. They could do the same thing to me if they wanted to, and it wouldn't bug me. "Hey, give me some of that. Here, make me a sex object! Let me be one!"

I was promiscuous as possible and was developing a different attitude toward women. I started out from a real clean place and just wound up wanting to fuck as many girls as possible. Me and Joe Wright, in our blue blazer days, we'd drink up twenty dollars in fifty-cent tankards of beer over weekends, looking for new girls to fuck, new ones. More than one or two weekends. He liked being with me because he was better looking than me, so he figured he'd be chosen first. I figured I could get strays from him, too. And I liked him anyway. I was in love with the guy. He was clever and smart, beguiling and evil Irish charming. We were pals for a number of years, sort of grew into the counter-culture weirdness together, and we were sex fiends.

There's a sort of woman-hating thing in there, from a pop psychologist point of view. A promiscuous man is probably someone who resents women. That's what is at the bottom of promiscuity. We used to hear back then that the guy who never finds the right girl, and goes from girl to girl to girl, is really looking for a boy, but that's bullshit. I mean, you go and find a boy and stay with boys, if that's what you're meant to do. Men follow their dicks. I'm not saying that it doesn't happen. Some men are just too guilt-ridden to admit to themselves that they're homosexuals, so they don't even allow it to surface. Those are the guys who are married with two kids and turn into flaming faggots when they're 45.

But the majority of guys who are promiscuous have a deep resentment towards women. Why? Because, as Norman Mailer said, we are the prisoners of sex. We are self-imposed prisoners. They don't put you into this prison. Joe and I used to say, "Think of all the money, time and poetry we blow just to fuck chicks. It really is a shame. It's shame on us and shame on them. More shame on them. Fuck them! Let's just get our way."

It never was really an ugly thing, because we never fully verbalized it. But there was always this superiority, there was always this trying to score, to win over them, to conquer them. Wright used to say, "I don't feel like I defeat a woman, that I've beaten a woman, because I get to fuck her. I don't feel that way." But he did feel that way. Whenever he got into his dogmatic thing, he was rationalizing for himself behind that. And I suppose I felt that same way, too. That it was a war between the sexes, and the point of the war was to get into their bodies and as many of them as possible.

This isn't an attitude toward women that is conducive to get one to settle down. I'd go with a girl for six months to a year, two years sometimes in between, but it was mostly just serial girls, one after another, as many as you could get.

I don't know how to explain it. I was just pissing away time, never working to build anything. Reasonably happy, more than reasonably happy, being this way. I thought I was real cool. I was a fucking pain in the ass.

When you're young and you're real self-centered, you can get away with murder with women. I didn't eat too much pussy. Just kind of using them. Being charming to them in their ignorance, dumb ignorance. They're really better natured than they are submissive or masochistic, so really I was not being too nice of a guy. Not being really mean and ugly, but not being fair, not really being a man. This isn't the way I look back at it. This is the way it was. I really wasn't a man towards them at all, but getting what I wanted—getting laid fairly easily and reveling in the ability to do that.

I wish there was a rutting season. Although it might make life less exciting, it would make life much easier. I am distracted by women all the time, on a moment-to-moment basis—women on the street, women sitting in a window, driving by in a car. I'm very attracted to women. I'm very attracted by what they look like, constantly. This is a burden. I could think better and concentrate better if there was a mating season, instead of this biological signal all the time to spread your seed.

It seems to me it would be less distracting to have all your sex in May and June. Then you could have the baby in the winter or the spring. Men would be less tormented, and so would women, if they weren't constantly being distracted by sex. The world would probably work better. People would kill each other less. There'd be less physical abuse, if we all knew that in May and June we were all going to fuck each other—a lot. Then we were going to go back to work or back to wine or back to whatever it is we do. And then the babies would be born.

I haven't had sex with anybody but my wife since 1978, and I would like to. I don't want another marriage. I don't even want a relationship. I want sex.

Our society is set up to discourage that sort of thing, to tell you that's selfish, male piggish and in many ways just simply an inappropriate thought. I would say it is a perfectly natural thought, and there's nothing wrong with it. Going through with it, actually having sex with somebody else, is something that I haven't done, and I don't know if I will. Right now, it's certainly not likely, because for the sheer pleasure of it, I would be betraying a trust that's implicit and explicit. I would feel just waves of guilt. I don't know how I would handle that sort of guilt without confessing it, and then the whole thing gets blown all to pieces. I don't want to feel guilty about that, because the pleasure would be transitory, but the need is real.

If you express these feelings, you are considered by women to be the largest pig raised outside of the Midwest. Of course, many men who feel this way are enormous pigs, gross and disgusting persons, and the most amoral, selfish guys you've ever seen. But in this particular area, I feel the same way they do.

I do look at beautiful women and imagine what it's like to fuck them. I don't imagine what it's like to have tender love scenes with them. I'm not lacking in tender emotions. This need for variety is not so much an emotional need, as far as I can tell.

My wife will, on occasion, notice me staring at a woman. I will notice her noticing, but we never say a word about it. What is there to say? When you come down to it, you're not going to have a rational discussion on the advisability of my running after this woman and waving a hotel key in her face. So, why discuss the fact that this woman is younger than my wife is, and in better physical shape, and maybe dressed better or is prettier? That's just pointless. But I think about it.

There's nothing wrong with rolling around in your mind, but society will tell you there is something wrong with your marriage if you want to sleep with other women. That's just not true. I have a good marriage and I'm really lucky to have Kathy.

There is another fact that is a major consideration in this whole equation: these women don't want to sleep with me, as far as I can tell. Nobody said they would. I haven't been propositioned for years.

My wife even gets mad when I beat off. I get a lot of enjoyment out of masturbation. It's very easy. I certainly don't do it nearly as much as I used to, but I still do it, maybe a couple of times a week. There are just certain circumstances where I'm completely in the mood. Maybe I've been out to the beach, seeing a lot of hot women, and Angie is working. I come home and I just beat off, because I really feel like I need to beat off. Or maybe if she's working at night and I get tired, I'll beat off before going to bed, because it's just easier to go to bed that way. There may be any number of reasons. But she gets upset with me whenever she finds evidence that I've beat off. It makes it a little weird. Sometimes it's almost like she's looking for the evidence.

Masturbation is a lot easier than sex, for one thing. All your fantasies are jumping on you. It doesn't take twenty-five minutes to please your right hand. *My* right hand doesn't take twenty-five minutes. Hey, he's easy.

My wife and I are trying to figure out our sex life at this point. It got bad for a few years. When you have kids, you're just so tired all the time. "How come we're not having sex?"

"Do you feel sexy?"

"Nooooo." Falling asleep at nine o'clock in front of the TV set is a real turn-on.

A few years ago, there was a period when our sex life was just dead. We couldn't understand people who would have another kid right after they'd just had one, because that meant they got to have sex right away. It's hard to do that.

I went through this time where every weekend, starting on Friday afternoon, I would get real anxious about, "Are we going to do it this weekend?" By that time, having sex during the week was out of the question. Both of you come home from work. You get dinner, play with the kid and put up with her, feed her and put her to bed. Then you sit down on the couch, and zonk out. But on weekends we were still somewhat getting it together to have some kind of sex life.

On Friday afternoon I'd get this real anxious feeling and be tense all weekend about trying to get laid, and my wife, too. We were both getting real tense about whether we were going to have sex this weekend, or for that matter, have anything at all to do with each other this weekend. It's like the anxiety you feel on Sunday night when you have to go back to work on Monday.

That ruined it for the weekends, too. That's about the time we got into therapy and started working on it.

Sex is a real obvious indicator. It's not the most important part of the marriage, and certainly not the part that occupies a great deal of time, at least in our marriage, but it's such an obvious indicator of the state of the union, how intimate you are. We could both sense that we just weren't having sex anymore, and there's got to be a reason for the fact that there is no intimacy of any kind. In a lot of ways, there was no desire. We both wished we had a sex life again. I had more desire to do it once in a while and Becky didn't. That was how we identified the problem: she doesn't want to have sex. But I think we both knew that wasn't what the problem was.

Now, as we talk more, there's more real intimacy. We're having sex again. We're trying. Still, during the week, we're real tired in the evenings, but we don't turn on the TV as much as we were for a while. Sometimes just making the conscious decision to sit and read the paper together is okay, and is better than just drifting in there and reading the paper together anyway. There's more of a connection if we just spend two minutes saying, "What do you want to do?"

"Shall we sit and read the newspaper together?"

My only flaw was adultery—that's what it's called after all. It's one of those things that goes back to my original environment in an Italian-American neighborhood where all our heroes were wiseguys. The wiseguy has a wife at home. She cooks, takes care of the children, she does the wifely duty. Then you have your mistress and your mistress you fuck. That's what she's there for. You take care of her. She's probably got the IQ of lint, but she's different. She looks different, acts different. I knew guys whose mistresses were dogs and their wives were beautiful, but the mistress had a certain attitude, a certain provocativeness to them. That was the real difference. If you wanted to put it into a category, most of these guys, no matter what the wife was, their mistress was different, a different menu that they got.

You had respect for your wife within the framework of the street rules. No respect for any other woman, especially the girlfriend—they don't call it mistress. If you chose for that kind of life, then you're going to get your fur coat, you're going to get your car every two years and your apartment is going to be paid for, but what you are is just sort of a one-on-one hooker. And you're going to be treated that way.

One thing that stood in my mind from all these years is when I used to wash this wiseguy's car. He had a girlfriend and his wife knew he had a girlfriend. He lived in this building with his wife, then there was a two-family house next door, and then there was his girlfriend's house. His girlfriend had a rule he gave her. She left her house, no matter where she was going, she had to make a left turn. She could not pass his house, because that would be disrespectful of his wife. Can you imagine this warped sense of bullshit? There's your wife, there's your girlfriend. What are you talking about disrespect?

One day for whatever reason, she made a mistake. She came out and she turned right. Obviously, she did it when she thought she could get away with it. This time, she got caught. I was washing the car. He came out and he grabbed her. He turned her around.

"Why can't I walk this way?" she asked him.

"Because," he said, "you're a whore. You come out of your house, and you got to go to your left, because whores go to their left." And she accepted it. You grow up with that kind of example and you are not going to take women too seriously.

For me it was just somebody who would fuck. I could never say no to a girl who made it obvious that if you pursued her, you'd get her in bed. If I knew that, it just seemed like something I had to do. Once it came into my mind that I could screw this girl if I went after her, then I'd have to. Not a compulsion. Just something I did.

I never neglected my family. Anything important I would do, but after I got laid. If I had to get laid, I'd do that, and then, when I got home late, I'd do the important things.

I could never understand a monogamous husband for the longest time. I thought it was like a character flaw in men. If you and I were out ten years ago, we met two broads, and we could see something would happen, I'd say, "Come on. Let's go for it."

"I'd rather not," you'd say. Or, "I don't."

"What the fuck?" I'd think, "What is wrong with him?" It made no sense. I mean, what's the difference? Your wife's not going to know, so what's the problem?

We were married for a year or two, and she had an affair with somebody else. Not an affair—she'd done it with somebody else. And you know, you've got to see those signs coming at you. She says to me one time, "Do you think other people find me attractive?"

"Sure," I said, while I was munching up my moo shu

pork. I remember we were eating Chinese food with those pancake things. "Yeah, yeah, you're attractive." I had this whole I'm-married-I-can-take-it-for-granted thing. I had just gone back to school, so I was working and studying and doing well. Moving and grooving. Then one night about a week after, she tells me she's done it with somebody in the office.

"Whaddaya mean?! Whaddaya mean?!" I went crazy, but I went crazy almost because it was the thing to do. I didn't go crazy because I wanted to. I actually had to sit there and drink enough to get myself to go crazy. Inside, I was saying to myself, "Okay. I guess this marriage is over." That was my gut reaction, a calm, "Well, I understand that. You slept with somebody else, and you told me about it. The marriage is over. It's time to leave." But there's something— and I still don't know what it is, maybe it's some macho thing—it's just a thing with men where it's easier to get *nuts* and crazy than it is to own up to the fact that, hey, this happened.

I drank a lot of booze and systematically picked out things that I was going to break. After I knocked back my third drink, I made sure that my next swing of whatever I had in my hand was going to hit that hanging lamp in the corner. It did and it broke. So, go figure. There was like this map that I was following. It was the you-mother-fucker-you-can't-do-this-to-me map, instead of really owning up to the situation—"You did this? Fuck you. I'm gone."

I think I smacked her once. Didn't hit her or beat her up or anything, but I felt that was a part of it, too. I felt I had to work myself up to a pitch where I could actually hit her. It was some half-assed shot anyway. It certainly wasn't a belt. It was all these things I thought I have to do, that I *should* do.

And there was that incredible embarrassment of, "How

can I tell people that this marriage is over because she fucked around on *me?*" You know what I mean?

Plus, all during the year and a half that we'd been together, I'd been working in a music store where old girlfriends would come by and just sidle up and say, "Hey, you want to go for coffee?"

"Oh, no. I'm married." I was really into this marriage thing, which meant, "Hey, I don't even *think* about that stuff. I don't even look anymore. Women? Ha-ha. Forget about them. I'm *married!* This is my life *forever.*" I really bought that notion. She was a virgin, too, when we got married, so it was the typical scenario. You got to be a virgin when we get married and we live happily ever after. It ain't true.

I stayed married. I went through this big thing, didn't tell anybody what had happened. That was the weirdness about it. Told no one. Not my friend, not my parents, not her friends. Nobody knew that this happened—except me.

Not too long after that there was this little chick at work. That's what she was, too, a little chick. I was 23, so she was maybe 20. At the time I felt like I was the "older man." We had a little thing there and it was fun. This was before I even started acting, but I played the part of the jilted husband. It was, "Oh, woe is me." All this crap. A certain amount of it was true, but I wasn't going anyplace. Which was fine, too. She didn't ask me to leave my wife, but I always had this in the back of my mind that I was going to stay here in this marriage no matter what. There's nothing that's going to make me leave this marriage. I could never own up to something like failure.

After my little affair, I felt like the score was even, and we got back on a kind of even keel.

I am a really jealous person when I'm going with a woman. If I'm going with her, I don't want nobody touching my woman, nobody giving her nothing but me.

I'm not going to take no woman to no club. No, no. What you going to do? If I'm going to a club, I'm going looking. So if I got a woman, I don't have to go to no club. Going to ball games, movies, or church, that's legit. But you take a woman to a club, man's going to want to dance with her. Next thing you know, he's got his hand on her butt. Apparently, you're not happy with her, because just as sure as you go to the club, you're going to look at another woman. Or you're going to get in trouble, because somebody is looking at her.

If we walking down the street, sure, she going to look good. But I ain't having no woman with no dresses way up her legs where when she bend over you can see way up to her butt. I'm not having that. My woman going to have a nice dress, at least to her kneecap. Not these bikinis, don't be on no beach in no two-piece bathing suit. Not mines. Not mines. I don't want no woman like that.

I don't like for my woman to go out and spend overnight. She mine and she's going somewhere to spend overnight, and don't tell me? There's no excuse for a woman not to stay home, if she got a home, unless it's sickness.

"Oh, I just decided I'd stay over my daddy's house."

"Nah, let me stick my finger in it and smell it." I ain't lying, that's what I tell her.

"Smell what? You ain't smelling nothing here."

I tell any girl I deal with, "You going to hang out somewhere, if you going to do something, I don't give a damn. But when you come home, don't come in and run straight to the bathroom, go washing it and taking a bath. Don't do that. If you going to do something, you better clean up before you get back here."

"What you mean?"

"Exactly what I said. If you go out and fuck around, you come in the house like you got an attitude, you try to ease in the shower and get a bath and want to go to sleep. Then you been out fucking around, that's all there is to it. Don't come in the house like that."

Back then, if my wife tried to give me a blow job, if the woman I married tried to suck my cock, she better not know how to do it. She better have to have a book in front of her explaining step by step how to do this. If she does it real well, where did she learn to do that? She didn't learn it in the last two minutes.

I remember going with women who did this, but no woman I cared about did that, until I got older and had a more mature outlook on things. The only women who did it were a certain ethnic group, we thought. Only Jewish women did it and they only did it until they got married. After marriage, they stopped altogether. The only truth in that was that they were generally brighter and read more, so they were more open. That's all it was.

The Italian girls that we grew up with wore all the heavy make-up and the stockings and the spaghetti straps that wrapped halfway up to their thighs, and had absolutely no sex, although they appeared very sexual. They could screw, you know. But all the ones that I've ever known had a real aversion to any kind of extensive foreplay or oral sex. Do anything a little bit "strange," and they say, "I don't do that. I don't do that. Why would you want me to do that? Go get some Jewish broad, if that's what you want."

It was a curse word, for Christ's sake. "Suck my dick."

"He's a cocksucker." "Putana." It's something that's dirty. You think your mother sucks your father's dick? You say that to guys and they'd fucking shoot you.

What I found as I got older was that the better educated the woman was that you were with, the better she was in bed. There was no comparison, and they were generally less flashy. They were more secure about what they looked like. So I grew up around a lot of these neighborhood girls who would strut their shit, but they didn't know what to do with it.

I have a friend and we're sitting in a bar one night. It was one of those three o' clock in the morning things, which is generally when people tell the truth. *In vino veritas* is not even close to what we're talking about here. We're talking about *In Puke-o est Truth-o.* He's on the rocks, and he turns to me and says, "The only difference between men and women . . ."

"Oh, God," I said. "You're going to tell me something important. Jesus, let me like have a glass of water and get straight for a second, so I can hear it."

"Men have sex, because they like sex," he says. "Women have sex, because they want something."

I'm not sure that he's not right.

Women are not as passionate as men. Women think it's exactly the opposite: Men are people who go hump-hump-hump, turn over and go to sleep. I hear that constantly. It's in the newspapers, on TV talk shows.

I resent that stereotype, that blanket condemnation. I'm not like that and I find it hard to believe that most men are like that.

I'm 36 years old. I've been to bed with a lot of women—as stupid as that sounds—and I find women *less* passionate than men, either through lack of experience or lack of feeling or inability to relate on that animal level.

Maybe it's the women I choose. Maybe it's the women who choose me. Fact is, most of the women I've been to bed with are in need of instruction. They're not terribly competent at sex. Not that sex ought to be a game, like it ought to be something you have to go through classes to learn. But it should be something that anybody who's in touch with their own feelings ought to be able to deal with. They ought to be able to say, "I want this," or "I don't want that."

A lot of women I've been to bed with aren't like that. They are confused beyond belief about things sexual.

One thing I don't want to hear when I'm making love to a woman is, "I've never done that before." Especially being somebody who is 36 years old and has been around and is not going out with 12-year-olds.

"I've never done that before."

"What? You've never heard about it? You don't like it? You know, tell me the truth."

We're not talking about arcane stuff here. There's no handcuffs, there's no leather, no blindfolds. "Okay, you're going to be the fireman and I got the hose. You swing from the chandelier and then . . ." No, we're not talking about that stuff. This is normal stuff that people who are attracted to each other do. We're talking about normal fucking sex.

"I've never done that before."

"Where have you been?" I feel like saying. "What have you been doing?"

They tell me this afterwards. I find that weird. It really throws me. I always feel like apologizing, but there's nothing to apologize for. This is not a forced situation at all, believe you me. They have to be lying in bed with their clothes off saying, "Come here, come here, now," before I even get involved with them.

I would hate to think there is an entire generation of women out there who think that normally interesting sex is weird. If that's the case, then we're all in a big shitload of trouble.

Certainly, they have more orgasms than we do. Tiresias was right about that: "Sex feels better for women than it does for men." More and various kinds of orgasms—big ones and little ones and intermediate ones, *groups* of them. Guys, it either happens—bang!—or you slip, and you're trying for it not to happen yet, and then you move wrong, and she moves some way, and you go, "Ah, shit! There it goes!" And that's it. You don't have another one for at least fifteen or twenty minutes. Most men I know don't want to start again for an hour. By then, she's had five or six, and she's sleeping.

We got into this whole wife swapping thing. It was the middle of the '70s, and all the men's magazines were talking about it. The seeds of the sexual revolution were planted in our heads. People were looking at sexual mores and saying, "What are we going to do? Shall we see what this is? Foursomes and fivesomes and sixsomes. Here's a nice couple. Let's see what's going on with this."

Sure enough, my wife goes off with her husband, and I'm left here with this girl, Nancy. Basically, we're both like, "Duh? So what now?" Finally we decided, "Let's just go in the bedroom and see what happens there. They seem to be off on their own. Should we kiss now?"

There was no real passion and no real lust either. If there's lust, there's something to go for. You see it, you want it, and you have that feeling where your dick does all the talking. But this was an exercise in futility. Not to say it wasn't nice. It was nice.

We did that and everything was fine. And it went on, not on a continuous basis, but there was this sexuality and tension in the air after that, innuendoes and asides. We went on to other people. My cousins were interested in talking about it. So my cousin Randy ends up having a crush on my wife, so he's really horny for her. It starts off with everybody taking their clothes off and running around in the country, to everybody doing it in separate apartments, to everybody doing it in the same apartment—but not really because everybody couldn't be in the same room, so who goes into the bedroom?

At the time, I felt, "Yeah, yeah. Let's do it!" I remember telling his wife things like, "Listen, after Jim leaves in the morning for work, why don't we just go into the bedroom and do it with Greta, the three of us?"

Hey, that sounds like fun. Yeah, let's do it. All right. Sure enough, we did it. Jim gets back from work in the afternoon, finds out that we did it without him, and he was so angry. It was anger and jealousy just because he missed out on the fun here—and I got the two women.

Then I remember this one time where we were all together, and everybody was making it there. We're all in the same room this time so it's really hot and really heavy. But I'm not interested in this group thing anymore. I'm interested in Nancy now for something real easy and enjoyable without all this craziness. I don't want my wife and Nancy's husband there. So as soon as I finished and had an orgasm, I remember going to get my glasses, going to the corner of the room and sitting there smoking a cigarette.

It was a great picture. Greta is fondling Nancy, the two of them are in an embrace and Larry is in back of them hugging them. I said to myself, "Well, that's it for this scene." Seeing the fantasy come to life killed it. All of a sudden it was over. What is this? What exactly are we doing here? What exactly is this, because it ain't doing it for me anymore? I was always missing something. It wasn't fun.

Sex is a positive thing, but you have to be able to govern yourself, and don't let sex be a problem for you. I could jump up and down in a woman every night, if necessary, but I learnt that is destroying me. It's not helping me. You try to fuck every night and work, too, you going to die. You going to die *soon.* I feel for a guy if he gets a woman who likes to fuck. Every day she want to fuck, you got a problem. You got a big problem.

I had a lot of sex growing up. I'm sure I had more sex than my son has, but it was all touching and having intercourse in a car. It was never really nice. It was always tough sex. It was difficult for the girl, I'm sure, and difficult for me.

I talk to my children and things seem to be different now. There seems to be less pressure. I'm not sure. I hope there is, because I have a daughter and I worry about her. I tell her all the time how evil men are, how evil I was and I know what I would be thinking if I was going out with her. She's a dynamite-looking lady. She tells me, "I don't know what you're talking about. I've never had any experience with what you're telling me. No guy has ever done that to me or said that to me."

"Oh, okay," I say. "Forget it."

I came home several years ago and my son was having a party at the house. My wife was upstairs and my daughter was gone. I walked into the recreation room, and there is my son and seven or eight guys—high school seniors—sitting around on the two couches, with their hands neatly folded behind their heads, leaning back. Their sneakers are open and they have their sweatshirts on. None of them are saying anything to each other, just sort of rocking back and forth. They're watching this heavyweight porno flick. I came in and all I heard was, "Hmmmmmmmmm-slurp-slurp-slurp. Uh-hummmmm." They're just looking at this woman give incredible head to this guy.

Now, when I was their age there was nothing like that. At best, you could imagine what it was like. There were some French films, but you could hardly make out what was happening. There were guys with black socks on. Everybody looked really sick and bad and perverted. Things have changed. Hopefully, for the better.

My son is almost 10 and has not been interested in girls—or so he says—for the last several years. But girls seem to like him. He gets phone calls from girls. Something is occurring now, and I'll tell you how I know.

It was seventeen degrees out yesterday, and the school bus was on the way. We can stand in the mailroom of our building and watch for the school bus to come, and then go out to get it. But there were two young girls, one of them in his class, each of whom has called on a number of occasions about, "What's the homework?" These girls are standing outside in the weather, waiting for the bus.

I'm with my 10-year-old and my 5-year-old. My 10-year-old looked out the door and said, "Let's go out."

"Too cold," I said.

"I'm not going," the 5-year-old said.

Disappointment was written all over the 10-year-old's face. I said, "You can go out, but it's seventeen degrees."

"That's okay, Dad," he said, and went across the street to chat these two girls up until the bus came. I could see it on his face. There was that real euphoric feeling of flirtation and the attention of the female of the species. He was digging it. Ten years old.

Four: **Love**

Ask a man about love and he'll either tell you about first grade or about his divorce. There is a vague childhood memory of that strange visceral accompaniment to love—the feeling that a few hundred feet of tinsel Christmas tree garland is being threaded through your small intestine—then for the next twenty to thirty years a hormonal fog descends on men's brains, and they are almost incapable of discerning love from lust. Complicating matters further is the fact that men are terrible romantics, haunted by cultural vestiges of the chivalric code, the knight in shining armor routine. As one man put it, "Men are the ones who think something magic is going to happen, and if it doesn't happen, they should go look someplace else. Throughout time, women have made homes, and they've adapted to their circumstances, because they've been forced to stick with it. It's men who are not very reasonable and want the relationship to always be full of flowers and champagne."

This combination of testosterone blindness and romance can make them do some silly things, with very serious consequences. A doctor in his late thirties described his experience this way: "It was an impulsive, rash comment made at sunset with a glass of wine in hand. Not being particularly serious about it, I said, 'Why don't we just get married?'

" 'Yes!' she said, and then she immediately got up and ran to the phone, 'Mom, I'm getting married.' All of a sudden it became a reality that I couldn't get myself out of.

"We had a pretty good first year. But after the second year, when things were going downhill rapidly, what neither one of us was capable of saying was, 'This is really wrong. What can we do about it?' "

A 36-year-old executive, one of the top businessmen in his field worldwide, with a penthouse, a chauffeured limousine, and a salary that verges on a million dollars a year, explains how love affected his life: "Sixteen or seventeen years ago, during my last years in college, I fell in love. I've never really been close with people, so to admit that I was actually in love is a major statement. I just saw fields of flowers, and there was music in the air. It was real. I thought I was going to get married.

"After a year and a half, her parents told her to dump me, because I wasn't the right ethnic background, and she did. I began to pour myself into my work, seven days a week, virtually twenty-four hours a day. In retrospect, I can see that most of what I was doing was proving to her and her family that they made a big mistake, that I was worth it. Now I wonder, 'What did you do that for?' I haven't had time for people in over ten years. I lost a lot of friends. I was almost crazy and reclusive.

"Through old friends I know where she lives, that she married some salesman and has three kids. It's 1991 and there's not a Sunday when I'm driving home from my beach place and I pass the exit nearest the town she lives in that I don't look to see if she's driving on that highway with her husband and three kids, going from her parents' house to their house. Isn't that weird, all these years, two or three Sundays out of every four, I look on the highway to see if I see her."

Men have problems with commitment. In our culture, rightly or wrongly, the old attitudes about marriage still hold sway. For women marriage is often seen as fulfillment, while for men it is perceived as a limitation. A bartender, who has avoided marriage until his late thirties, expresses it this way: "You take a perfectly fun female, just a hoot. When she gets her man, then that's it. A wild woman and a wild man, you put them together and the wildness is gone, because the woman will get conservative. She'll tone down, and then, by God, she expects the man to tone down, too.

"I've been married for about a year. I love my wife. Of all the people I've ever been with, she's probably the best bet for making a go of it. But I'm not crazy about marriage. It's changed me a lot, to be real honest. It makes it hard for me to be completely myself. I'm certainly not as wild as I used to be, but that's still an integral part of who I am, this kind of wild, silly, crazy person. Around her, I can't let it out. When I finally do let it out, I break things and go to extremes."

When pushed to more completely define what this "wildness" really means, men talk about hanging out with the guys and drinking and mild disorderly conduct. But finally it comes down to a matter of sex. The bartender continues, "A large part of it is freedom. If I see a woman that I'd like to pursue, I don't feel like I can. Oh, I could. But I have this view of what it means to be an honorable man. It's not a real moral thing. I'm moral in some senses, but not very moral when it comes to sex. I've fucked other men's wives, other guys' girlfriends. I have fucked other women when I've been in the middle of a major relationship. I have no problem with that. It's just that I know how my wife is, and if she found out, it would devastate her, it would ruin our relationship. That would be a bummer."

A 50-year-old police officer recalls a conversation he had with a psychologist who happened to be the coach of his son's Little League team: " 'You know, Hagar,' I said, 'You're a psychologist. Why can't I be faithful?'

" 'It's easy. Neither can I. There are certain guys who can be, and there are other guys who just can't be. Now take that guy, the manager of the other team. He'd love *not* to be faithful. But look at him. The guy's three hundred pounds. He never has to make a decision. He never has to deal with it. If he was an attractive guy and still was faithful, then he was a special kind of guy. It's not easy for men like us.' "

What is most interesting about the cop and the bartender, and almost all the men I interviewed, is that they did not mention the effect that a wife's or lover's infidelity would have on them. The typical male delusion is that women don't face the same temptation, much less give in to it.

Of course, some men do have long-term, rewarding relationships with women. Even in "marriages made in heaven," there are two stumbling blocks that at first glance seem so small but which men can never seem to surmount. The next two voices belong to men in their early forties, both of whom have been married for approximately twenty years, both of whom are successful in their jobs and in their relationships.

"Her birthday was in May. 'Happy birthday,' I said. No cards, no flowers, no nothing. We're now into June. It's probably that early influence in my life that said it was faggy to send birthday cards. Roses and stuff wasn't tough-guy shit. The tough guy stance is that you ignore women unless you want them around. When you're dating, when it's the chase scene, then it's okay. What's interesting is that I did send roses to my daughter on her sixteenth birthday. But not to my wife." For all their insistence on passion in love relationships, men are terrible when it comes to maintaining the romance.

The other stumbling block is the age-old shibboleth, "communication." The following quote comes from one particular man but will sound familiar to every man in America and could have come from almost any of the men interviewed for this book.

"Women want you to read their minds. Women want you to know what they need without asking for it. I don't really understand why that is. But it's true in my life.

"You're arguing. No, excuse me, you're 'discussing' something. You think you're doing fine. The end of the argument, you suddenly realize that you haven't done fine at all. There was something that you were supposed to say that you didn't say.

"Now, the woman thinks it's because this thing you were supposed to say that you didn't say is something you don't feel. But you didn't know the conversation was about the thing that you didn't say that she didn't tell you that you had to say, because you're supposed to know that *thing,* whatever it is. I don't know what any of that means, but I find it to be true all the time.

"I don't think *any* man has ever won an argument with a woman. Even when you win an argument, you really lost, because now you're a heel. You made her feel bad, because she lost the argument. How could you be so insensitive? I think I'm zero and ninety-nine. There's always something you have to be wrong about."

The media image in America today is focused on women who can't find "a good man," as though they were the only ones looking for meaningful relationships. What was striking in these interviews was how similar men's complaints were to those voiced in women's magazines and on television talk shows. Single men, divorced men, men in unhappy marriages are all lonely and longing for true love. Their longing for companionship is as plaintive and often as despairing as women's. Here's the wealthy young executive again:

"It's hard looking for a relationship. Now, I'm at a point where I'm thinking, how much do I want to be with this person? Is this the person I want to have kids with? It's not, how great is the sex going to be? I don't want to fool around, so is this forever or what are we doing here? I'm too old to not know what I want to do. But I don't. I think I want to have kids, though. It looks like fun. I'd be good at it."

A public relations consultant in his thirties, who has been divorced for several years, said, "I miss women. I know this is going to sound weird, but I find it hard to believe that I'm not with a woman right now. I've had girlfriends—heck, I've had hundreds of girlfriends. I go out with women. I talk to women. I don't have a wife. I don't even have a steady girlfriend. I find it amazing that what was considered pretty natural when I was growing up—a man and a woman together—is no longer the case.

"Men and women are so fed up that they've retreated. I may be one of them, but I won't be for long. I guarantee it, because I like women too much. I want to be married again. But that's not the point. The idea is meeting somebody that you love, that you want to spend a lot of time with, and you want it to be official. I don't know what went whacko."

In first grade, I had a crush on this girl called Jane. Our mothers both went the same way to the school, and I would see her walking with her mother on the other side of the street. I didn't know why I had a crush or what a crush was, or why I should even like girls. I was barely out of infancy.

I'll show you the picture of my first grade class. Here's Jane, the woman I loved. She always wore her hair the same way, in pigtails. This is Paul, the little scumbag that she loved. And this is me trying to figure out, "What the hell has he got that I haven't got?" He's got a tie on. I have to wear these checkered flannel shirts.

At the little dances when the parents tried to put the boys and girls together for the cuteness thing, she wound up with Paul, the little scumbag. I didn't get the girl back then.

I was in love with her and she was an unattainable goddess. She was physically beautiful, sophisticated, the coolest girl in the school. I would make jokes, and she liked to laugh. She just had some cast inside of her that if you could make her laugh, you could get to her. So I would do anything and say anything to make her laugh. When everyone was laughing, and I was basking in my punk triumph of disrupting a class, my eye dwelt only on her to see if she was laughing.

In eleventh grade, when her boyfriend was off in the Navy, she told someone to tell me that she wanted to go out with me. I didn't jerk off and I had diarrhea for a week just from hearing this. I was terrified and joyful. That was my first love.

She asked me out, one of those Sadie Hawkins' Day numbers. I didn't really date, I certainly wasn't getting laid. I was too shy. My stock rose with all the lover-boy types at school when they saw that she picked me.

One date, she wore a safety pin on the side of her skirt and we were sort of making out in the front seat of her car —she was teaching me how to kiss. I didn't know shit. She pointed out that the safety pin was easy to open up. I still couldn't get around to doing it. I was so fucking shy, plus my heart was in my throat every time I was around her. To even think about her, I would get butterflies in my stomach. She was a total and complete goddess to me.

She finally broke that down a little bit. We didn't really have intimacy then. She was the first girl I ever touched, and it took her about four or five dates to convince me that I should do this. She let me touch her. She almost *made* me. I didn't even know how to go into her underwear. She had stockings and a garter belt on, and I tried to reach underneath. I touched my first cunt, and it was the girl that

I loved, you know? I didn't know what I was doing. I probably could have done whatever I wanted, but she didn't ask
for it. It was a beautiful thing, really.

But it was the same story. A few years after high school,
she wanted to get married. I didn't want to get married. I
ran away from it.

That's a beautiful memory in recall. If I was ever pure
with a girl, it was certainly then. Completely and totally, so
it's nice when you're a retired rake like me to think back
on your relationships with women and know that at least
you did start out from a place that was completely and
totally pure. My feelings toward her were that way, you
know. It gives you a frame of reference. I know I was capable of that kind of love at one time.

I knew I was serious about her when one day I was
walking out of the dorms with my baby, arm in arm, and
Q.T. came up. He's one of my oldest friends, all the way
back to grade school. Q.T. pulled me aside and said,
"Oooo, King. Got you new gash, eh?"

I run back and just punch him. Knock him cold.

"Oh, my God," I said. "Q.T., you shouldn't do this to me.
Please come back."

He woke up on the ground and said, "What'd you do
that for?"

"I don't know why I did that, Q.T. I'm sorry." I'm still
slapping his face, picking him up. "Let me carry you back
to the dorm." Girlfriend is screaming hysterically. "Go back
to your room."

Wow, these are new feelings. I've never hammered a very
close friend of mine. The next day, I'm there at seven-thirty

in the morning. "Are you okay, Q.T.? Is there anything I can do for you?" He couldn't talk. For the next three or four days he was drinking through a straw. Then I was buying him beers and his lunch in the cafeteria.

I wanted to get married, because I wanted a ritual. Language seemed to me—and still seems to me—so useless in making sure we really understand one another. The ritual of marriage was all built toward a moment in public and between us in which we both knew what we were talking about, and we agreed. This moment, when we said something that was indisputable to one another, was what I wanted. I wanted the security of feeling, as illusory as it might be, that in that moment we were going to make a promise to one another that would be very clear.

It was funny. Since language and making a promise were so important to me, I wanted to know what we were saying, since it was going to be in Hebrew. So we went to see the rabbi who was going to marry us. The rabbi translated what we were agreeing to. It had something about obeying. She was supposed to obey me. She didn't care to the same degree as I did about the specific words. But it was important to me, so I jumped up and said, "How come she's supposed to obey me and I'm not supposed to obey her? What is all this stuff?"

"Look," the rabbi said. "This is a tradition that goes back five thousand dollars." Instead of five thousand years. That pretty much ended the conversation. I felt at that point that I wasn't going to get any satisfaction, and that the promise had to come between she and I.

Immediately after the marriage, I was depressed, because it didn't seem anything had happened. I was the same guy the next day.

We didn't have money to have a honeymoon. We were going to take all the money from the wedding and go to Europe for three months and live like paupers, so we could make it spread for as long as possible. So we didn't indulge or have the opportunity to go to some fancy hotel and have a big weekend.

Instead, we walked around New York City where we were living. We went to the top of the Empire State Building, looked around. As we walked home, to the Lower East Side, it suddenly hit me what I had done. What I had done was make a decision about my life. I couldn't have done that before. I had made this very important decision that I was going to live with this person, that I was going to share my life with this person, and that I wanted her to share her life with me. Everything that I did from now on was going to involve her. I'd never made a decision of that magnitude before. I decided that now I was an adult.

I don't really believe in romance as it's constituted in romantic novels, in songs and movies. Yet, I feel very romantic. When I decided to get married, I got confused. I had been in love before, and I was in love now. "What if I fall in love with someone else? This could be possible."

The big lie in romance is that there is only *one* person for you. I don't think this is true. What is romantic is the decision to say, "Okay, it is going to be *this* person." What is baloney is to say, "This is the only one." Romance is not only a matter of the heart, it's also a matter of your head, your will, and your decision to do it.

There is something to be said for monogamy. The thing to be said is not the great thing of romantic literature that you will now have a fulfilling, romantic, amorous life forever. The thing to be said is that, if it works out well and you work hard at it, you will have a companion who will understand you better than anyone else will ever understand you, who you can be committed to and who will be committed to you, who you will trust and who will trust you, no matter how difficult things get. That comes from being together through trials and crises. It doesn't come because, "You two were meant to be together in the *stars.*" The stars don't give a shit and there could be someone different that you could fall in love with.

Most men are romantic. I'm not. I'm not at all. Like this guy sits at the desk next to mine always sends flowers. I hear him on the phone, "I love you so much." I've never spoken to anybody like that. I don't think there's anything phony about it. But if a guy has to be romantic to screw his own wife, he's got a problem. It may work, but if it's a necessity, really a necessity, then it's going to be a problem.

I wasn't ready for it. But the biological imperatives were such that it was the thing to do, and there was mutual pressure from her side. I was going to law school, and it looked like I was going to be a success. She was a sharp

girl on her way to becoming class president, which made
her a real achievement symbol for me. It had all the ear-
marks of what everybody thought would be an ideal situation. Only we didn't get married for the right reasons.

The morning of the wedding I almost took a Greyhound
bus out of town. I didn't have much money on me, but I
thought I could swing a bus ticket in some direction. I was
drifting at that point in my life. I really didn't want to become a lawyer. I didn't know what I wanted to do. It was a
bad time to be married and assume that responsibility as
well. It was just one of those things. I thought I was in love.
As I look back now, I realize that hormones probably had
more to do with it than anything else. It surely wasn't a
whole lot of brains involved. Anyhow she was a nice
enough gal at that particular time.

We had a sit-down dinner for three hundred people at
the *second* reception. The first reception was for about a
thousand. The last day of our honeymoon we spent in a
hurricane in Bermuda. That was a portent of things to
come.

We came back to live near her parents after I finished
school. I was fairly happy in my work. The marriage was
all right at that stage, too. We had family support for raising
the kids who came along before long. It was a life. I can't
think of any real highs or real lows. Just going on existing.

Reflecting, you'd like to think that your life has these
great moments of revelation, of something or other. Up
until the time of my separation, when I turned 40, there
was nothing really exhilarating other than the birth of the
kids, nothing terribly traumatic other than realizing that the
marriage wasn't going anyplace.

We'd been in counseling—Hell!—for about six years
learning how to communicate. Learning eye messages,
preparedness effectiveness training, and all that sort of

stuff. It's funny; here I am in a field that deals with communication a great deal, and yet we don't communicate in feelings, which are important in a marriage.

She and I were communicating on a material plane rather than a spiritual plane. I became very passive. "You want to do this? We'll do this." When she wanted to redo the house, we spent thousands of dollars and wound up with a Polish whorehouse—ultramodern throughout. It was chic and stuff like that, but there wasn't anything warm about the house. I enjoy modern things, but there's modern with personality and there's sterile modern. We got into the sterile mode, just like our lives were terribly sterile.

It just wasn't emotionally satisfying. I'm sure from her standpoint it was the same problem. She had gone to graduate school and become a psychologist, learned all about feelings and caring—at least from a certain perspective. Here I was in my practice dealing with criminals, people who were scumballs and slimebags. She viewed these people as poor, deprived unfortunates. I saw them as people who were making things work for them. They'd had some pretty conscious choices to make along the way as to which way they wanted to go in life. Not entirely, but certainly there were paths they could have taken rather than end up in the criminal justice system.

So our professional lives started to diverge as well. Once the kids grew up, coming home was almost torture. But you can't stay at the office forever.

You just have to shuck it. Of all the acts in my life, that probably took the most courage, because here I was throwing away everything that my life had been pointed to for years and then taking off in a new direction.

As I recall the situation, I had bought a motorcycle. I'd had one before, and had gotten rid of it. I was sitting on the motorcycle when she came into the garage and said something. I just sort of bopped it to her, "It's quite obvious that we're not making it. Let's not keep up the charade anymore."

With that, she went to her friend's house in San Francisco, called me, and said, "I want you out of the house."

"Fine, good-bye," I said. "If I leave the house, I'm not coming back, ever." She thought with all her psychological skills this would pass over. I think she still had some hope for the marriage. She's never remarried, and the break-up was more traumatic for her.

When her attorney made his first demand, he asked for one hundred twenty percent of my income. "She needs this to live on," he said.

It was a chapter of my life that I don't look back upon with a great deal of pride or pleasure, aside from the kids. You look back and think, why do we do these things? You'd think we'd know better.

As I view things now, from what I'm enjoying now, I realize how sick some of the things we did were. I regard the upper part of my life being finally able to form a warm, loving relationship with Elizabeth.

Elizabeth and I come from different backgrounds, different worlds. She's addicted to Bingo and smokes. After my first wife, I said, "I'll never marry a woman that smokes. Never." Elizabeth said, "I'll try to give it up." Brains here, I married her first. When I ask her when she's going to give up smoking, she says, "When you give up eating." That's the kind of crap you get.

Elizabeth has the same sense of right and wrong that I developed. Because she is so terribly loyal—God—and so giving of herself, it was very easy to fall in love with her and get married. Had she come along twenty years before, it wouldn't have been the right time for those kinds of things. I was into an achievement mode rather than a satisfaction mode. I was trying to accomplish things and find security and happiness, not realizing that it wasn't the achievement that brought the happiness. It was yourself that brought the happiness.

You think you can coat over it by buying a new car and new clothes, buying fancy things to put on the wall. I bought a motorcycle, a symbol of freedom. It turns out it was kind of a stupid purchase, because I got one that was really too small for me. I was afraid to get back up on a big bike, and I didn't want to spend all that money on one. This little shit didn't give me what I wanted anyway. I wound up selling it.

The house I live in now with Elizabeth is small and comfortable. I probably could have bought something three to four times this size and still afforded it, but there's still some insecurity I'll be working on throughout my life. Elizabeth has made it easier for me to relax and get more comfortable. Maybe you get there anyway just by getting older and not having the same drives that you did as a kid. I like to think it's her.

The first few years we were together, we just laughed all the time. I remember telling my brother, probably in the first year that Diana and I were together, that was really what was different and special about being with her—that we laughed all the time. Somehow our sense of humor was just on the same track, and we'd laugh about everything.

You get to the point where the teasing moves down to the complaint level. Even if it *is* just teasing, there's also this feeling that you know too much about each other. We don't fight much, we don't argue, and there's really something wrong with that. We *never* argue. There's got to be something to disagree about.

We got into this pattern of just not talking, not arguing, not anything. We wouldn't even discuss something to work it out. We both thought we should be happy together all the time, and avoid things, put things off that we didn't like about each other. That hasn't worked, so we've been working on finding some better way to live together.

We see this therapist every week now. The funny thing is, we both don't like her very much. We don't think she really gets at the important stuff. Sometimes, she just seems to miss the point altogether. But we both agree that it's doing some good, because it's getting us to talk about things. If the therapist brings something up, or suggests some explanation or insight that we both think is just full of shit, completely on the wrong track, so what? It's something to get us talking about it, and we're both pissed at her instead of each other. She's either smarter than both of us or dumb as a rock, and either way it works.

We're trying real hard to find that intimacy, to get back to the thrill of discovering that we have something in common or don't have something in common. We are actually able to tease each other again about things and laugh at each other. For a few years there it was like we couldn't quite remember why we got married in the first place. That's bad.

I dated a woman for about four or five months a number of years after I got divorced. She was divorced, too, and had two kids. Her notion of a father and a husband essentially boiled down to somebody who brought home a paycheck and basically took care of her. I was fully expected to be out of the house at least one night a week. She had a real hard-core '40s and '50s traditional type view: the man ruled. Period. The man was right, and the man could do whatever he wanted to do, as long as he was loyal and loving and brought home the bacon. Then everything was fine.

Boy, that scared the shit out of me. I mean, it did. It was the one time in my life with women that I knew for sure that this was wrong; this ain't going to work at all. I don't mind making decisions, but I'll be damned if I'm going to make all of them. And I'll be damned if I'm going to watch my partner only deciding which napkins to use. That doesn't cut it with me.

I really believe in this whole business of the virgin, the mistress and the imaginary woman. The virgin is your mother, your wife and your daughter. Your mistress is the woman you always want to be with or want to go to and have sex with. The imaginary woman is the perfect combination of those two, if you could ever find it, but nobody ever finds her, you know?

As I've gotten older, I realize that you can fall in love with that virginal image of your wife, this wonderful woman who is sacrificing and giving. It's a self-love, because she loves you so much and pays this huge price to have you in her life. So I can't help but love this person for what she does.

As years go by, that love turns into a sort of anger. You find all these faults in that person. You rationalize your running around by saying, "She never really took care of herself."

Well, she was too busy taking care of me.

"She never grew with me."

Well, she didn't have time to grow. The kids grew. It took so much effort to take care of me and my children.

But nevertheless, she ends up this product of what she is. Years and years go by, and she's this house mother.

There was a time, certainly among our parents' generation, when you just didn't get a divorce. You lived with that. So what? You settled for that life. You fooled around once in a while. You had a girlfriend here or there.

Amongst the men who I know now, almost all of them have gotten a divorce. They are now with a woman they feel more in community with. In almost every case, the woman is ten or fifteen years younger. Their wife is this older woman.

One of my dear friends, a guy I know since sandbox days, he had been seeing someone, running around on his wife. He had money, so this woman he was seeing was everything we had talked about when we sat on the stoop when we were kids. She was an absolute fucking knockout, but not a heavyweight intellectual, could barely string a sentence together, but could cook very well and is gorgeous. His wife on the other hand was smart and extremely tough.

When his wife came down with cancer, he had a terrible feeling of guilt, but is in love with this younger woman. Then his wife died. We were talking about it. He was weeping, crying. We were *all* crying, because her death made us all feel so vulnerable, since we are the same age. And he said, "You know, the worst feeling about this is, I'm so happy."

I don't know what he expected from me. Maybe he thought I would be shocked. But I said, "I understand how you're feeling. That's really natural. I understand that you're happy." Because he never would have been able to face his wife and say, "I want a divorce." She relieved him of all that by dying.

Women are different than men in dealing with this business. If there is a time in their lives where they are in a situation where they are unhappy, they are capable of incredible coldness and have the ability to confront it head on. They say, "I don't love you. And you're leaving, because I don't love you anymore, and I can't stand this life."

I have a friend whose wife told him that in their twenty years of marriage she had never once had a satisfactory sexual experience with him—in *twenty years.* Now she's met this guy, and she's found out what sex is all about. It devastated this guy. She ripped his heart out and bit it in front of him.

I know some callous guys, but I don't know a man who could sit down and say that to a woman. What we'll say is, "I don't understand what's going on with me. I have to leave. I have to try something else. I'm confused, I'm fucked up. My head's on backwards. I'm walking down the street bumping into things. I have pains everywhere." We have to rationalize our behavior. Is it because we haven't got the courage? I don't know if that's the right word for it.

I know in my case, I'm still in touch with every single woman I've ever been involved with. All of them. They don't call me. I call them all. We talk. It's like extending your arm behind you and keeping a finger hooked in the collar of one—always hanging on—and reaching out to grab the next one. Saying, "Let's stay in touch, let's stay in touch."

When men say that, they really mean, "I want to be your friend." Women have said to me, "I don't want to be your fucking friend. I have plenty of friends. I don't need you as a friend. You're either in my life or not in my life."

I just want them to still like me.

If you have betrayed a woman in some manner, you would probably expect not to be forgiven, but it is possible that you would be forgiven. However, it will come up again at another time and place that you've sinned.

With most men in a personal relationship, they either decide, "Okay, we had a deal, you cheated me. We're not having another deal. That's it. Good-bye. Forget it. Never again."

Or they say, "All right, fuck it. But don't ever do it again." And it won't come up again. One or the other, but not both like women have. They'll forgive you, but they'll remember it and bring it back up to you.

Women say men can't commit. I can commit, but I don't want to commit for eternity. I may not want to commit more than a weekend. I'll commit for this weekend, and I'll commit for two weekends from now, but I want you the fuck out of here tomorrow. I want all of you out of here tomorrow.

What's interesting about that is, there are women who have met this kind of man, this kind of revolving door, so they know what's going to happen. You're there for that first night and the second day, and by the third day, they're packing your bag. They don't really want you to go, but they know you're ready to go. They're not going to give you a hard time about staying. They can be very sad, but it's also a tremendous relief for both of you.

The women that I've most enjoyed being with are women who are married. We have this prescribed time that we are together. We know there is arrival time, familiarizing ourselves with each other again. There's the lovemaking time. Then preparing to leave and leaving—and swearing undying love. "But don't put marks on my body, don't scratch me. I'll call you tomorrow, or maybe we'll skip tomorrow."

Maybe I won't hear from her for three or four days. But the next telephone contact is really warm and wonderful. "How have you been?" It's wonderful again, because I don't have to be there when she's not feeling well, and she's got a headache. It's like going from one date to another date, so you never have to go through any of that middle territory.

What's so horrible about all this, and the truth of why we were meant to be monogamous to a certain extent, is that if you're not with one woman, your life becomes just a series of beginnings and endings. That's very sad. Each of those endings takes a toll. After a while, you are constantly beginning and constantly ending. How many times in the course of your lifetime do you want to sit and really suffer over separation and a divorce? How many times can you take that emotionally? If you're going through this on a regular basis once every three or four months, you can start losing your mind.

If you're running around with decent people who want a commitment and then become committed—you can become committed even for that short period of time—then there's the beginning, the middle and the end. Every relationship has a natural course. The end in most cases is marriage or living together, or separating. You can't go on dating forever.

The girl I married, I met when I was 15. We got married when I was 24. I've had a lot of women since then, no relationships. Up until recently, I was never monogamous the way I should be. There were very few people who even know I'm married. If they knew I was married, they thought I didn't take it seriously. Raising my family, taking care of my family is very serious business. I never was an absentee father or husband. I never was uncaring. But I ran around on my wife all through our marriage.

Somewhere around 40 or 42, I realized I should get my priorities in the right order. I reached maturity. Now I understand things like trust. It was no big decision, no great effort on my part. Nothing happened to turn me around. No fire and brimstone, no apparitions or anything. I didn't get caught and almost lose my family. There was absolutely nothing that you can point to, even with a lot of soul-searching. In fact, most of the time I wonder what the fuck is going on with me.

Rather than something that happened, it's that I sort of lost the desire. It's not loss of sex drive. You start to see more things than that. You lose a lot of ego, that's part of it. As the years go on, you start to realize that you're just not going to be what you were, or what you thought you were going to be, or what you hoped you'd be. You're going to be a survivor. Most of us are survivors. Then you start to look at the little things that make a marriage and you appreciate the little things that you didn't beforehand.

Most of the time if you sit and think about it for a few minutes before you go off with some girl, you would walk away from it. As you get older, you think more. You act more than you react. I find that in myself. But most people show maturity sooner than I did.

At least I didn't have a mid-life crisis that most men go through. If anything, now I enjoy going out with my wife on weekends, which is something I never did. I used to hate her friends. Her friends and my friends were distinct, because most of my friends were guys from my business. I hated going out with her friends. They would talk about how they're going to paint the living room and how they're going to put tile on the floor. Fuck, I didn't want to be there. Now I'm sitting there talking about how to paint the best way and how to install the tile.

I figure if she put up with me through those years, now it's just a snap. She even laughs at the old days. She wasn't raised in the same environment that I was. She wasn't raised to be an Italian housewife, pregnant and in the kitchen. So it was strange that she put up with it. I don't know why. Some kind of warped affection for me. She put up with a lot of shit in those days, nasty shit. Girls calling the house, because I gave them the phone number. What kind of nonsense is that? But that was the things you did then. Girls were just things you did.

Now I just don't have the energy for running around. Tonight, I could go down to the corner from the office, where we all hang out, fuck around with that barmaid, and probably take her home. Instead, I'll call my kids, and say, "When I leave the office, I'll drive you guys home from class," rather than go try and screw around. If somebody a few years ago had told me that's what they were going to do, I would have told the guys I hung out with, "I like that guy, but he's fucked in the brain. There's something wrong with him. Instead of screwing what's-her-name down at the bar, he's driving his kids home." I would've put my kids in a cab. But now it's the right thing to do and I understand.

I had always wanted two wives. Why not have the option? The funny part is that the two women aren't weird at all. They're very normal girls. One might even say conservative. They were best friends and worked for the same outfit.

Here's what happened. Kay and I used to go out on dates. It was no big deal. I always had more of a need to go to town and do something—like go to the movies, maybe—than my wife, Millie, ever did. So I'd call around to see who wanted to go. Sometimes I'd go with Kay's husband, sometimes I'd go with Kay. We were just friends.

Then one night, she and I were out, and all of a sudden she threw her arms around me and told me she loved me, had loved me for a long time. I thought about it for a minute or two, and said I guess I always sort of loved her, too. Always had a lot of warm feelings for her, whatever that means.

Nothing happened for a few days. We just sat on it. Then I said, "I guess I am in love with you, and you're in love with me, so I guess we have to do something about this, because it would just be kind of frustrating not to. Can't have that."

We found this trashy little hovel that some guy was willing to rent for a hundred dollars a month. We had to go and meet there at times. We did that for a little while, not years and years. It was kind of fun and exciting. Emotionally, I never thought of it as an affair. Emotionally, I felt absolutely equally committed to both women. The idea of an affair implies that you're fooling around on the side with somebody. I never ever, ever, ever considered leaving my wife. That was absolutely not part of any thought. Most men have affairs without any intention of leaving their wives, but most of them end up doing that or dropping the other person. In my case, there was no way that I would do either one of those things.

Number one, I couldn't see it going on forever, and number two, I have a real strong need to take care of the people I'm around. I didn't feel like I was in a position where I could really take care of Kay or Millie by splitting up my time so drastically. It occurred to me that the only way to solve all this was to propose this grand experiment.

I presented it first to Kay as an alternative, because she was having nothing in her relationship. She was married and still lived with him, but there was nothing real. She'd left her husband before for five years and then came back. They existed together because of their kid who they were both concerned about and in love with. The relationship was built around the kid. That was very frustrating for Kay and I know it was frustrating for her husband, although he wasn't very expressive about it. But it had to be, because she's a maniac and he's this calm guy.

It was all very difficult. Tons of upheaval, just thinking about it. I've tried to reconstruct when I actually broached the subject with Millie, and I can't even remember that. So it must have been extremely emotional. I don't even have a clue as to how I pulled that one off. I can't even think how I did it. I swear to God, I don't have a clue.

At some point, I worked out how Kay would move in with us. Millie had accepted this and was willing to be a participant, because the deal was that Kay was going to leave her husband, because of incompatibility (and there was a lot of that). Millie was asking me if it was okay if Kay came and stayed with us a little while until she got resettled. I reluctantly agreed. This is our story, which sounded plausible to the rest of the world, knowing all the personalities involved. Of course, Kay's husband was fairly thankful about all this. He's always thought it was really nice that I would take care of this asshole that he had the misfortune to marry.

So Kay moved in. It was kind of weird, because she brought her kid out. Now we had my two kids and her kid and the three adults. But it was a big house and we managed to squeeze people around.

From the very beginning it was too hard emotionally for them. The first day she came out there, we all tried to sleep together and have sex together, but it was just too weird for Kay. Millie was so intent on making sure she and I were still married and that she didn't lose me because of this, so she was the one who ended up much more willing to accommodate. Immediate bad reaction. That idea stopped. It's not going to be a harem. I really didn't have that concept in mind to begin with. I assumed that if that could work it would be the best approach. Then everybody could be intimate with each other.

They immediately came up with this alternate plan: we would all sleep together, but there would not be any kind of a sexual time. We'd have times during the day when you have your "private time" with the other person. We did that for a couple of years, and then we'd all sleep together at night.

If Kay had been disposed to take care of everything, actually make it work like Millie was, we'd probably all still be happy doing it, one way or another. But Kay's this real emotional girl, which I liked, since it was sort of the opposite of Millie in many ways. She was more expressive, and a lot more outgoing, demonstrative. Talk about a mixed blessing.

She was from the outside of this thing and that was rough. Kay felt like she was coming into something, interrupting and having a giant disastrous effect on this relationship that already existed. Plus she and Millie were best friends and worked together.

Also as tempestuous as Kay was, she'd get really, really angry and act out emotionally. Then Millie and I would have to deal with that. We were always having to protect Kay. So Kay was the one who got taken care of, and Millie would be the one getting the shaft in terms of fairness.

I worked my ass off, because I assumed that it would work, since we were all intelligent people and had decided to do this. But that wasn't good enough for either one of them. It very slowly got on their nerves.

Mine, too. The pressure to provide both of them with intimacy and reassurance built and built and built, until finally they both decided they could do it, but only if they each had their own place. That's when the concept of building Kay a garage apartment came in.

When it got to the "two residences" point, I lost hope. It's never going to work out. If I had to be two people in two places, nobody was going to be happy, including me.

That's when everything fell apart, even though I built the garage apartment. By then they were both angry and disillusioned. They were both feeling the same kind of jealousy. And it was a very unique situation for jealousy to occur. Neither one of them could go out and talk to their other girlfriends about it, so they ended up falling together and getting very close. I don't know if it was a matter of finding fault. That was never really expressed to me, but I had a feeling that might be the case. And if, in their minds, there was a fault involved, it was *mine*.

They live together now, and I'm gone. They never developed any kind of lesbian relationship at all. That would have been good. I probably could have fit into that somehow.

I wouldn't try it again. Given ostensibly who they were, as much as you can know a person without having gone through this, we were pretty much ideally suited to try being a triple. People who've known each other all their adult lives and really got on well with each other. I would have thought that Kay would be the one who was the most liberated and adaptable to it. But as it turned out, it wasn't even close, so I don't think it's a real possibility.

I have no regrets. We did it for four or five years, which is a lot longer than many simple little marriages. I think if Kay had been just a little bit calmer—just fifteen percent more calm—then it probably would have been okay or at least manageable. But I don't recommend it.

One of the things I have learned about myself along the way, which is both a gift and a curse, like most things are, is that I have a way, almost like a chameleon, of blending in and mirroring the person that I'm with or that I'm close to. That's real nice for the person that I'm with, because it makes them real comfortable. The flip side is that a lot of times I start to wonder what's in here inside me, what am I, and why am I so flexible? The pejorative word would be wishy-washy. The place where it's the most dramatic is with women I'm with in a relationship.

It started off with this really nifty woman who is wonderful in many, many ways, talented, likes to do homemaking, really interested in being a wife in a more traditional sense, which kind of bothered me a little bit, but it's okay. Frankly, I didn't like being taken care of so much. I can live with it. It was a nice change after the feminist wars I'd been in.

She decided she wanted to marry me the first night we went out, and she started on a program of making sure this was going to happen. During all that first two years, I was being pursued. It was fine and I liked it. She was the one who was sensitive about rejection, in the sense that anything that could be interpreted even remotely as rejection was interpreted as a rejection. I was stuck in a relationship where it was impossible for me to say anything negative. I sat on it, whenever I found something negative to say or even a problem to work on. What I saw was that we had problems between the two of us and problems with our kids and no mechanism to make it work since everything was so sensitive. Catch-22. You can't get out of it.

My saying, "I'm pulling out of this relationship a little bit. I think we need to back off. I'm not going to come over for dinner every night anymore, and we're going to kind of cool it for a while," was taken as this horrible rejection.

Then she started rejecting me, and said, "Okay, I'm getting out of this." An interesting thing happened that never had happened to me before. I became really obsessed with her. Maybe that's pretty typical. The person who is leaving all of a sudden is being left, and the tables have turned. The obsession she had with pursuing me immediately became my obsession. Not only that, but I became obsessed in the same way she had been. I had watched her enough to start doing it to myself. The dance started up again, but it went the other way.

It got almost addictive. A missed meeting would cause great anguish and anxiety. A phone call that was supposed to happen at ten o'clock at night that only happened at 11:30 was, for that hour and a half, just sheer hell.

About the only place I could get some relief, aside from having the addiction itself which meant getting the phone call or seeing her, was to go to places like Al-Anon. The only connection is that those are people dealing with out-of-control issues, like a spouse who is an alcoholic, for example, learning to let go of that person and not try to fix or change them.

Ironically, the relationship with my children suffered during that time in a funny kind of way. I pulled back out of the relationship in part in order to protect them from something, and then became so incapacitated by the result of my actions that I actually hurt them as much in some ways. I often became sort of absent, I was so uptight about what was going on.

In a strange way, the obsessive behaviors I went through with this woman may have been there all along with me, but I would have kept them under the surface, never daring to express them, if I had not seen them modeled in her. If I had been with an assertive woman who had finally said to me, "Hey, look, I'm going to go do my thing. Don't worry about it," I just never would have pursued her again. But with this woman, there was this dance, this ritual, and this agony that you have to go through.

We're still dancing that way, although it's cooled off. This is a five-year-long saga. There for a while I thought she was really gone. That was fine. I was beginning to adjust to it. But every time I begin to heal, she calls and the whole thing starts up all over again.

I still get calls. We still talk two or three times a day. I have no idea what kind of status I've got, whether we're lovers, boyfriend/girlfriend or what, but we're still connected somehow. So the agony may yet go on.

I'm sure in another month or two or three, somebody's

going to call her and ask her out, and she's going to disappear. Then I'm going to go through some of that same
tizzy that I've gone through. I hope not. God, I hope not.

Having obtained a certain lifestyle and a certain level
of possessions makes you vulnerable to what's out there.
I've really been taken advantage of. I'm a romantic. I'm very
easy. I get very involved in people's problems.

I've been sort of destroyed a couple of times. I swear I'm
not going to fall in love, then I meet someone and I get that
great time in the beginning. It's very rosy and idyllic, like
out of the movies. At first, the person could never do anything wrong. Anything bad is "cute." It's all beautiful.

But in that period, I become very vulnerable. Things
come up about her situation in life, and her problems lend
themselves to monetary solutions. I buy things when people start singing the blues. What happens is they need
bailing out, and I feel like I'm being taken for a ride. I don't
think I'm stupid. But I should be a little bit more assertive.
I should act more intelligently, instead of emotionally. I
never learn either. I really never learn.

Sometimes I feel there are women who prey on me.
There are women who totally expect to be taken care of. I
fall for them. I'm a caretaker. I get that from my father. He
was extremely into and promoted the idea that women
need to be taken care of. You always open the door for
them. You always pick up their chair. You always are on
the outside walking down the street. He gave me all this
knight in shining armor stuff, and I've always lost. I've always gotten fucked.

So, I met someone with a lot of money. I figured that's

safe. We have major conversations about how it's very hard to trust people, and how you're easy prey if you have money. She has the same problems. So Glenda and I develop this relationship. We traveled a lot and had a great time.

Then what happens is you become subservient. She's the type of woman who snaps her fingers all day, so when she comes home at night, she's still snapping her fingers.

That doesn't work either. It's like, "Excuse me, you want me to hold the door for you, pull out your chair, *and* let you snap your fingers at me? No, it don't work that way."

It was a disaster. I love, admire and respect her in business. I really admire ambitious women, but I do find that most ambitious women, unfortunately, are not very good at equal partnership. I find them very demanding. The bulk of them are *always* challenging you *all* the time. They think they're in the office. They don't know that at six o'clock it turns off. You're supposed to be a female person now. It's this constant challenging, challenging stuff. I have the ability to say, "Excuse me, it's six o'clock and I'm off duty." I have said it to her. Oh, she's so sorry. "Sorry. Sorry. I'm so sorry."

"When do you stop?" The other night at dinner she's going on and on about work. I said, "Glenda, it's Friday night. It's eleven o'clock. Do I have to hear about your job all night long?"

She looks at me a little disgusted and says, "Oh, well. I really value your opinion."

"Yeah, you do. But not in this situation. You're just talking. You're not really putting anything in front of me for an opinion. You're just rambling on and on and on."

I'm trying to get away from my business. Who cares? I don't care. It's just business. I hear my friends talking about projects and clients, and I think, "Who gives a shit? Why am I doing this? I don't care anymore."

I don't want to be 70 years old and look back and see that I was by myself. I see people all the time in business, men and women, who are very successful, but by themselves. "What are you doing for Thanksgiving?"

"Oh, nothing. Nothing." They have no family. They have friends, but the friends are all married and are going to be out of town. There's this bunch of executives who are these lonely, pathetic people. I don't want to be like them. That's what I'm afraid of.

But as you get older, you get much more picky. Very picky, very critical. I have become much more critical of the way a person looks, the way she dresses, acts, what her attitude is towards things. Younger people are a lot more open towards another person's eccentricities. When you're young it's, "Okay, we'll go to the country or the mountains."

Now with me it's, "What do you mean, you don't like the beach? Fuck you. I don't want to go to no mountain. I want to go to the beach for the weekends." I'm not ready for compromise. I want interesting conversation and beauty. You know what I'm saying? You become a little more fickle. Definitely fickle. It's hard.

I'd like to find a girl and fall in love, but I can't find one. They're all shopping at the holistic market and pretend they want to be organic and spiritual, but they're really judgmental. They drink coffee, they drink alcohol. They wonder why you're not out there being Barney Social at the racquetball club. How come you're not getting your contractor's license and striving for the ultimate dream?

All the single girls in this town have known a guy who

owned a yacht in the harbor or a Ferrari or an airplane or condos he's renting out. Or they all say they do or have. It's always in the back of their minds that they want some materialistic stuff to grasp on to. Presently, I don't really have any "stuff," besides my truck and hang glider, a motorcycle and a guitar. But I'm content with that. Really content. It's in their energy in this town. Everyone's in *Vogue.*

It's just shocking that so many want to be married and have kids, stay home and take care of the family. For all these years I've known girls who said they wanted that career. When I got to my thirties, and I meet girls that age, it's amazing, they all want a family, instead.

Another thing I notice about women that I meet in their thirties is that a lot of them that are single have gotten hooked on perming their hair like a poodle, watching videos and drinking wine. It's sad. They come to a point where they've given up looking. Video has locked them into their homes with a bottle of wine. I've met so many like that.

I've tried looking for women in acting classes. I've tried swing dance class, churches, whale boat trips and self-esteem classes. Adult education stuff, city college, gospel singing, hang gliding, glass blowing class. I've tried them all. There's always girls looking in the self-help programs. I've tried bike paths, hiking trails, the beach. Shopping malls sometimes work, cruising in there. Talking to hostesses and waitresses wherever I meet them.

There's a real coldness in bars now. It's hard for me even to go in, so I don't go there anymore. But there are good ones there, because they're looking, too. Somebody found my ex-wife in a bar.

I had to go out of town on a business trip. My wife and I had been separated for three or four months and she called about two days before I left and said, "I don't think it's going to work out. I'm going to come up to the apartment and take my stuff."

"That's fine," I said. "We're pretty clear on what we own and you can take whatever you think is fair." That's how we operated. She's a very decent person, so I had no problem with her pulling a moving truck up to the apartment while I was out of town and taking everything she thought was hers.

When I came back, she hadn't taken anything big that I thought I owned and she didn't, but there were two things missing that I thought were strange.

It was a hot August afternoon. I'd just gotten off the plane. The first thing I did when I walked into the apartment was get into the shower. When I stepped out and looked into the closet for a towel, there were no towels. None. There were no towels in the apartment. She had taken every single towel. How can we own twenty towels together and when we're separated, I don't have any left? It sounds like such a small thing, but when you're wet and dripping, it's a big deal. Anything would have been a help, even paper towels. I had to air dry.

Later that afternoon, I had some new stereo equipment I was moving in and needed some tools to hook it up. I have a tool kit, nothing special, the Sears model. It was gone. This woman does not know how to sew. She doesn't know how to screw in a light bulb. Why did she take the tool kit? I looked and looked and I finally called her when I couldn't find it anywhere.

"Hi, hon. How're you doing?"

"Good. I'm good," she said. "I came to pick up the stuff that we agreed on."

"Yeah, that's great. That's fine," I said. "Why did you take the tool kit? What *possible* reason could you have for taking the tool kit?"

"I don't know," was all she said.

I don't know for sure either, but I believe that she still loved me at that point, and it was like the "boy thing." She wanted to keep a little part of the "boy thing."

Having been through my divorce experience, I don't see anything wrong with a marriage of some length, whatever seems natural. I'm glad it's relatively easy to get divorced in this society. Most of the complications arise from sorting out property and making life reasonably secure for children. The only real problems come from ego involvement.

That's because marriage is viewed as so sanctified and necessary. The longevity of it is supposed to be paramount. It is perfectly natural for people to be attracted to one another at one stage in their life, and then suddenly not be very attracted to each other at some other point. I used to not think that divorce was a very cool thing, but now I have no problems with it whatsoever.

Perhaps it ought to be more matter of fact, that there's no way people would go into marriage without a premarital agreement. But the culture makes it just the opposite. "You don't love me if you want a premarital agreement. If you love me, you love me no matter what I do for the rest of my life, you asshole."

That's how it is. When people get married they have to say that they love this person no matter how things change, no matter what goes on. They're making this commitment to feel exactly the same forever and ever and ever, here and now and hereafter. It's so ludicrous.

My divorce was just finalized, but the end of the marriage happened a long time ago. The divorce was nothing. I thought it was supposed to be some giant trauma the day it happens. I couldn't even tell you what the date was. I couldn't tell you if it was a month or two months ago—it _was_ real recent—mainly because the emotional shit happened so far in the past.

Look at me. I'm not bitter at all. I have nothing but good memories. I'm pretty purposeful about that, too. When I went through the pictures, I didn't take any pictures of my wife. I've got a pile of pictures that I took, and they're all fun events or pictures of my house. Purposely, no pictures of her. Boom, she's gone. I'm a Communist at heart, a Brezhnev: "Khrushchev is out! Get me the airbrush! Aaah, he's a cloud now."

While I was partying, I met this chick and got married when I was 20. We had a little girl when I was 21, named Harmony. That's her picture right there.

A couple years after we had her, I was working in a full service gas station. I was the manager. I worked morning shift, and I had people to work the second shift, but it was hard work. The cars come at you quick and you had to make change. There was a lot of people couldn't do it. Sometimes, they didn't show up or whatever, and I had to work it. The night shift was busier than the day shift.

I come home one time after working a couple of double shifts, and she'd made me some spaghetti. Come to find out, she'd put some Quaalude powder in it, which is a down. It knocked me out. I was tired anyway, so she probably didn't need it, but it knocked me out. She wanted to make sure that I didn't wake up, because when I did, the only thing in the apartment was the bed I was sleeping on. She'd taken everything. She took both cars.

Later on, I found out she'd been planning this for some time, because she hadn't paid the rent for three or four months or the light bill or the gas. I was working a lot trying to get something, and she thought I was out running around when I'm at the gas station. She had buddies and her buddies were telling her, "He's doing this. You don't need this, you don't need that." Their lives were screwed up so they screwed up hers and mine in the process. I wasn't doing anything. She knew where I was at all times. All she had to do was drive into the station.

I drank, too, and she brought some of the blame on the drinking. But I was working hard, earning money, and when I wanted to drink, I drank. We didn't fight or nothing like that. I wasn't beating her all the time or nothing. She wasn't complaining or nothing. She just had a girlfriend who said, "Hey, you can do better than him."

So anyway, she left. At four o'clock in the morning, I woke up and had to have the gas station open by six. There's nothing. So I walked about two miles to a buddy's house and cried the blues to him. "Can you believe it? This shit?" I had to tell somebody, so I told it and went to work. I was devastated. Heartbroken, you know? But there wasn't nothing I could do about it. I didn't know where she was staying or nothing. I really didn't want to know, because if I found her I'd be afraid I'd want to hurt her. Especially after a couple of weeks went by, and they were going to throw me out of my apartment, turned off the gas and electric. She was planning this all along and just smiling at me. She took my daughter and I couldn't see her.

I missed my little girl, and I was real vulnerable at that time emotionally. I was lonely. I quit my job so I wouldn't have to pay no support. I was damned if I was going to pay when she was being a bitch and wouldn't let me see Harmony. I started hanging out with this guy who was into coke, so I got into the drug. Got to stealing radar detectors to go to the rock houses. It was awful. Didn't pay my rent, didn't eat, didn't care. Busted and bailed out, busted and bailed out.

Finally I sat in the workhouse for four months. When I got out of jail I went to a drug program and got clear. A buddy of mine let me stay with him and his family. Debbie was a friend of his wife where she worked. Over a period of time, I got to meet her. I asked her out and she started going out with me. She's got a daughter, so we just got together and said, "Hey, well, let's move in together and start a household. Get it together." We did and everything is going good so far. I don't have any problems. Everything is like your regular, normal life. I've been up and down, so I know the differences, I know when things aren't going exactly right. We're trying to save up so we can maybe buy a house. I'm paying my back child support, and I got a lawyer trying to help me get Harmony back. Her mother ended up deserting her and lost her to Children's Services out there. But I don't have the greatest record in the world right now, so it's a problem for me.

There's a kind of bitterness in me about women. I'm not perfectly happy with Debbie, and I'm sure she's not perfectly happy with me. I got to get along with Debbie, so I work at getting along with Debbie. Every day is pretty good. You get in moods and stuff. When I'm in a bad mood, I try to avoid her. If she's in a bad mood, I try to get her out of it. You can do little things that will make her smile. Other times, no matter what you do you're not going to make her smile. She's working six days a week, so she's really trying, too. She deserves the best that she's able to get. I work on that.

She knows I was in on the drugs. She don't know nothing about my childhood, except that I wasn't raised by my mom and dad, but that's about it. Especially to me, that's like crying to somebody. That's softness, and I'm kind of hard when it comes to feelings, because—I don't know— mine have been jerked around so much I'm afraid to put them out there on Front Street. It's hard to smile, hard to laugh, hard to get any kind of emotion. It's all straight, business. I try to loosen up a little bit. But it'll take a little while.

Finally, I've got one I can live with and that's made me hold a whole different opinion of them. I'm finding out that the lady I'm involved with is probably the best thing that ever happened to me. We were talking last night, and I remarked to her, "Isn't it nice that we've been able to find someone we really want to spend some time with and we don't have to compromise?" Yeah, it is. It's real nice. But she is a combination of all the other ladies I ever looked for.

Most people spend a lot of time compromising. A friend of mine once told me, when we were talking about this stuff, "It just gets to the point where you settle for what you got. You get tired of looking." His *wife* was sitting right there. The first thought that crossed my mind was, "This guy's not going to see tomorrow with a comment like that."

"He's right," she said. "You just settle for what you got." For a lot of people, it's not a question that you've found the best. It's just the fact that you ain't going to look anymore.

I don't have the depth of feeling to want anything enough. I've locked myself off against failure by guaranteeing myself failure in my doings, because somehow failure is less painful than success.

With this girl, Mary, I loved her from afar for about four years. When she was my girl, when she told me that she loved *me*—you know what I mean?—it was a feeling like none other that I've experienced in my life. It was completely and totally unworldly.

But it wore off, you know? Somehow being happy is like that line from a corny Dylan song, "This must be what Paradise is like after a while." That was sort of me.

I think back on Mary and she haunts me. I remember going on Sunday night dates. I haven't done anything on Sunday night in twenty years but psychic suicide, but then I was so clean that we did Sunday night dates and they were some of the finest, closest and most wonderful memories that I have. Going to the movies when the whole world was sleeping and freezing in my car because I had no heater. Walking out of "Flower Drum Song" and singing in Chinese to each other for half an hour riding around in the car. Wonderful, wonderful memories.

Then towards the end of the tenure, when I was starting to take myself seriously, and my friends were starting to say, "Graham's no fun anymore. He doesn't want to be the clown anymore. He's taking himself seriously," Paradise was getting to be a drag a little bit.

I had sex with her one night, came home, and jerked off thinking about sex with another woman. That frightened me at the time, but I was compelled to do it. I wasn't satisfied and this was the love of my life.

I suffered as much as I'm capable of suffering—a great deal—after she finally threw me over. It was the only thing the poor girl could do. She wanted to set an engagement date for us to get married. I saw myself backing out in slow motion.

My predicament isn't that unique. "Happiness" makes me more uncomfortable than "unhappiness" as these two states of being are understood to be. I'm more comfortable with lonesomeness and unhappiness than I am with a permanent happiness. There is a closed-endedness that reminds me of the Flash Gordon sequence where Ming the Merciless has the walls, the ceiling, and the floor close in to crush the hero. Tune in next week! The walls start closing in on me in an intellectual sense that stifles me.

Maybe it's not that there isn't the depth of feeling there. Maybe it's just some pathetic little flaw that makes me like this. Or I don't have the guts or the strength to endure it. Most men really see the married life, the social life, the integrated life lived with other people as something that is oppressive to them, too, a good deal of the time. But it is less oppressive to them than the idea of being alone. So I think to myself, "Maybe you just don't have the guts to horse it out."

But that's not it. I'm just a loner. I enjoy my life. I seem to have so little. I'm not a success at anything specifically. I don't have any money. I'm not making girls happy, in other words a relationship. That fucking nags at me. Making another human being happy, serving another human being is a very strong grade of manhood, and I don't do that. I have to live without that. I don't need a man or a woman or even a fucking hamster on an everyday basis. To me that's always grating. That's missing in my life.

Five: **Physical Education**

Growing up male is a combination contact sport and endurance test. Walk through any elementary school playground and witness the blindside tackling, the clumsy imitation-karate kicks little boys throw at each other's heads, the inevitable bully twisting the arm of a weaker, smaller boy. Some of the horseplay is simply the expression of youthful exuberance. But there is something else going on as well—competition, a physical testing and mental tension that almost never stops. Who is the biggest, the strongest, the fastest, the meanest? Who has the most power?

American culture encourages this constant conflict. Fathers smile while they admonish their sons not to fight. The one piece of advice every boy hears is, "Stand on your own two feet. You're going to have to fight your own battles sooner or later." So men grow up very physical creatures, whether they swagger or slink; men sniff the air for a warning of the smoldering violence that might be just beneath the surface of the next challenge or dispute. From their youth on, men spend all their lives grimacing and posing, whether it's in corporate battles over turf, or the barroom one-up-manship that escalates into a shoving match; whether bowling team rivalries or gun-waving disputes over freeway driving. As misplaced as it may be in our technological society, men still respond pugnaciously to territorial instincts buried deep in their genetic codes. Men still have a primitive urge to try to dominate other men, to be the undisputed silver-backed gorilla at the head of the troop.

Our earliest sports began as training for young men for hunting and for battle. The classic Olympic sports—running, jumping, boxing, wrestling, archery, the javelin and discus throw—all hark back to the violence of combat or the chase. As civilization progressed, sports became a more or less bloodless substitute for combat, and a relief valve for male aggression, which, unchecked, could destroy the fabric of society.

Boys are introduced to team sports to channel some of their excess energy, to teach them about compromise, cooperation, about "life." With just the right combination of physical talent, challenge and compassion, playing a sport well can be one of the most exhilarating experiences of a man's life. "There is nothing else like it," says a 40-year-old philosopher and inspirational writer. "I can still remember the feeling of executing a perfect cross body block when I was playing high school football. You focus on the other guy's numbers on the front of his jersey and launch yourself at them. Just before you get to him, you turn your body sideways in the air. You hit him at the waist. He just folds in half and you both land on the ground. It was great."

But not everyone is cut out to be an athlete. A 38-year-old photographer who is successful in his job and the rest of his life puts it this way: "Growing up a non-jock, when most of the boys were into sports and seemed to know all about football and baseball without having to be taught, made me have this feeling that something was wrong with me. I was one of the weird kids. Like, you're not a real guy. There is this whole feeling that you have to live up to a certain definition of what a boy is, or what a man is supposed to do. You don't meet it. In fact, you never get a clear idea of what it is, so you're never quite sure anyway. Even the guys who were captain of the high school football team were never quite sure they were doing it right. But I *knew* I wasn't doing it right. I always knew that I wasn't quite what I was supposed to be."

Although many men give size, strength and the ability to throw, catch or hit a ball excessive importance in the definition of what it means to be a man, those physical qualities are fleeting. A slight 41-year-old newspaper writer from the Rockies explained his experience of this phenomenon by telling about his twenty-year high school reunion: "The biggest revelation to me was that those gargantuan guys, who always loomed over me in the hallways and had a five o'clock shadow by the time 3 P.M. rolled around when I wasn't even shaving, turned out to be normal-sized men, with regular jobs and families and bald heads just like me. They weren't giants, I just wasn't grown yet."

A 47-year-old insurance adjustor from the Southwest added another perspective: "I was eighteen years old. We won the regional championships that season and I was a bona fide hero in the little town I grew up in. My picture was on the front page of the newspaper more than once that year, everybody knew my name, kids on bikes waved to me, girls wanted to go out with me. By the middle of the following summer, I came to the startling conclusion that that was the high point of my life. I'd had it and it was over. Barring a miracle, it was all downhill from there."

As men grow up and grow older, their personal participation in sports quickly dwindles. The majority of American men drive cars to work, literally or figuratively punch buttons all day (or tell someone else to punch them), and spend most of their recreational time on their butts, flipping around the television dial with a remote control. They have almost no physical contact with other men except for handshakes, which are sometimes overly firm, bordering on painful, but hardly qualify as sport.

"The thrill of victory, the agony of defeat," goes the introduction to "Wide World of Sports" every weekend. This is the call to prayer for the millions of fanatical male sports fans. On weekend afternoons and Monday nights in the fall, most wives know exactly where their husbands are—in front of the television set viewing the ritualistic battering of a pigskin ball. Then there are boozy summer afternoons spent sitting on a hard wooden seat in an open air cathedral, eating hotdogs, drinking beer, eating peanuts, drinking more beer, and standing up for two songs: "The Star Spangled Banner" and an organ recital of "The Mexican Hat Dance." Every morning millions of American men grab a cup of coffee and begin the day by deciphering the hieroglyphics in the sports section of the newspaper, the bible of the exclusive male religion dedicated to competition, with its own coded language.

Men worship competitive sports for two reasons. First, the game on the field is an idealized version of men's lives, and represents a kind of hope for a higher plane of existence. The competition is man to man, the goal is manifest, winners and losers are decided quickly and fairly, and everybody generally plays by the rules. Life for men is almost never like that.

Secondly, notwithstanding a few female journalists in the locker room and a couple of little girls suing to play baseball, sports is the last bastion of male camaraderie, a de facto men's club where males idolize and envy other men whose physical superiority has won them fame and multi-million dollar professional contracts. In the relative privacy of male companionship, men can yearn for youth and indulge in a nostalgia for that physical side of themselves which is so important to self-image, but which is virtually useless in the modern world.

And there's one more reason, which needs no explanation, or at least has none. Sports is fun.

My most powerful visual image of my family comes from a time in about 1961, when we were living near the coast and my parents were building a house in the mountains. We would go out as a family to work on it. That meant that the children were usually sent out to pick up rocks or some other inane activities to keep us busy and out of the way. We would travel there in this huge station wagon. All of us were present the day I remember: five kids, my parents and my father's mother as well.

We are driving through town, and my parents are having one of their arguments, going back and forth at each other. My mother is not being confrontational so much as being antagonistic or negative or irritating. It isn't whining, she just isn't allowing him to have his way at this point. I remember my father just exploding himself. He stops the car in the middle of the street. He leaps out of his side, goes over to the other side and pulls my mother out. He starts kicking her and hitting her, physically requiring her submission.

That image of their violence and the potential for what male violence could do to someone who was at a disadvantage was very, very powerful to me and quite frightening as a child.

Very quickly after the divorce, my mother began a not horribly intentional campaign to keep me in line by using my father as a very negative image and using the characteristics of my personality that she could label as potentially explosive or violent as very negative ones, ones that needed to be controlled to an extreme degree.

When she was being sort of neutral, like if I was to try to give her a hug, she would say, "Oh, you're real strong. You better be careful about your strength. You have to watch that." She didn't really want or encourage any kind of physical contact or affection between us. It was constantly the message, "You have to control your strength. It is not a necessarily positive characteristic."

Then when she would get angry or I would misbehave, it wasn't, "You're just like your father." It was, "I'm going to send you to your father and your father is an evil man. I'm going to send you off to this hell."

She gave me a very good indoctrination that men are not trustworthy. Men are all potentially violent. Men are not responsible. You are a loaded gun with a hair trigger. I just didn't quite have the personal strength to remain rebellious. I feel like I was eventually humiliated into being cooperative and into being the good son. I just shut down. No interaction was the safer course when you had to be afraid of your own impulses.

My father just didn't believe in hitting a woman. The only time he whacked *me* was one time when I gave my sister a whack.

"Whatever they do, you never hit them. Never, ever, ever."

One time, my mother hit my father. He said something that needed being said real bad, because my mother could get out there, you know? After he said it, she was at a loss for words, so she slapped him. I saw this from the top of the stairs and was getting very scared. My sister was crying.

"If these children weren't here . . ." he said. But he didn't hit her back. It was lots of verbal fights that would just well up in the course of the day, like a storm or a snow flurry, then it's gone an hour later, automatically. But it kept me on edge a lot wondering when it was going to happen next.

He beat my mom up. He didn't beat her too terribly. Just a slap or two. The yelling freaked me out. It was weird to see my mom get knocked down, fall on the piano and tumble off the bench.

I ran to the Norwegians' house next to ours and banged on the door. She answers—the mom—and I asked her where her sons were. I went running through the house, down to the basement, crying, and told them to call the police on my dad.

"What? Ya? Ya?"

They didn't call. I came back home, and she was just crying, talking, taking her curlers down from her hair that were knocked out when he slapped her around. That's what made me decide I'm not going to be like my dad. I'd never be mean to a woman or punch them out or slap them around.

When I was five or six years old, the excitement was all around what was forbidden, the monstrously evil things. The older kids—they were 12 to 14—allowed us to tag along with them when they "went hunting." There were garter snakes all over the woods down there. We hated snakes. Somebody lit a kind of torch-like lantern, they'd catch the snakes and burn them alive. Meanwhile, we would dance with glee, screaming and yelling, at the evil of it all.

We'd catch these huge yellow and brown locusts in the summertime. They were big, ugly grasshoppers that could fly and jump and spit brown juice at you. We called it spitting tobacco. There was real sport in hunting them, spotting them in the dried grass, sneaking up, the pounce, and then a wild, manic chase.

But when we'd caught a bunch, then the game changed. It became a sort of Nazi holocaust for insects. We'd pry their legs off one at a time and then watch their legless bodies squirm around. We'd break open firecrackers, light the loose powder and let it fry a grasshopper alive. We'd tie a rock to one of their legs with a piece of string that was just short enough to keep them from getting to the surface when we dropped them into a bucket of water.

We couched all this in terms of experimentation. And I guess there was a real element of curiosity involved. But some of it was just fucking nasty, the kind of bad that even makes you feel creepy when you're doing it, but you just can't stop yourself.

In my neighborhood they had stores and stoop fronts. This is a series of steps, usually four, going up to the front door of a house or apartment building. I was 6 or 7 the first time I walked down four or five houses from my house. This was a big exploration. I hid behind this huge sycamore tree and looked over on the stoop. I saw all these guys sitting there, just as it was getting dark. They were in semi-shadow. You see guys sitting on the bottom step, the second step and the top step. The older guys were on the top of the stoop. The younger guys, who were a little older than I was, were on the bottom step. There were some guys who couldn't find a place on the stoop. They would never sit there, even if there was a spot. It belonged to somebody. They might sit there until that person showed up, but then they immediately got up, especially if it was one of the higher seats on the stoop

When I was that age, as soon as dusk came, my father would whistle this two note whistle and I had to be in. But the accepted progression in the neighborhood was from the house to the stoop. The expectations of your parents are, is he going to fit in the group? "Go make friends." "How are your friends?" "What do your friends think?" When I'd catch a ball with my father, he'd ask, "Did your friends ever see you throw a ball like that?"

For an entire summer, I was standing and never had a seat on the stoop. But during that summer, I was a pretty good athlete, and I made comments they thought were funny. I went from standing, right to the second step.

One evening I came back home and said, "I sat on the stoop tonight."

"Oh, really?" my mother would say. "You should bring something to drink. Doesn't anybody drink anything out there?"

"No, Ma."

"Well, tomorrow night, I'll give you something to bring to all of them."

"No, it's not like you're inviting people over to your house, Ma."

They were glad you were sitting there because they were worried a whole lot about the fact that there were some kids who never got invited to sit on the stoop.

The guys on the stoop were good-looking guys, good athletes and tough guys. Tough guys sat on the top, and it didn't matter what age they were. You could be a tough guy and sit on the top step at 14. If you were a ladies' man you could sit wherever you wanted. That's the truth. Of course, you had to be a certain age before anybody appreciated that you were a ladies' man at all.

What was interesting was that we really admired attractive guys when we were very young. You look at some guy who was thin and well-dressed, and he took care of himself, he was an admired guy. As I see those guys through the cloudy view of memory, most of them were also good athletes. God really is a prick in his heart, because what he does is give these guys so much. Not only is he a good athlete, he's good-looking, he's got money in his pocket somehow or other, parents and teachers liked them, everybody liked them.

On the stoop, you just sat and talked and looked at the stars and really wondered about life. There was lots of talk about sports and athletic prowess. The young guys on the lower steps mostly just listened and laughed a lot.

It was a time when young men were still being drafted, so it was always talk among the older guys in the neighborhood about being in the Army or the Navy. Anybody who went into the Navy was really a big deal. Those guys really traveled and they brought back matchbook covers from whorehouses in Valencia.

"Wow, what do you think happens in that place?"

The girls who were around during the day were just unseen once the sun went down. They stayed in, because their parents wouldn't let them out of the house. It was strictly a boys' place.

Still as children we'd play games at night—nighttime games. We'd play ringelevio, which is a kind of hide and seek in the dark, except you have to wrestle down the guy you find and bring him back to the base. That's how you found out who the strongest guys were, who were the fastest runners, the toughest guys. The fastest guy would run back to the light pole and free everybody else. The fastest guy on my street was this guy named Pepe. "Pepe's going to come." He'd yell for everybody, come zipping out of the darkness and free us. Everybody would split into the shadows.

It wasn't long before you made the progression from the stoop down to the corner. This is around the time you reach puberty good and strong. You stand around in the circle of light under a street lamp and play a little tougher game, like Johnny on the Pony, which is a game that has to do with strength and meanness. One guy stood up against the light pole. Right in front of him, some guy would bend over and put his head alongside of the pole and wrap his arms around the first guy's waist and the pole. Then that guy would brace himself with his legs spread. The next guy would put his head between that second guy's legs, and wrap his arms around the second guy. So you'd have a series of six or seven guys bent over, and one guy up against the pole as the buffer. He was to keep the pole from cutting into anybody's head.

In the middle of the street would be another group of about the same number of guys. The first guy in that group would be a quick, light guy. He would run as fast as he could, dive into the air and land as close to the pole as he possibly could on the back of the first guy bent over. Then the second guy in the street would dive and land on his back, and the third guy, hanging on to each other all the while, giggling, all kinds of shit. Pile and pile and pile. The last guy's job was to jump on so hard that he'd bring it all down. Crush!

If you brought it all down, you got to get up and do it again. If they could hold you up and call out, "Johnny on the Pony. One, two, three," then you had to get down and they'd jump on your backs.

Now there were guys who would run and hit with their knees first. They were real pricks, really bad guys, and these guys turned out later in life to be real sons-of-bitches, you know what I'm saying? You run across the street, jump, come down on your knees in the middle of somebody's back, that hurt. But there was also camaraderie, because you would hang on to each other, even when everybody was falling over onto the pavement.

We'd hang out and think about next summer or two summers from now when some of us are going to be able to move up to the _next_ corner, directly across the street from the bar, where the lights are on till three o'clock in the morning, and people are playing shuffleboard, drinking and flirting, where everything was happening.

But they wouldn't let you near that place. If you went up there, the older guys would chase you. "What are you doing here? Get back to the street."

The price for hanging out with the older guys where I grew up was that if some young punk from another part of town gave them some shit, you had to go and beat them up. That was part of your job for being allowed to hang out. They couldn't go and beat the little shit up themselves, because they were too big. They'd send you.

There was this Irish kid who was fearless. He was right down the street yelling shit back at the older guys. "Go get him, Billy."

So, I went down there to do my job. This red-headed kid took one punch and knocked me on my ass. I couldn't believe that one punch. He didn't even hit me hard, he just caught me right and I went right onto my ass. I got up, dusted myself off, and . . . uh . . . walked back to the older guys. This was in the third grade and he and I became friends for a bunch of years.

The only way to be protected was to be real honcho, and people stayed away from you. Nobody messed around with Clint because he was in the Jokers. The Jokers were cool, because the Jokers had cards–you know, the Joker cards from a standard deck. There was the black gang, the Mau Mau Chaplains. There were the Skid Row Gents. There were the Testors from the glue because they were glue sniffers, like the guy called Whitey because he'd be all white in the face from sniffing glue. I had friends who were all of a sudden walking down the street with that vacant look on their faces, their nose is all red and their eyes are running. You look like shit when you sniff glue, and you get glue on your face from the bag.

Just by sheer luck, I skirted all this stuff. I said I was going to join this gang, but then I didn't show up for initiation. Naturally, they had to reciprocate. They met me after school and got around me. All of a sudden, one guy hits me in the back of the kidneys as another guy hits in the front and I just went down like a sack of beans. I was this blob on the sidewalk. I tried to get up again, and somebody took another shot at me. But one of the guys was my friend, too, so he watched out for me that I didn't get beat up too much. They weren't going to kill me. Joey's going, "No, no. Don't hit him in the face."

I remember not being able to get up and saying to myself, "Well, somehow the right thing happened. I wasn't meant to join this gang stuff."

I really never left my part of town. I would go and visit relatives sometimes on a Sunday. I'd sit in the backseat of my father's car, we'd drive over the bridge and I didn't even look out of the window. I'd get there, go into my relatives' house and I didn't want to leave the house. I didn't want to go out into that neighborhood. I didn't want to be on that street because I didn't know anybody on that street. I recognized that each neighborhood had the same kind of set-up. When a stranger comes in, you're in serious trouble, because you could get the shit kicked out of you. They just beat you up. They'd get the toughest guy in the neighborhood to show you how tough he was, which meant beating up somebody from your neighborhood.

It happened to me a couple of times, and after that I'd just stay in the house and watch TV. Once I got back into my neighborhood, I'd run around like a dog you just let out of the car. "Whoa-ooh, back!" You really felt safe.

The tough guy in your own neighborhood never picked

on anybody, because he didn't have to pick on anybody. It was his block. Nobody bothered him. By the time you were ten, you knew who not to fuck with.

When I went to high school, it necessitated that I take a bus and leave the neighborhood, which was scary beyond anything that I could imagine.

On the first or second day, coming down a flight of stairs, carrying books, I met these black guys coming up the stairs. They were older guys, juniors and seniors. They just knocked the books out of my hands. I was scared to death of them. They were black, they talked this language that I'd never heard before, and they were using words like motherfucker. Whoa, these guys are tough. When I went to get my books, a guy banged me on the back of the head and knocked me down these steps. The guy says, "I'm going to be here tomorrow when you come down these steps. When I see you, I want 25 cents. My name is Harold."

That's all I got, 25 cents for lunch. I was shaking like a leaf, walking to the cafeteria.

This cafeteria looked like there were thousands of people in there. Seemed like there were hundreds of tables and they were set up in a way so that seniors sat on one side of the room and freshmen sat somewhere else. The guys from my neighborhood were sitting at one of these tables. I walked over there and one of them got up from the table and said, "Where are you going? You can't come over here. You've got to go back to your side."

"I want to ask you something," I said.

"What is it?"

"Let me tell you," I was half crying, "I was coming down to go to lunch and this black guy knocked down my books and said he was going to beat me up tomorrow if I didn't give him money."

"Where? What black guy?"

"Harold."

"That Harold over there?"

"Yeah, that's him."

"Okay, don't worry about it. Go back to your side."

I went back to my side. Four tables of guys get up, half of them from my neighborhood. They walk over and I see them talking to this guy. One of them reaches over and pulls this black guy out and they got into a fistfight. All the black guys just watched while this big white guy from my neighborhood beat the shit out of this guy. Literally, he beat the shit out of him and then came back to me and said, "You know, if you have any trouble here, don't you start anything. You come get us." He told me, "And we expect you to take care of the next guys." It was a great, unbelievable feeling.

Everybody had one of these guys in high school, red-headed fellow, freckle-faced, a little overweight. The English teacher was sick, so we had a substitute and a study hall. There was a group of Future Farmers of America in the class, too. They wore these blue corduroy jackets, and up there in Potato Land it was a solid club of guys. Movers and shakers in that school belonged to FFA. They were kind of a gang. They moved their desks into the back, and one at a time they came out of this group, went over to this red-headed kid I hardly knew, and they were harassing him, doing things to him, shoving his books off his desk or poking him in the back, each one trying to be more creative about giving this guy shit.

I really took offense at it. I waited until the smallest guy got up to do his thing to the kid. Logically, it was because he was the smallest guy in the group that I chose to make my move. I intercepted him before he got to this guy, and I said something like, "Why don't you fuck with somebody your own size." I probably was two inches taller than he was. The guy turned around and went back to the group. I went back to my desk.

There must have been five of these guys. They all got up as a group and surrounded me at my desk. This is all with the substitute teacher sitting there like a log. The ringleader, who was a big guy who had been held back a year or two, was their spokesman. He's saying, "You got a problem with this?" And he kept shoving his fingers down on my book.

I had one of those 99-cent fountain pens that you buy cartridges for. I took that in my hand and turned it up like a dagger and I said, "You put your hand on my desk again, and this is going to go right in the back of it."

You could see it in his face. He could have torn me up, but he had to stop. He just sort of melted and thought, "What am I going to do?" But now he was also surrounded by all these guys. So he grabs my wrist. The fountain pen is above his hand. I turn my wrist, so the pen is on his hand, and I drive it down between his thumb and forefinger. Just buried it. And he lets go, by God.

By that time the substitute is next to us going, "What's going on? What's happening here? Get back to your desk."

At the end of class, the big guy meets me before I can get through the door, and he says, "I want to see you out at the bus stop after school."

"Okay, sure. No kidding. Yeah, no problem. I'll see you, buddy."

The next thing I know people are coming up to me from all over school. My sister who is a junior says, "Jimmy, you can't go meet this guy." I was trying not to worry about it. My rationalization was that I've always been able to talk myself out of everything, doesn't matter what it is. My life has been a nice comfortable life. I can talk myself out of this. No problem.

It was a bright, sunny, clear winter day with the reflection off the snow and ice just blindingly bright. I delayed my entry into that blindness, because I was looking for gloves. I thought that I needed gloves to fight. Basically, I was going to go out there and talk to them about it and that would be it.

I got out there a little late. Here are these guys with the blue jackets from the FFA in the snow, being real amiable. I walk up to them and I say, "Where's this guy?"

"He got tired of waiting for you and went back into school to look for you. Oh, there he is. He's coming out of school now."

I turned around and looked back at the school to see him. Then I turned back around to talk to these guys. That was one lesson that I learned: If you've got an enemy, never take your eyes off him. He walked up right behind me, wheeled me around by my shoulder and decked me. For the next ten or fifteen minutes, I got up and he hit me. I'd get up again, and he'd hit me again. There was this crowd of students around us. I just kept getting up. I was trying to kick him in the balls which felt so absurd, because my feet were just going out from under me and not getting close. He was coming over and hitting me at will. I was falling down.

From what I understand, my sister went to the basketball hero and told him to go stop this fight. He was the one who stopped it. I went home that day on the bus and I was just hurting and hurting. When I went to sleep that night, I was in such pain.

If I could define the one thing that seemed to be the big neon sign in my childhood, I found out early in life that I was really good at sports. I was very competitive, the sort of win-at-all-odds thing, the American Way. It was all either black or white. You either won or you lost. Your heroes were defined by winners or losers.

That was the dominant thing in my life. Locally, the majority of people were working the mills, and the ultimate achievement was playing professional baseball, or going to college to play football and making the NFL.

All my friends were completely into sports. A second tier friend might be totally into drag racing, but that was okay, because that was win or lose, too. Winners and losers.

There were steps up the ladder, and these were fervently followed. There was Little League, Pony League, then Babe Ruth League. It wasn't so much that your team won a league championship, but that you were good enough to get into the next league, because everybody was looking at the bigs in every league. Then there's junior varsity and varsity. That's all I was looking for was the next notch up. Then I got to college and figured out that this was the end of the line.

My love of sports is the same as the *Soldier of Fortune* type's addiction to war, because it's this incredible miniature life you can act out in an hour or two.

I went to the racquetball club tonight at 5:30. Through the course of several games I was forced on numerous occasions to decide whether to lie on a close call or not. There are so many value judgments, so many tests of your character. Am I going to blow this lead? Can I come back? You've got so many little things that you can interpret as *life*. Some people wouldn't, but I choose to do it.

"God damn it, I'm behind this guy 12 to 8 and the game's

to 15. If I'm anything of a winner, if I'm anything of a *person,* I can beat this guy."

If you do, you say, "Hey, I'm really something." That's a wonderful feeling. "I just kicked the shit out of everybody!" Where else can you go and in an hour have victories and losses, come from behind, putting your mind and body to the test? I was winning tonight and I was on a high. That's a quick and easy high to get on. At the end I was standing around saying, "Doesn't anybody want to play?"

"Wayne, we thought you had to be someplace at 7:30."

"That's okay, he can wait. Doesn't anybody want to play?"

What a world that teaches you the wonderful lesson, "Well, I got the absolute dog shit kicked out of me, but there's always tomorrow." There are very few areas in society where you can learn these little lessons and parables and stay in one piece.

I wanted to be a jock, but I was always the weakest and slowest kid. If we ran the hundred-yard dash, I would always come in last. I would do the fewest chin-ups. I wasn't down at the bottom. I *was* the bottom.

I would come home from playing baseball in an empty lot with kids, and I would be really mad and unhappy that I struck out a few times. I wanted to throw the ball all the way to home plate from the outfield, but I had to hit the cut-off man, because I couldn't throw all the way. I just couldn't.

In seventh grade I joined the school basketball team. We won one game that year, and I was the worst player on the team. I scored one basket that game. My father was there. He was at all the games. He saw my one basket. Then we argued about whether it was straight in or off the backboard. It wasn't a big stupid argument because we were feeling pretty good, but we still couldn't manage to avoid arguing over something. It was off the backboard. I was there. I shot it. He was sitting in the stands and he said, "No, it went right in," as though that were a better shot. That's the way things were with us quite a bit.

At one point, they give you IQ tests in school. Normally, they don't tell you the results unless a parent asks. My mom went and asked. Mine was high. She told me, in part to inspire me and in part because I wanted to be an athlete and I wasn't cut out for it. But she let me know she thought I was special. After that I always did feel special.

High school for me was pretty bad socially. My anxiety was about going out in the world and surviving the emotional trauma of dealing with whatever might come up. I remember just being scared, not so much picked on, although there was that, too, because I was a skinny little boy.

P.E. was nothing but team sports. You would think that a good gym teacher would emphasize physical fitness, and would help kids like me get a little stronger. Maybe teach us how to enjoy some of the games and some basics: how to run and how to throw. If you're going to play team sports, they ought to take the kids who don't know the games, or don't play them very well, and help them get better.

I never seemed to know the details of how to play. I assume the other guys were watching TV with their fathers, maybe playing catch and baseball with their fathers. I wasn't. My father had a physical handicap, so he wasn't out there playing sports a lot.

I went through a lot of years where I got bad grades in P.E. because of my health. That meant that some days I just wouldn't put on my gym suit, because I said I wasn't feeling well. There was a whole group of us who seemed to be sick an awful lot. My parents could never figure it out. "Honey, why does this say that you've got bad health?"

"It's a long story, Mom."

The coach would always pick a couple of team captains and no matter what the sport was, basketball or baseball, every time I was the last to be picked. That really hurt. It didn't make me want to get any better.

The first thing I ever really loved was baseball. In third grade, I'd be in class in the afternoon, and if it was cloudy, the only thing I could think about was the weather. If it rained, nobody would show up at the field after three o'clock to play. So I'd sit there praying that it wouldn't rain, so I can go out and play baseball. The biggest bummer in my life was rain. The sense of joy when I did play was as pure as any I've ever had.

I was totally unmotivated in everything but baseball. I was a slightly above average athlete who became an excellent hitter out of sheer will. It was like English class in school. The reading I loved, but the grammar I resisted completely. Fielding for me was an exact corollary. I was a great hitter, but they stuck me at first base, because I couldn't field and was sort of disinterested in it.

Little League was my great love of baseball coming to fruition. When I was 10, I went out for Little League and didn't make it. At 11, I made it and was sort of scrub, learning how to hit. When I was 12 years old, which is the last year of Little League, I led the league in hitting with a .476 average. I led all *three* leagues. I was the best hitter in town. I had no power. There were better hitters, because they could hit homeruns, but on the average I was the best. I was real good at it. Boy, I loved that. I really loved that.

But there was a rule that said the cut-off date for 12-year-olds was August 1. My birthday was in late July. This kid—Dick Jinks—he's a little bank vice president now, but he was a pinched-faced cocksucker even back then. I used to hit the living shit out of him when we played stickball even before Little League. So one day, between games playing stickball in the school yard and he's facing me, he says, "Vince, when were you born?" I didn't even know about this rule, so I told him.

This is the end of the season. The All Star Game was coming up and I was the first baseman. We have to play a tournament here in town for three weeks, and then we go to other towns to play. I come to the dugout, dressed, ready to play that day. The managers who were running the team came up and pulled me aside and told me that I could play in the local games, since I was the best hitter in the town, but I couldn't play in the other games because I was four days too old. Because of Dick Jinks I couldn't play in the All Star Game either. So I went over and sat on the bench and cried. I didn't want to cry, but I couldn't stop it.

The next year I had to go out with the 14-year-olds and I was barely 13. I made it through two cuts. Then I got cut on the last one. I cried then and was consoled by one of the coaches. That's the last time I can remember just blubbering for about five or six years. Then once over a girl, and then that was the end of crying.

I played midget football for a team that was the best in the metropolitan area. Every year they won all the championships. These guys had been playing together for four or five years, so they were pretty cliqueish. One of the coaches' sons was the star of the team.

I saved up my money, and I bought elbow pads. One day, I had to leave practice early to go to some appointment, which I hated to do, but my parents insisted. This kid who was the coach's son said, "Listen, you're leaving. Can I borrow your pads? I'll give them back to you tomorrow."

"Sure," I said.

The next day when I came up and asked for my pads, he had written his name on them. He said, "What pads? What are you talking about?"

I went home and told my dad. He essentially said, "You're going to have to fight your own battles."

There was no way to get any justice. I went to the guy's father. The guy's father just shrugged me off. "What are you talking about? My son wouldn't do that."

So I went to the guy. He was in the midst of his four or five friends and said, "Hey, you saw me buy these pads, remember? You were with me." Yeah, yeah, yeah.

It was one of those places where I had nowhere to turn to. Not only was I lost. No one could help me out. If it was just me and this kid, I would have fought him. That would have resolved it, but it wasn't like that. I was far away from my own neighborhood where I had my own friends. I was the only guy on this team that I knew except for one other kid, who really wasn't going to help me. I was left with it completely unresolved.

I felt powerless and humiliated. As far as manhood goes, it was like being emasculated. It was one of those things that's over, but for years you're asking yourself, "What's with me? What's wrong with me?" I felt like a failure, like an asshole.

Have you got a list of "The Two or Three Worst Things I Ever Did"? You know, when you were lower than a low dog. Every man has got a few of those. There's a few borderline acts that you can kick off the list from time to time. Then you do something else. You set up the hierarchy when you're a kid and these are things that nag at you. Jesus! Most of them have to do with letting down somebody else, imaginary as that was.

Here's one of the things I keep running through my mind. I was a jock when I was a kid, because I'm very physically adept and I'm a big guy. We didn't have a swimming pool at my school, but there was this great guy when I was growing up who started this little YMCA swim program. He talked to kids who were fairly good at it, and started a swimming team. He collected this ragtag bunch of kids that nobody else wanted, and we had a great little swimming team and we won all the time. This went on all through school. By the time I hit high school, I was the greatest thing in the town, swimmingwise. In fact, practically in the whole state, and that's fourteen million people.

Finally, we were the division champions two years in a row. Nobody was winning anything else, since it was a small school, so all of a sudden we were the heroes of the school. Three-quarters of the kids in that high school didn't even know how to swim. They could pitch hay and do a whole lot of other things, but swimming wasn't something they'd thought about too much.

We went to the sectional championships and I had a lock on winning the 100 yard backstroke. The only kid that was any good, I had beaten twice that season. Twice. Beat bad, too. By a long ways.

I swam up and swam back, made the turn. I was swimming along, and I closed my eyes. I got hung up in the ropes. Only takes you a second to get out of the ropes. I never got out of the ropes. That kid swam past me and I came in second.

I'll never understand why I lost that race. It was a big thing to everybody. It was a big thing to the coach, a big thing to the other guys on the team. I was so far better than the other swimmers. That's the only thing from my childhood that I regret, that I lost my concentration. I've always wondered all this time, if I did it on purpose, sort of, because there was absolutely no reason for it. In all the eighteen years before I left home, that's the major thing that I think about—my failure. Very weird.

One of the things sons of divorced people do is they are constantly looking for male role models, for heroes. At 15 and 16, I was trying to identify my coaches as heroes for me.

In my second year of playing football there was one

practice in particular that sticks in my mind. We'd lost the week before, and we were evidently not pleasing him in practice. It was hot. He chose to direct negative comments to everybody, but for some reason I heard this one and took it very personally. "Conroy, you're a *puke bucket.* You can't do anything. You're some sort of *wussy.* Get up and go throw yourself at that guy! Just bash your head in!"

The message was, "Go be self-destructive. Be out of control." I tried to do that, and got up from tackling this person who was forty pounds heavier than me and saw stars. I was devastated emotionally. I was crying, but not making that obvious to anyone. A helmet and face guard hide a lot of things.

This somehow meant that football had lost it for me. I was not going to be able to be successful at this. I just couldn't buy into the physical aggression. I couldn't be this coach's image of what a football player and a man should be. Realizing that I was never going to be able to be that represented a real emotional loss. You think that you're male. You've got the right anatomy. You're going to try to be whatever you buy into at the beginning as the image of a man. Being physically competent was one of those images. It became clear that I would never do that, never be that. It was extremely painful.

I continued to play football after that, but the heart went out of it. I was no longer looking up to those people as heroes or father images. It was one of those dawning realizations that life is not fair, that you don't necessarily reach your dreams.

The first three years of high school, I started and played. I was a defensive end. By the time I got midway through my junior year, I wasn't growing anymore. I was just much smaller than the guys I was playing against. They moved me over to offense, but I ended up being second or third string.

My senior year, I didn't go out for football, I wasn't going to bother. The most fun I ever had from football was in the practice my junior year, because they'd make me a ball carrier. During the week, we would scrimmage, do the other team's offense, and I would always play a key position in the other team's strategy. So I had a lot of fun practicing, but sitting on the bench was no fun at all.

It was one of those things that was about my manhood more than anything else. Machismo. I wasn't going to be someone on the bench on the Glory Day.

I was literally dating the girl next door. We grew up together and went out together and were best friends throughout junior and senior high school.

But in high school, Vivian was being strongly courted by Bob Wick, who was in football. He asked her out to something I had already asked her out to. She said, "Maybe." That pissed me off no end. I had possession, right? Even though I was still very ambivalent about her, I didn't have a burning passion for her, never did, but the territory had been staked out, I thought. Here comes this contender from left field. What the hell is going on here? Jocks? You mean I got to worry about jocks, this guy from the football team coming and snooping around her?

I got real angry. We got into a huge fight about it, so I didn't walk her home from school that day. I just left.

I had to walk through an elementary school play area on my way home. Like most playing fields, it was just dirt and rocks. There was no grass. Who meets me on the way home but Bob Wick. He came up and said, "Listen, I don't care what you think, I'm taking her out to this."

"Wh-wh-wh-who do you think you are? I been going out with her."

He just hauled back and smacks me. I was stunned, because hitting was not something I grew up with. You don't hit people. What's the point? I wrestled with him. To me that was fighting. He was punching, I was wrestling, and I got the snot kicked out of me. Big, bad time. I thought, "She agrees to go out with this guy and then he comes and beats me up. So this is what's so wonderful about dating?"

When you're in the reformatory, everybody made you learn how to fight, because if you could fight you didn't have to worry about nobody robbing your stuff or taking advantage of you, or nothing like that while you are confined.

I can get real angry, but when I learned how to fight, I learned I had the power in me. You might hit a person in the arm and it won't do anything to them, or I hit them on the arm and break it. It's no theory or nothing. What really brought it out was when Bruce Lee was in the movies. I started seeing where not only could I throw a punch but I had strength. I used to rassle two or three guys. I would like to let them get me down, one on each arm and trying to hold me. I would say, "To the Ultimate, All Power, Come In!" And I could just throw them right off me. They couldn't hold me. It may have been a make-believe thing, but it gave me power. It was like mind over matter.

But just because you're large don't mean you can go around beating on people. Sooner or later, people get a group together and kill you. Once I learned I had the power, I started slowing down and getting myself more together into life. "You're a man now. You've got responsibilities. The most important one is to yourself."

When push come to shove, I did my share of shoving back. I never went out picking on people, but anybody that jumped on me I defended myself and I defended myself good. I wasn't afraid of going in and getting my ass kicked. I was lucky, though, I never did. It could have been a lot worse. I'm not the biggest guy on the street, but I beat up guys who was two or three times my size, just because I had the instinct of not being intimidated.

My buddy, Eddie, was getting married and that same day his sister was moving out of this apartment. There was these two guys in there that were heckling her, two big country boys. Her two brothers was there, but they were scared because these guys was huge. So they come down to where we were at the reception from the wedding. They said, "These two guys are getting on your sister."

So we went down there and I walked up to the dude who'd said it. I turned to the sister and I said to him, "I understand you said this woman here stinks. Is that right?"

"Yeah," he said. I turned like I was going to walk away and I come around and just blasted him. He hit the wall and just slid down to the floor. As he was going down the wall, I was just beating him. A big guy like this wanting to intimidate a woman and a couple of kids. So I got pissed off, and I had a temper.

He got up, went next door and got a gun, a little .22. I walked out on the porch, and he stuck the .22 in my face. I said, "Hey, look, buddy, if you don't pull that trigger, I'm taking that .22 away from you, and I'm shoving it up your ass." Looked him dead in the eye.

"Damn, you must be drunk," he said.

"Hey, I'm not drunk, but if you don't put that gun down I'm shoving it up your ass."

I was scared shitless, but I wasn't going to let him know. Just stupid, but I knew he didn't have the guts to pull the trigger. He put the gun away and they left. My friend's sister moved out, and everything was said and done. It left an impact on the people around there. It takes a bit of craziness. I grew up with a lot of craziness. As long as I don't use it to intimidate other people or hurt anybody else, I feel that everything is okay. You got to have a little craziness to survive.

When I was 16, I wanted to be a gangster. That was what I was going to do. I went to work for the Gallo brothers. I was making money you couldn't believe. Two, three hundred dollars a week cash. I was still in a parochial school with such high academic standards that we did not have to take the college boards to get into a university.

It was a great feeling to walk into a joint when you're connected. You get treatment that you don't normally get. You don't pay to drink. Everybody looks at you from the side. Nobody dares look at you straight. All kinds of whispers going on, but you know they're not bad whispers.

"Oh, wow, he's with Joey Gallo."

"He's one of the guys."

You're driving cars and you don't even have a license. And they're Cadillacs. You park a convertible and leave the top down in a neighborhood that was as bad then as it is now, and nobody would bother it. You knew damn well pigeons wouldn't shit on it.

Then I'm 18 years old, just out of high school, when the shit hit the fan. It's a funny thing to wake up one day and realize, "You know, you could get killed doing this shit." It's no longer pretend. Now when you walk, you look all around. It's gang war. People are getting killed all over the place, getting shot.

So I go from something that's fairly lucrative and sort of a charade for me, to something that's frighteningly real. I was crossing the line from playing the tough guy to being the tough guy. There's a big difference from intimidating somebody who really is not going to go against you to trying to intimidate somebody who will probably pull out a gun and pop you.

I started in my mind to say, "What is all this shit about? What is happening? What am I doing here? Is this really what I want to do?" That was the one thing that separated me from a lot of the guys around me. The thing that made me feel vulnerable was that I could think a little better. Most of these people cannot think. There is no reasoning. If you're taking the profile of a gangster, you're dealing with a narrow mind and it's made of cement.

Somebody gets killed, that's murder to me. I don't care

if you call it "the right t'ing," or if you say, "He had it coming." You take a guy's life, it's never going to be replaced and this is wrong. You're ashamed to use the words morally wrong, but you still know it's wrong. This isn't about war. You're making your own rules here. You're not defending a country. If anything, you're defending a criminal enterprise.

I spent a year in jail for assault on a police officer. He was trying to lock me up and said something about my mother, so I took his gun and hit him with it. When I was in there and when I came out, I started to realize that as much as I tried, I did not have the stomach to be a tough guy.

Somebody assaults your family, you defend against them. That most people can do. You can build up the adrenaline. But to hurt somebody, just because you have to go out and hurt somebody for whatever reason without that kind of anger, I didn't have what it took.

When I used to do collections, I'd send other people, because I just didn't have it in me to go beat somebody up. Nobody really knew it because I was doing enough posturing and shit. Sometimes you had to do it personally to keep your reputation. But it turned my stomach when I had to do it.

I started to come to grips with it after I got out of prison. You can wear all the pinky rings that you want, own lots of featherweight shoes. You can talk about being a tough guy and you can pretend. You can say you're a tough guy, but someday you got to be tough. Then you learn what that really means.

Believe it or not, since I'm so big now, when I was a kid I was always small and not too athletic. I was always trying to prove something to myself. I had three older brothers. A couple of them were in the band, and one of them wanted to play football, but my mom said, "Aw, you might get hurt." Then he rebelled, so when I came along and decided to go play football, she let me do it.

I remember my aunt saying one time, "You wouldn't let the other boys play football. Then this little puny guy comes along, and you're going to let him play football? It doesn't make any sense." That stuck in my mind and I said, "I'm going to excel in this thing." It became an obsession for me. I had to work at it hard even though I had some natural attributes—I had good explosive power and I could jump real high as a kid.

It paid off. When I was finally a senior in high school, I made All-State and got twenty-four scholarship offers. That made my dad happy, saved him some money. My dad worked in a factory. He made a decent wage, but he wasn't flush for money. So it helped out the family.

When I got to college, I was at the bottom of the totem pole again. I was smaller than most of the guys there. I hated double sessions. It was like being in a concentration camp, I imagine.

We'd get to the campus two weeks before the rest of the students. They wake you up in the morning about six o'clock with the fire alarm in the dormitory. After the second or third day, everything just hurt all the time. You'd get up in the morning, and even when you brushed your teeth it hurt. You thought, "Gosh, is this all worth it for a scholarship?" But the alternative at that time was Vietnam if you quit school. I thought, it can't be too much worse there, but it lasts longer.

I'm sure all the other guys hurt all over, too, but the receivers, they just had sore muscles. Every once in a while they'd get hit, or they'd accidentally block somebody. As a lineman, everyday you were pounding, pounding, pounding. You were taught to head block, so you were hitting your opponent with your forehead. In those days, we had the suspension-type helmets, so you could tell all the linemen. They all had a black and blue ridge across their foreheads that was kind of puffy and a big gash over their nose that would start to scab, and then all of a sudden you'd get hit and your helmet would come down and knock the scab off again. Then you have your other injuries, your sprained fingers, maybe a pulled hamstring. Your knees hurt, because you were down on them all the time. In those days, they also only had one type of football shoe, and they usually put the big, long cleats on. Just in case it gets muddy, that'll give you extra traction. But we'd have a dry period of two or three weeks, and the field would be like walking on cement with these cleats that hurt your feet anyway. Your feet always hurt.

Then you go down to breakfast. Your stomach is a little upset. But you'd eat, because you didn't want to lose too much weight. You were losing weight anyway, because you were sweating so much.

You always had to get your ankles taped. If you didn't, they'd make you run laps. I think the trainer was in on that. He wanted to keep his job and make himself important, so we'd go through like fifty or a hundred rolls in one day just on ankles. Everybody had to get their ankles taped. They taped them real tight and at a weird angle. It probably kept you from getting sprains, but it just hurt all the time.

Even though they'd wash your stuff, there's certain things they didn't wash. Like your ear pads inside your helmet. I'd always get these big, huge zits under my ears from this old sweaty pad. I'd change them once in a while, but it was always rubbing. The pads on the inside of your shoulder pads always smelled like old sweat. All these things started weighing on you.

You walk to practice and see steam coming off the grass, so you knew it was going to be a hot day. Especially as a sophomore, you were cannon fodder. Guys weren't as big in those days. I went into college as an offensive guard at a hundred and ninety-two pounds. You would hit every session. Hit! Hit! Hit! You hit so much you didn't want to hit anymore. Game day you felt like, "Oh, no, another hit day." We had ninety-three guys on scholarship. They didn't care about injuries. One guy would fall, break a knee or something, they'd come out with a stretcher and take him off. Call the next guy up. So as a sophomore, I was 205 pounds, and I'm hitting against these seasoned guys who are getting ready to go to the NFL that outweighed me by forty or fifty pounds at least. I was lucky I didn't get like a neck injury.

Then you'd get over the first session, and you'd be so thankful. You'd walk to lunch. By that time, you were so thirsty, because they didn't have water breaks like they do now. They thought water was bad for you. Make you throw up. Now they found out that you can die without it. So they have water breaks all the time. You were on training table, and they had all this pretty good food, tasty stuff, but you'd load up your first tray with Kool-aid and iced tea and Seven-Up. You drink four or five big glasses of this stuff and then you say, "I'm not really that hungry anymore."

Then you go back to the dorm and take a nap. I always fell asleep in a snap. You're 19 or 20 years old and you were always tired and sore. Fall asleep immediately, you'd have your alarm set. All of a sudden, it was time to get up and do this all over again.

You get up and you had to go wait in line to get your ankles taped. All along you'd be thinking, "Wow, this is another whole afternoon of this kind of shit."

You'd leave the field house where you were getting taped and walk up this big hill, which was also the thing they'd make you run for punishment when you were bad. You'd get up there to the field, and do the same thing again— Hit! Hit! Hit! Everything is sore, and first thing you know it gets numb until you stop. You go eat at the end of the day, go back to your room, bullshit with the guys for a while and then fall asleep. Pretty soon the fire alarm would go off the next morning.

This only went on for two weeks, but it seemed like two months. Guys would count them off. Every once in a while, a guy would quit. He's say screw it to a full scholarship and throw it away. You could understand it. I could relate to why he did it.

Soon as the season started it got better. You only hit at the game on Saturday. Then on Sunday you'd go into the real dehumanizing part. We lost almost all the time. The fans would cheer if we won the toss. Most years I played there, we'd have one win or maybe a tie which was great for us. We'd call that a victory.

On Sunday, they'd get us into the film session. They run it back and forth and back and forth and yell at each guy. "Look at yourself here! You look like a wimp! A pussy! This guy is killing you!" Then they show it over and over again. You get embarrassed in front of your peers. Then they would be talking about another guy and yelling at him, and you'd see yourself screwing up in the background of that shot. You think, "God, don't let them see that. Don't let them see it." They run it back and forth. "Maybe they'll yell at him long enough that then they'll go to the next play."

Four quarters of football would take you about three hours, because of all the yelling in between each play.

Sometimes when a coach was really mad he'd run it back maybe twenty times. You see yourself screw up over and over again. They're yelling at you and calling you names. And you're men, young men, you're not kids, but in some ways you are. You see guys cry. This one coach would take the projector, break it and throw things. I mean you could hear a pin drop. You got all these 230- or 250-pound guys afraid of this little shit that any one of us could have broken in half. But he had us.

I'd always go out of that place and say to myself, "We lost a game. Here we are in a little midwestern town and we lost to another town within two hundred miles of here. There are millions of people all over the world starving. Do they give a shit if State lost one and if I missed a block? I'm not that bad of a person. I didn't rape or kill anybody. I didn't hurt anybody. I hurt our team I guess, I missed a block. Maybe we would have won." But they tried to make you feel like you were responsible for the deaths of fifteen thousand children in Biafra.

Finally when I was a senior, I was on the All-American team and got to play in the East-West All-Star game. Everything started clicking together again. I got a lot of free agent offers. I got a sizable bonus when I turned professional. I made it a pretty long career. It lasted eleven years, which is longer than the average player for sure. Contrary to popular belief, the average professional football player's career is about three years.

Once I got into pro football, it was like heaven. You're getting paid a lot of money. You only hit once a week. They have beer in the locker room after the game. You got all week to heal up after a game, plus all the drinking and partying. If you won, you usually didn't have a curfew, so that was always fun. Then you come back on the plane all hung over and bandaged up.

I'd usually give my mind a rest the day after a game. Just

going somewhere and doing something with my wife. Get over the hangover. Then the next day, all the guys would get together and we'd all go downtown, sit on the main drag of this beautiful city and drink draft beer. We were the big heroes, sitting right in the middle of town, and everybody would come up and talk to you. You were King Shit. And unlike my college football career, we won most of the time when I was playing pro football. That was a good change in itself.

Then on Tuesday I'd start getting psyched, especially if I had an opponent that I knew was really tough. For me, it was a personal battle. This sounds a little selfish, but it was more important for me to have a real good game and do my job even if we lost than if I didn't play well and we won. It was like a boxing or collegiate wrestling match where it was one on one. A lineman can feel that more than a running back, who's got eleven guys trying to tackle him. But as a lineman, most of the time, there was one guy that you had to worry about the whole game. He was your personal foe. So I would develop respect, hate, intensity for this man. I would start on Tuesday to develop a little bit of tension. It would grow on Wednesday. By the day before the game I was ready to eat nails. The game day, I would hardly speak at all. I was very intense. It was war. I was getting ready to go to war. War was game day.

The only thing is, as an offensive lineman, you had to have a very controlled type of violence. A defensive lineman could kind of go crazy. It was a street fight for them. I had to have a somewhat controlled feeling. If you got too much of this hate type feeling, you would do things that were stupid. As soon as you lunge, even a little bit, there were a couple of little guys who were like bullfighters, he'd be by you and Olé! So you couldn't do that.

Pass blocking was an art, because you had to back out

of your position. The defensive lineman is just trying to get by you and maybe hurt you as he goes—that's even better. But he just wants to try to get by you as quick as he can. I was trying to keep my body between him and the quarterback. I would go into a game and no matter who my opponent was I thought I could never be beaten on a pass rush. Sometimes they did.

The head game was more than half the battle. I've never been to prison but it's like that. When you go to prison, you got to be tough, you got to act tough, because if you're not, you're going to get shit on some way or another. When you're playing a contact sport like football, the intimidation factor is a big thing. You're always acting a little tougher than you deep down think you are. It's a macho thing.

It was violent. But somewhat controlled. Once the game was over, you had respect for the guy you played against most of the time. Sometimes, you didn't like him personally. We had coaches who didn't want you to have any contact with players from other teams. They wanted you to be going to war all the time. I'm from the old school. When I see these guys, no matter what level they're playing at, high school, college and the pros, when you knock a guy down, I don't think you should help him up. It doesn't mean you hate him or disrespect him, but you're at war out there. After the game, okay, then go up and talk to him. But I don't think you should help him up. You got to keep that game face.

My personality is pretty mellow. I'm not a violent person. But I was violent for eleven years. It was almost schizophrenia. I'd become a different person game day. But that's the way it was and the way it had to be, for me at least.

I was up for Lineman of the Year my last year. I was the biggest I'd ever been, between 250 and 255. I was strong. I never did any steroids, but I could bench press 440 pounds. I knew I was going to do well. I knew that I was better than most people, in all modesty. I thought I was good, and I *was* good. You have that air of confidence about you. You know you're going to do well, and if you don't, it's because of a mental lapse, not because you haven't been physically prepared.

Unfortunately, I was in a major car accident about halfway through the season. I was the passenger. I was thrown about a hundred feet from the car, landed in the median of an expressway on my rear end, and broke my pelvis. If I'd landed on my head it might have been real damaging, and if I'd landed on the pavement it would have killed me, but God was with me, I guess. I landed in the median in the grass. The guy driving the car had a broken back and was paralyzed for life. So I was very fortunate.

But it was the beginning of the end. I was at the peak of my career at 29 years old, which they thought was old back in those days. I was having a great year. I was team captain and leader of the offensive line, so to speak. As a result of the accident, I didn't make the finals for Lineman of the Year, and I know I would have probably gotten it.

The following year, they didn't count on me coming back. They got some young guards and stuff. But I wanted to play again and I made a statement not long after the accident, "I'm going to be here again next year even though everybody says I can't play again." I did make the team and we won the championship that year.

By the next year I was 31. The coaching staff we had was really on a youth movement, and I was the oldest guy on the team then. They kept making statements like, "He's losing a step." They wouldn't even use my name sometimes. "We're real concerned about our interior linemen." The other guard was old, too. You got to see it in the newspaper the next day.

I got cut during that season. I probably wasn't having my best year and if we had been winning at the time I might have still been there. It doesn't matter how great you are. If you play long enough, you're going to get cut. You can't play til you're 90. I didn't want to face the fact that maybe I was getting old, especially at 31. I wasn't going to retire. I liked it too much. It was a love-hate thing, but it was a love affair that I never wanted to end.

There was a feeling of relief when I got cut. There also was the hurt to your pride. It was like being jilted, the pain emotionally. People treated you a little different. They'd see you on the street, and you weren't the big hero anymore. Some of them would piss you off if they felt sorry for you. Then you'd have the people who'd say, "Well, what are you going to do now?" Like you were some sort of invalid.

The egotistical stuff of having people and kids idolize you, people respect you even though sometimes you maybe didn't deserve it, that was neat and I can't lie about that. I miss that a little bit. I miss the money and the lifestyle.

Violence as such, I don't miss it. It used to get so competitive at times in double sessions, especially on the professional level, where your job was on the line, when management had to get down to a certain number of players on a certain date, that it would get pretty hairy. You turn animalistic. There's fights and blood and guts. I didn't really like that, but it was a necessary means to an end. At a certain point if you didn't fight for your position, it wasn't going to be there. I used to hate the insecurity that somebody younger and stronger and faster was going to come along and get your job.

I'm not a masochist. I didn't enjoy breaking my own bones, or anybody's else's for that matter, but especially mine. When you're out there with your fingers taped because one is broken, or a separated shoulder, or a pulled hamstring, it just hurts.

I miss that certain gratifying feeling you get when you knock somebody on their back. As Cro-Magnon as that may sound, I think it's in our roots to want to overpower somebody. It makes you feel neat at the time. I'm not going to go into a bar and pick a fight. But when you're on a playing field in competition with your peers who are basically your same size and same strength and the same mentality, it gives you a sense of accomplishment to knock somebody down. This is a throwback to the caveman days when you dominated with physical power and a little bit of mental superiority, too—I'm not saying you have to be a genius to be a football player, but you have to have a certain mentality, intelligence and control so you can beat somebody. And when you pull around the end and there's a little defensive back there, trying to make a tackle, and you run over him like a truck, yeah, it's kind of neat.

I miss the camaraderie. You had that in sports like you don't get in any other profession. Maybe guys in combat have the same type of thing. We were brothers.

The only thing I regret is that my aunt didn't live long enough to see me grow to 255 pounds and bench press 440 pounds and knock people down on the football field. Even though I thought it was a little cruel when she said I was puny, and it sort of pissed me off, maybe she did me a favor. She planted a little seed in my mind to say, "I'm going to beat the odds. I'm going to show 'em that I can be big and strong."

Six: **Homophobia**

"The first time I ever heard the word *queer,* I was in the fourth grade, playing dodge ball. I put my arm around my friend. As kids, you put your arm around a buddy. He turned to look at me and said, 'Hey, are you queer?'

" 'What is that?' I asked him. He didn't know, but he had learned it somewhere. So I went to a Webster's dictionary and looked up the word *queer.* It said something about abnormal behavior and that was it. There was no real definition, sexually speaking.

"As I got older I realized what queer was. I grew up being a jock and playing football. If anybody was considered a faggot, you know, queer, immediately he was an object of ridicule. My God, as a freshman in high school, this one guy got caught masturbating in the shower, and he was accused of being a queer the rest of his life. Of course, all the rest of us were doing it too, but we never got caught. 'Playing with yourself. That must mean that you *like* yourself and *others like you.'*

"This one guy on the football team said that another kid who was very effeminate tried to give him a blow job. So he beat the kid up. We all sat and watched it. I felt real bad afterwards, because the kid getting beat up had an expression on his face that made it clear he hadn't tried to do anything. Unfortunately, he was just one of the bad lot. He was different."

This quote, thrown out in passing conversation by a 35-year-old actor, born in Texas and raised on the West Coast, is like a poem about manhood, full to the brim with meaning and significance.

Almost every man sometime in his adolescence or young adulthood has been called a "queer," has been the butt of a dumb joke between friends about his sexual identity, or at the least, near the end of an inane teenage dispute, has been confronted by a cupped hand holding an invisible penis to his face followed by the taunt, "Smile when you've had enough." During those formative years, every pubescent boy wonders whether or not his problems with dating, masturbation, and acne might be due to the fact that he is secretly, even unknown to himself, one of those mysterious homosexuals. The wondering may last ten minutes or ten years, but it can be excruciating, whatever the final conclusion. Once sexual identity is resolved, that should be the end of the problem men have with homophobia. It's not.

The latest Kinsey Report on sexuality in this country states that fifteen percent of the men interviewed had had homosexual experiences, yet there is still what amounts to total denial of homosexuality in the public mind. Gay bashing—a hollow coinage that doesn't come close to expressing the pain of emergency room stitches and psychological terror—is rising precipitously. The more conservative men I interviewed were vituperative on the subject of homosexuality. Men with much more liberal, enlightened viewpoints began to display their fear and contempt for gays once they ran out of politically correct slogans on the subject. The great middle would just like to ignore the whole thing. As a 40-year-old lawyer put it, "Most modern men are prepared to not actively oppress the gay community. You just don't want to be confronted with it, and if you screw up and tell a fag joke, you don't want to lose your job. That's probably about it." Even two of the gay men I interviewed—a legal secretary and

a political analyst/public relations executive—admitted to having trouble accepting aggressively effeminate men. One called
them queens, the other, sissies.

What are men so afraid of? Religious qualms, moral indigna-
tion, eugenic arguments, revulsion at "sexual perversity," and
especially in our time, dread of contagion and finger-pointing
about the source of the AIDS epidemic are only stalking horses
for a deeper hatred, a more insidious fear. Homophobia focuses
all of men's insecurities, failures, and disappointments with
men and manhood like the magnifying glass that transforms the
diffuse light of the sun into a pinpoint of searing heat.

"Unfortunately, he was just one of the bad lot. He was different." Men who display more of the feminine side of their personalities are associated with women, and it's already been
demonstrated in this book how much some men fear women.
These men have gone over to the enemy, and if they are homosexual as well, then they must be doubly despised as traitors in
the war between the sexes. They have the freedom to lay down
much of man's psychological armor and weaponry. They don't
have to be infallible anymore, and they can be afraid. They can
be wimpy, i.e., creative and emotional. They no longer have to
shrink from touching and being touched by other people. So they
must be hated for that.

There are gay men of my acquaintance who are different from
other men in their sexual preference and little else. Yet, even
these men, by following what for them was the natural course,
acknowledging this difference and openly living with it, have
managed to jump out of line, break the lock-step march the rest
of us are in toward some impossible apotheosis of American
manhood. It may be a relentless, impossible task to become that
ideal pneumatic John Wayne, toughing it out alone, denying all
emotions, but men are resentful when another man abandons
the straight and narrow parade. He makes the rest of us look
stupid, flexing our muscles and posing for one another's benefit

in our constant, if pointless, competition to be King of the Mountain.

"Playing with yourself. That must mean that you *like* yourself and *others like you.*" I believe there is more fear and hatred due to the similarities between gay and straight men than to their differences. Much of what we hate is simply what we know is inside of us, too, but which we refuse to accept or which is denied us.

Homosexual men are perceived as being able to express the voracious sexual appetite that many, many men recognize in themselves, but which they are taught to subdue and subvert. Men learn early in their lives to be afraid of sex. It means losing control of oneself and it deteriorates the brain. Men are control freaks, and sex—at least good sex—makes one feel out of control. The disgust expressed for the so-called perversity of the homosexual act is just another repudiation of the polymorphously erotic self—the testosterone troll—that frightens men and threatens our culture.

Perhaps the greatest resentment—albeit unconscious—is that gay men can have men as lovers. I don't mean lovers in the sexual sense, but in the sense of intimacy and caring, a higher level of communication and ease with other males. The vast majority of men are excluded from that kind of mental communion and physical rapport with members of their own sex by the time they are 10 years old, when their fathers start shaking their hands, instead of kissing them, and schoolyard friends find an arm around their shoulders embarrassing. Men are cut off from other men and that depreciates their lives, and makes it even harder to be a man. "Hey, are you queer?"

The fact is that gay men are still only men, prey to the foibles and self-delusions, the one-track thinking and self-centeredness that all men are prone to. They are no better and no worse than other men. When men are afraid of homosexuals, they are fearful of their own maleness, terrorized by the impositions of man-

hood. When men hate them, they are hating themselves. "We all sat and watched it. I felt real bad afterwards, because the kid getting beat up had an expression on his face that made it clear he hadn't tried to do anything. . . ."

I hung out with a whole lot of tough guys, tough and dumb in at least half the cases, so there was lots of banter.

"You're a fag."

"This guy's a fag."

"Hey, fag."

But it was all the manhood thing of growing up and not that uncommon across all kinds of socioeconomic strata from the time you hit puberty and running up to the age of 16, 17, 18, when you actually got to get your hands on a girl.

I'm not even sure that sex is a factor. Maybe it's just male rites of puberty for boys to show how tough you are. Black urban kids ride on the back bumper of buses. I dare you to do this or that. Hate the right things. So the effeminate kid at school gets picked on.

"You're a faggot."

"No, you're a faggot." That's common parlance for kids. But if you don't really feel that you, yourself, are a faggot, what's the problem?

What makes a homo a homo? No one knows how you get to that. The fantasy carousel is really what makes you what you are, right? Whatever spins around in your head is what your dick follows in life. If you don't imagine something or fantasize about it, you ain't going to wind up in that predicament. Randall Cooper and I were trekking into

Times Square to buy nudist magazines when we were 14, just to get any kind of heterosexual porn we could in lieu of getting our hands on girls.

When I hitchhiked as a kid, I was picked up by gays. "Uh-uh, not interested." Didn't have any problem. I never would have admitted it at the time, but there was some sort of satisfaction that this person came after me, found me attractive as a 14-year-old (I don't think I've ever said that out loud before). So there wasn't a hatred ingrained in me as a result of that. It was more a factor of amusement that somebody was in this predicament, and wanted to take it up the ass or give a blow job rather than chasing girls.

Why you don't hate them is because you're not really having an identity crisis within yourself. Somebody who is an adult and hates them is afraid of his own manhood in one way or another. I know that's just pop psychology, but what else could it be?

When I was in high school, I had this terrible fear that maybe I was gay. It was just part of my own insecurities. I'd hear kids talking in the locker room, and you know how kids lie: "I boffed her last night and I was hanging from the chandelier and I came fifty times." The exploits sounded so magnificent that I'd find myself sitting there thinking, "I'm not doing that. What's wrong with me? Maybe I'm a fag." Everybody is calling everybody else a queer. Then it became popular to say, "Well, you're latent," which seemed to mean everybody was homosexual. I can't say I gave it serious consideration, but it was one of those peripheral thoughts that was difficult to totally assuage.

Then at one point in my youth, I was hanging out with this lesbian girl, and she and I would go occasionally to these homosexual bars. A couple of times, I started dancing with guys. Of course, they press you close on the dance floor and try to kiss you. As part of what I considered an experience and an experiment, I kissed this guy back— this is pre-AIDS, by the way. I would never do anything like that now. It struck me as so ridiculous, I had to laugh. There was no question in my mind that there was nothing for me in any of this and the issue was resolved.

As a youngster growing up, I had an uncle who was a homosexual. Back then it was labeled dirty, very wrong, sinful. You know how parents can make things. "Don't go near him. He's a . . . I ain't saying what, but you can imagine." So you imagine all sorts of things. If you have that implanted in your brain at a young age, you feel that way.

I'm going to give you the straight way I feel about it: basically it ain't right. But I don't feel no fear. To me it's a sin, but they're the ones that are going to pay for it. If you want to look at it animalistically, then that's the reason the good Lord put women on the Earth, for that type of thing, childbearing and all of that kind of stuff.

Maybe it's a little Bible study I've had in my life. I feel that the way you are made is the way you ought to end up.

It might be kind of hard for them, but I don't feel that anybody should try to change their life in the way they are put together.

Most Southern Baptist and Pentecostal people, they believe that it is Devil's work that people change their sex or if they're gay or lesbian, which it could be. Who am I to say?

People like the Jehovah's Witnesses take parts of the Bible and use it the way they want to, and the gay people do the same thing. They say, "It's all right to be gay. Paul was gay because he never took a wife." Course, I'm not a scholar on none of that, but I don't think that's true. Paul wrote that if it would take away from his loving and praising the Lord, he'd rather live without a woman. Lot of people try to mix that up with homosexuality.

The really big question for me is, "Why are we *still* homophobic?" The only good answer I've come up with on that is that you have to have a science fiction history as well as science fiction when you're dealing with questions for which all the possible explanatory data cannot be retrieved, and that's true of history.

In my fictional reconstruction, at least 15,000 to 30,000 years ago, at the time when human beings were doing such spectacular things as making the great drawings in the caves at Altamira and Lascaux and elsewhere in France, they obviously had some members of the population with an IQ of one hundred fifty or more. What else were they doing besides drawing in caves?

Maybe they had a group of people who were rulers and

priests and also psychologists who actually invented behavior modification. They found out that you could get
immense degrees of control over people while they were
growing up as little children if you forbade them to
do something that is, in the normal course of events, to
be expected in primate development—I'm talking about
primates because of us being humans. That is the invention of taboo. You take something that the organism ordi-
narily does and you forbid and punish it. That puts the
lever of guilt and shame into position, and then for the
rest of life, when you pull the lever, the person jumps to
attention.

Now in all primate species, there is a developmental
period that the young ones go through in which they engage in sexual rehearsal play. You can see it in humans as
young as 3 or 4. By the time they are 5 or 6, they will
actually play at the positioning of copulation and that's the
point at which we, as adults, switch to automatic pilot and
go berserk, beat them up, humiliate them and actually can
become brutally abusive in the punishment. We have carried on this very ancient tradition of imposing a sexual
taboo on our children and that gives us an immense
amount of control over people. The fund-raisers for the
Moral Majority know exactly which buttons to press on the
subject of pornography or homosexuality to raise millions.
But some people use the taboo and get no gain from it
whatsoever, except for the satisfaction of being cruel.

If you was a farm boy you could put this all together.
Sometimes you'll have an animal born that isn't the right

sex for the organs it's got. It might be a male, but it has a female way of acting. Somewhere along the line, Mother Nature made an imbalance.

Take chickens. We had an old rooster that never crowed, never had much of a comb, but he had the tail of a rooster. All the other roosters that we had would chase this creature off, because he wasn't right.

I don't see why it's not that way with people also. Maybe that's the way they are and they can't help it. Somewhere along the line something has got unbalanced.

Phil Donahue had people on TV not too long ago, males that had female things done to their bodies, like breast implants and their organs changed. They looked better as a woman than they did a man, even acted more like a woman.

There's two brothers of my acquaintance, raised the same way. Bailey, he's straight as an arrow. He likes the women. But his brother, who is two years younger, went the wrong way. He went all through high school and girls were crazy about him. But after he was 18 years old, he jumped on the other side of the fence.

I think one of his girlfriends might have told him off or refused him or rejected him so many times that he might have got frustrated. Then maybe it's not a sexual problem anyway. It might be convenience. He may rather be strapped to a man than he would to a woman. About that same time he was running around with a homosexual person and maybe he got influenced or sucked in. I believe gays recruit young people.

You talk to him and he's normal as anybody else. Well, you might put your pants on one leg at a time, but I don't call you normal.

There's an immense proportion of people who really believe that homosexuality is contagious, that you can catch it by seeing one or touching one, especially having sex with one. But that simply isn't true.

A homosexual act is totally different from a homosexual personality with a homosexual orientation. Anybody can engage in a homosexual act and it does not turn them into a homosexual, but most people don't accept that. That gay people recruit is a shibboleth. When people have their backs against the wall they fall back on shibboleths.

The real question for those people would be, "If it's so easy to catch homosexuality if you're heterosexual, why isn't it just as easy to catch heterosexuality if you're homosexual?"

Some years ago I had a patient write to me and say that he had been subjected to a prison sentence of fifteen or twenty years for something or other, and he thought that he would be better off if he could be homosexual while he was in prison. He was sure he was going to be deprived of his sex life and not be able to cope with it. If you could cure homosexuals, could he be cured of heterosexuality to become homosexual in prison?

With a certain amount of devilment, I sent a copy of the note to one of the very well-known sex therapists in this country who claims to "cure" homosexuals, and said, "Could you help me answer this?" I didn't get a response.

I've always felt uncomfortable with extremely effeminate homosexual men. That threatens me beyond belief. It's something I continually have to deal with. I have to tell myself that the real queens in the gay community have every right to be that way. If I have the right to be the way I am, they have the right to be the way they are. As a gay man, I have a personal investment in their behavior, because that extreme has become the stereotype for gay males. I can't justify divorcing myself from that. It's not a part of my community that I like or would choose to associate with, but it is nonetheless a part of it. So how do I deal with it? That to me is the big challenge as an adult now. So I wonder how much more difficult is it for straight men to deal with it?

I don't feel threatened. I don't feel they are plotting out there to come in and attack me. But you feel squirmish as hell when someone makes a pass at you in the sexual sense. Jesus, it's just so out of place and you've got no reference point. Immediately, you get a feeling akin to when you were a kid and had to kiss your cousin. Aw, no.

One time, my wife, Linda, and I were at the bowling alley. I went in the bathroom and this guy come in. Handsome guy, you might say. He approached me in an odd way and that set me off. I got upset, but I dealt with it. If I'd been a lot bigger, I probably would have kicked his ass, but he was bigger than me, so I just left it at that. I took care of my business and got out of there.

Linda made a big joke out of it and then it all blew over and was all right. She still rubs it in. Tells everybody about it. When the subject of homosexuals comes up, she uses that to get her little laughs. She thinks it's cute. I deal with it.

When I first moved to Key West, I thought I was really cool; I'd been a law student and thought I was a liberal. Down there the mark of heterosexuality is a pot belly. Having just been in school without enough money to eat very well and working out anyway, I had an okay body.

I'm walking down the street my first week in town and this older Cuban guy sort of sidles up to me. He says, "Hey, you wanna party?"

My first inclination was just to shove him. Nah, I thought, and he walked on past me. I took another step or two and I thought, "Now, wait a second. This is Main Street. The middle of the day. God damn it, what does he think he's doing?" I turned around, decided maybe now I'll give him that shove, but he'd already gone on down the road hunting for another person to cruise on. At that point, I realized that maybe I did have stronger feelings about gays, being confronted with it myself.

I had only been in town three or four months. I was looking at this apartment and although I didn't move into it, the guy who showed it to me was a real nice guy. He and I were interested in the same things. It was near Christmas, so when he asked me over for a holiday drink, I said, "Sure," dumb fuck that I am.

This guy made a pass at me. He grabbed my dick and I freaked out. It's funny, guys always say, "I'll punch those queers out. Kill 'em. Fucking queers grabbing me." This guy grabbed me and I was so shocked I froze. I finally spit out the words, "What are you doing?"

"Oh," he said, "I thought . . . I thought . . ."

"No, I'm sorry. I have to leave." And I left.

I'm walking to the subway and this little guy popped up on my shoulder like in the cartoons. He says, "Hey, let's go back and kill him. He's molested you. Fucking faggot."

"Yeah, I'll kill him." I didn't go back. It happened and I didn't know what to do.

I had dinner with these two gay friends of mine and one of them was driving me back to my hotel. It was like two o'clock in the morning and I had no idea where I was. He stopped the car in the middle of the road and told me that he loved me. And that he had always loved me.

"What are you talking about? You live with what's-his-name. You two have been together for years. Stop being an asshole. I told you I'm not gay. I'm going to get really upset."

He put his arm around me and when he did that, I belted

him. I thought it was the only thing I could do. I really hit him and he began to cry like a little kid.

I got out of the car and I said, "Just get the fuck out of here." And I walked away feeling very shook by it. Two things were going on. One of those was, it was sort of heady that someone would like me that much. But on the other hand, I found it so distasteful and upsetting that I was extremely angry at him. I was also angry at the fact that this would end the friendship and I really did like him. I was very ashamed to have resorted to violence. Also it was the kind of violence where you got no resistance. The guy didn't defend himself or anything. He said this and I belted him. It was horrible. I felt bad for him and I felt bad for myself.

I got back to the hotel and I didn't know what to do. Finally, I called the house. It was four o'clock in the morning. I wanted to find out if he had gotten back. He answered the phone and said, "Yeah, yeah, I'm fine. I apologize. I promise you it will never happen again." But since that time we've lost contact besides sending Christmas cards to each other. It's hard to explain what was going on. I sense in me a certain fear.

There are times I've become nervous, only because a person has started to become overt and I don't want to hurt their feelings. It's like the ugly girl who tries to pick you up, and I mean she is U-G-L-Y. You're in a bar full of people and the first thing you say to yourself is, "My God, I don't want them to think that I'm with this ugly girl." But she's really coming on to you and you don't want to hurt her feelings. There are those guys who can say, "You're fucking ugly. Get away from me." I can't do that. That's a human being.

For a while I lived in a group of cottages which except for three or four units turned out to be a lesbian colony. That was odd. I'm not much of a sun person, but on hot Saturdays and Sundays, I loved to go out to the pool area which we shared with the lesbian colony. As soon as I got out there, all the lesbian women would get up and leave, en masse. I'd wait till they all left and walk back into my house. I didn't want to be out in the God damn sun.

I'd stay there about an hour until they'd gathered back out there and I'd go back. It was perfect. Give me that kind of power and I'm going to abuse it.

I was involved with trying to put together a shelter for abused women with a coalition of people. The NOW organization in that place at that time was pretty strongly a lesbian organization. There were some gay men involved in it and some straight social worker–type women. Then there was me. I was the only straight male. Every time I'd try to open my mouth at one of the meetings, I would just get shouted down. "What do you know about it? You're part of the problem!" I was identified as the enemy.

I'm no gay basher and I've got no moral or religious qualms about homosexuality. As Tom McGuane wrote once, "I'm glad somebody likes it, so a possibility doesn't go to waste."

It's not a fixed policy with me, but I don't generally socialize with gays. Also given the choice, I'd rather not work for or exclusively with a gay person, although I have in the past without incident. I don't hate gays by any means, but I don't have a whole lot of use for them on a social or professional level. I mean that in the sense that I wouldn't have much use for a gift certificate for flamenco dancing lessons or for a job opening on board a Coast Guard ice cutter.

But mild aversion is not the same thing as active oppression, so does this make me a homophobe? Am I, as the ubiquitous phrase has it, "threatened by gays"? I say, no, because gays don't inspire fear in me. I've never been anywhere, including jail, where they declined to take no for an answer. I suggest that the phrase "threatened by" is overused by the powerless in order to lend themselves a significance which they might not actually be entitled to.

Gays inspire in me the mildest forms of pity and distrust. I pity them because they make an irresistible bayonet dummy for the Christian equivalent of Shiite Moslem fanatics, these dumb-guy theologians who inexplicably return to the American scene like cicadas. I thought we put them to sleep with the Scopes Monkey Trial in 1925, but in the words of the little blond urchin in *Poltergeist LXXIV,* "They're baaaack."

The misfortune of gays is that their off-brand sexuality titillates the *Deliverance*-style Christian at the same time that the private renovation of his own soul bores him silly.

He wants to claw off that tight necktie and make somebody squeal like a pig. He figures Jesus is going to be charmed and delighted by being presented a lei of infidel homosexual ears and usher him right into heaven like a bribed head waiter. The Shiite Christian is not nearly as good at setting an example as he is at staging a spectacle, unless he gets caught with his own finger in the K-Y jelly jar, in which case you've got Satan available for patsy duty.

Unfortunately, owing to America's ongoing cultural enfeeblement, these ignoramuses are getting away with it, so I pity gay people because they live in a progressively more ignorant society that persecutes them for celestial Brownie points and because it doesn't know any better. Not that I believe for one moment that the gays are above such tactics themselves. Most of them don't know any better either.

Why do I distrust gays? Two reasons. First, I believe heterosexual malice is nominally more forthright than gay malice. I mean by that that it is more predictable, it's easier to track on the old emotional radar screen and it does not have the Stealth technology that gay malice has. The reason for that is that most gays live in a Gypsy-like symbiosis with the straight world. They have to live among us—at least until the Lavender Homeland is proclaimed on Fire Island—and they quite rightly resent the fact that they have to cultivate our sufferance. Therefore, the sly roundabout quality of gay aggression and revenge which is so admired and imitated by our political leadership. Hmmmm. Maybe there's a link there. Congressional representatives, take notice!

The second reason I distrust gays is empirical—I'll say no more, other than I believe both genders of gay people have a vested interest in sabotaging straight relationships. I mean they tend to indulge in malicious gossip and agitprop against the heterosexual relationship when available as an easy and enjoyable form of politically destabilizing an unfriendly regime. It is really their own viable revenge upon the straight world which admittedly has much to answer for. It gratifies their love of intrigue. It is a vicarious form of sexual predation with varying degrees of toxicity, according to the degree to which they are embittered by their own treatment, and a lot of them have been treated real bad. Those to whom evil has been done, do evil in return. I read that in some comic book or other.

So to sum up: no to homophobia. Not crazy about gays, not afraid of them either.

I have friends who are homosexuals. If I harbored hostile feelings toward them as a group, I would be embarrassed and feel that I was betraying friendships which I value. But I don't think homosexuality is normal. It is politically incorrect or unpopular to say things about homosexuality that are generally perceived to be true by the population at large, for example that their sex practices are perverse, excessive, abnormal and sometimes dangerous. I get concerned when homosexual lobbying causes people like Andy Rooney to put their jobs in jeopardy, when the media is unwilling to reflect what people in general believe, statements that I think are basically accurate. If Andy Rooney can't say, "Homosexuality is abnormal," something is wrong. My quarrel with the gay community is only that there is a distortion of reality because of their lobbying. It's not just the gay community anyway. Women's groups have been doing the same thing for the last ten to fifteen years.

I do resent the taking of power, the forcing upon us of the attitude that we are wrong in not accepting them as an equal voice. Christ, they're still a minority. Maybe in places like San Francisco they are not, but it mars the beauty of that city for me that they have such an embarrassingly loud voice there.

I resent it when an aberrant group is able to make the rest of us feel so damned guilty about where our tax dollars go when it is clear from the facts that willful misconduct is what spreads AIDS. If you engage in anal sex without protection, you're going to contract AIDS if the person is a carrier. It's so black and white. It is willful misconduct that spreads AIDS and it will eventually hit the heterosexual community, who do not deserve it. So I do very much resent that these aberrant beings have to manifest themselves in the rest of us in such a fatal manner.

They are sexually obsessive. Sex is the overriding issue in their lives. You've heard the story about the big Hollywood star, haven't you? I've heard this story from people who know the guy. There is a new gay sex practice which involves sticking a gerbil up your ass in a condom. They put the animals in the condom in a semi-frozen state and they are inserted. Then they thaw out and start to move around and give the recipient some kind of big kick. It's one of those things that when I first heard it, I thought this isn't even possible. But I'm told by gay people I know and people who know this star that—oh, yeah—it's done. It's pervasive enough that I was thinking of going into the gerbil business.

Anyway, the star's condom broke and the gerbil got loose in his ass, so he had to go to some good and secretive hospital to have it removed.

Whether the story is true or not and whether the whole gerbil thing is true or not, it's indicative of the gay community—excessive and perverse, as a general rule.

When I was working with a French film crew in New York as a consultant, essentially I was escorting them around and showing them the "in" sex scene in the city. One of the places I took them was this gay bar down by the meat district in lower Manhattan. During the day when the meat guys were there, it was a go-go bar with girls. At night it was a gay bar. They would literally hang customers by the nipples from the ceiling. There were insanely perverse acts going on there. To me, this is indicative of homosexuality in general. That doesn't mean it applies to all individual homosexuals, but you've got to go a long way to convince me that fucking some guy up the ass is a natural act.

In our value system, it's moral for people to hurt one another and immoral for them to give pleasure to one another. One of the objections to homosexuality is that it is a source of pleasure which is not under the control of the patriarchy like the women the patriarchy controls and excludes. It's the idea of the promiscuity of the gay bar, stop off for lunch and get laid, stop in the so-called Tea Room —the urinals in the subway stations—and have pleasure. Are these people going to be under the reliable control of the patriarchy? Certainly not. They are on the fringe, unregulated by the sexual FDA as the rest of us are. We are attached to Mom and attached to wife. We are both repressive and bonded. They can get it anywhere, at any time.

I remember one of my ex-theatrical agents saying, "You know why we don't have any doors on the offices here? There's so many blow jobs given in this business that it interrupts work. So we took the doors off the offices." There's a concrete example where sexuality itself was being struggled against. Since many theatrical agents are gay there are many people who made that a part of their demands. Since it was in such ready supply, even the agency manager conceived of a way of frustrating it. That may be the larger issue. The availability of their sexuality is what is anathema to a Puritanical, Calvinistic, work-oriented society. That scares people.

I've never really known any gay people, because I try my best to stay away from them. Like blacks, I stay away from them, too. I'm just a country boy that's pretty old-fashioned in the way I think about things. I feel it's wrong and I stay away from the wrong things.

Most of the gay people are timid, feminine-type people. Do their nails and their eyelashes. In construction work you stand out like a sore thumb, if you're like that, and you won't last very long. As far as I know, I've never seen any gay people in the carpenter trade. They're probably there, but I've never run across any of them. I don't really think they get into the physical work that much. Hairdressers and decorators are different than men who go out and swing a hammer.

That wouldn't be the life for me. I love the women too

much. Maybe more than too much, but that's the way a construction worker is supposed to be: women and beer. What's left in life? That's the way I look at it.

He doesn't realize that I'm gay. I'm with him and other Yuppie guys are around and frequently something really, really nasty will come out, something jeering, like a fag joke. He's not a blue collar guy who works on a loading dock. This is no 30-year-old Archie Bunker that we're talking about. He's a professional man, talking to other professional people, and they say fag things all the time. It's something that's repressed for the most part, but when it comes out, it's very real.

These people would never think of making a nigger joke. Obviously, people don't make nigger jokes when they are aware that somebody black is around. Even if they are Archie Bunkers, they won't do that. But when you're gay, people don't necessarily know. I'm not identified by something as simple as skin pigmentation. So I experience homophobia a lot.

Maybe some of it is meant to be a joke. Maybe people misinterpret it sometimes and it's not as vicious as I think. We must have a sense of humor, too. We must be able to laugh at ourselves.

At my gym, these two guys were teasing each other and one of them hadn't wiped off the bench that he was using and it was very sweaty. The other one said to him, "Wipe those AIDS-infested germs off of there." Just joking with his friend. Buddies teasing each other. That's the big thing.

I've gone through it. I've buried a lover. A better half.

That's really devastating to me sometimes, because it was a real serious relationship. It wasn't one of these flippant things. He was a real nice guy. So I've gone through the whole AIDS thing with him.

I try and laugh about things, but where do you draw the line?

You know what I am afraid of is Winnebagos. One of those fuckers almost nailed me on the 405 the other day. So maybe I've got mobile homophobia.

Let me get this straight. Are we talking about Anglophobia or homophobia? Homophobia. Okay, that will only take a slight recalibration of my prejudices.

Other than a spot of trouble getting them to wear the lavender armbands to identify them in public—the little Nazis had a good idea there—I have no problem with homosexuals at all.

I get the sneaky feeling that unadmirable as this feeling is, it is shared. As we all know, things have tightened up a bit sexually because of AIDS. AIDS was brought to the fore by gays taking it up the ass, which started this whole sexual crackdown. So there is resentment towards gays because they closed down all the good times of the '70s and early '80s.

I'm not talking about I wake up in the morning going, "Those ass-fucking homos drove the pussy back into the woodwork." But sometimes in a dark mood when I can't find anybody else to hate in the old interior monologue, yeah, I do feel it sometimes.

My sister and her husband spent two weeks in Cherry Grove with some homosexual friends who have a house there. In all honesty, that idea just sent chills down my spine. I couldn't imagine doing anything like that.

At the same time, I have to say that my shrink out here is bisexual and I have nothing but respect for the guy. I wouldn't feel uncomfortable in *his* house. On the other hand, I might be reluctant to drink after him out of a coffee cup, too.

The AIDS epidemic has made people more afraid of them. Oh, yeah. Even their own kind. They're afraid of each other. They stay with who they brought to the dance, you might say.

This may sound crazy coming from a gay person, but it's too bad this fear exists, yet I kind of understand people's fears and apprehensions. My nieces are coming to visit soon with my brother and sister-in-law. Last summer we were at an ice cream parlor having ice cream sundaes. I had a banana split and one of the kids was going to reach over and take some of it. But her mother reprimanded her, just in case I might be positive—that's the way I interpreted it. But do you know what? I've got to admit, I can understand why somebody would want to do that. It didn't hurt my feelings when she pushed the girl's spoon away from the banana split. I don't blame her. I'm not a stingy person, but I would have pushed her away, but her mother beat me to it.

Early on in the AIDS crisis, I used to bump into a guy I knew around the neighborhood a couple of times a month at the grocery or the drug store. We'd just hang out and talk. He got really depressed over a period of time. I was walking with him down the street on a summer afternoon. He had a Coke with him and he was offering me a sip of his Coke, which I took. I said, "Why are you so blue, why are you so depressed?"

"My lover is dying of AIDS right now." Granted this was early into what was going on and now I've been enlightened, but I'll tell you I was taken aback about the Coke, that I was using the same straw as him.

So I understand people's passion when it comes to this.

It's damn scary. I don't blame them because I did the same thing with the straw in the Coke.

In all the gay men that I know, there is not anything like a choice involved in their sexual orientation. There is no issue of choice. They wake up to a sexual preference which the society doesn't approve of and they have a very hard time of it. They have to decide whether or not to deal with it and some of them do and some of them don't.

Recently at the firm, this guy died of AIDS, which was all hushed up. But in fact, his poor wife found out that she and their child had AIDS from the guy's secret love affair. That really is very painful and that's a direct result of repression. He shouldn't have to hide out as a married man.

I spend very little time dwelling on my sexuality. When I came to terms with it, I came to terms and it became a part of my life like any other part. I see so many gay men who never get past that and dwell on being homosexual. That consumes them.

They bother me in the same way heterosexuals who are consumed by their heterosexuality bother me. Okay, there are other parts of the body. Put your dick back in your pants and try to be a human being.

There's always been homophobia out there, and there's been beatings and attacks for years. Sailors way back when would go out to roll fags. But it used to be just plain old ignorance. That seemed safer to deal with because you can enlighten them of their hillbilly homophobia, that classic hick behavior. There are still people who are hicks in that way, but that homophobia is healthier than when people are vengeful and angry. I wish it wouldn't be vented with such animosity. People's bodies are being destroyed.

These young teenage boys live in a different world than I ever did. Sex is certainly much easier and freer. Gee, when I was in college, it was still a big thing to "score." They are able to have sex with greater abandon and frequency, but now there is the fear of death attached to it. They don't understand. Because of AIDS, they have the cumbersome activity of putting on a condom, which men never had to do since the invention of the pill. In the heat of passion, they may not come equipped and they feel robbed of whatever freedom or sexual independence they thought they would have when their time came. They blame the gay population.

"I want to score with this chick. I don't have my damn condom. She's worried about AIDS. It's the fucking gays who did this to me."

It happens to me frequently now. You'll get some young guys in a car. How they know or what they know, I don't know, but they'll call out names—"Faggot!" or "Suck my dick!"—as they go zipping by.

Young boys will look for bait. They'll look at you and wait for you to look back and then it's, "What the fuck are you looking at?!" They want the acknowledgment, yet when they get it, that's just the excuse they need to attack. There's a certain tantalization that goes on. They *want* you to look at them.

Let's face it, if a pretty girl is going to stare at you, you're going to think, "Wow, she likes me." You don't really know the score, but you may very well return the look.

For gay men these days, it's impossible. I try not to look anyone in the eyes, because something can happen. I'm afraid. I've had several incidents where I know that I've been pigeon marked, only to have it thrown in my face. They must get their rocks off on the humiliation alone.

I reprimanded this teenaged student who was really being obnoxious and sent him out of the room. Before the kid left, he said, "What's the matter, teacher, you worried about your HIV status?" It was said with such contempt. There's a whole new vocabulary going around today in young circles and a whole new hatred.

I've got a little better than a forty-eight-inch chest. I weigh 196 pounds. I don't look like Arnold Schwarzenegger, but I'm not your stereotypical sissy either. I look kind of "football." I'm a real big guy and a lot of guys like my body.

These little skinhead-type kids who seem to be invading everywhere, especially on the weekends, to them this big faggot here—me—is a real challenge. You walk by these trashy little white boys and you just sense trouble in their eyes.

I almost had a fight with a skinhead last week. This guy comes storming out of a store. He's stolen a handful of candy. That wasn't my concern. What was my concern was that as he was storming out he rams into me. "Careful there, guy," I said.

"What's wrong with you?" he starts screaming. "You queer? You queer? You queer?" It spills out into the street.

"Listen, you little fucker," I said. "You just shut the fuck up and get out of here. I don't want a hassle with you. Get the fuck out of here." I grabbed him and I pushed him.

I'm not a violent person. I don't like getting into fights. But it seems like a lot of these guys are egging me on. It's not fag bashing. "Let's get a little skinny guy and beat him up." There's a different look in their eyes when they look at me. It's like, "What are you doing being a fag? Come on, mother fucker, come on." It's a challenge. "Instead of beating up some little guy who can't defend himself, let's beat up this big strong queer and we'll really have done something."

I've never had to protect myself like that. You have to be concerned, because who knows how nuts some of these people may be. Not nuts, that's too much like an excuse. If you're nuts, you can plead insanity. A better word is hateful. The scary part is the hate in their eyes. It's not a game for them.

A lot of people have been slashed just coming out of a bar. I can't understand it, that somebody can do such wanton harm to someone else. I can see how you could kill your wife or your parent or your lover. You just go off the deep end and kill them. But to do harm to somebody you don't even know because of their lifestyle? What is the purpose of it? If you've got a bitch of a wife, maybe she should be killed, you know, there's a reason for it. This just seems so rude, to say the least, so God damn rude. That always amazes me and breaks my heart.

If it ever happens to me, I hope they take some money from me, so I don't feel like it's total insanity. If they wanted money and then did it, I can understand that. But just to lash out, it's shocking. It's a bad reflection on this animal that we are. It doesn't speak well of us.

We have a special problem with homophobia at the present time because we have a special problem with gay people having come out of the closet and deciding not to be persecuted anymore.

I just wish we didn't have this bad public relations problem with AIDS now. The whole movement is only twenty years old, from 1969 at Stonewall to the present. Now would be such a good time to fight all the old homophobia, but instead we've got this God damn AIDS thing, which is just a real bad public relations problem. I'm being very cynical and facetious, but it's true.

AIDS has also shown people a real strong side of homosexuals—the support, the kindness, the compassion, the courage that's out there. It's bringing people together. It's a rallying force. I haven't been a real big joiner of things, but now I find myself getting more politically active. People are riled up out there, and we in the gay community are not being so passive. Sometimes I wonder if all that power that's amassing is instigating things. Are we taunting people? Was it better to be kind of passive about the whole thing? Homophobia is escalating, but why is it escalating? Is all the publicity piquing a curiosity in other people and making things worse? Is it arousing sentiments in people just like it is arousing sentiments in me?

In this world, it's so difficult to find someone to love. If that person happens to be the same sex as you and I, what's the difference, as long as you are happy? That's what's important. If you're happy with a guy in your bed, fine. If you're happy with a girl in your bed, fine. If you're happy with a fucking dog, that's what does it for you, fine.

Tell me if I'm a bigot. Just as with my fear of homosexuality as a youth, I certainly fear being a bigot. But if I am, my attitude is the same: I might as well come to grips with it and accept the fact.

I'm not homophobic. Who's homophobic in our society? I hardly know anyone who's homophobic anymore, do you? Who's expressed to you homo hatred?

Seven: **Abortion**

"Once it was over, we never talked about it again. We kept our mouths shut."

"It's one of the few secrets I have from my wife."

"Besides her, you're the only one who knows this about me."

"Nobody talks about it. Even guys don't talk about it with other guys."

Men don't talk about abortion. Men who have been involved in an abortion don't stand up before political rallies and describe what happened. They certainly don't call home to inform their families. They don't whisper it to a best friend over one too many beers. Men don't even talk about it with the woman they impregnated and who had the abortion, much less the new girlfriend or wife.

Abortion is usually a young man's dilemma. A problem that should be approached with deliberation and vision is faced in a panic. One minute he's happily fucking, and the next his whole world is crumbling away under his feet. Confronted with adult reality, perhaps for the first time, he may just follow the callow impulse for self-preservation. His most conspicuous function is nail-biting, because, more often than not, the decision is made for him by the woman involved, anyway.

Afterwards, the relationship resolves itself or dissolves, but something big has happened. A line has been crossed—that is unmistakable—with a swiftness that leaves him off-balance and reeling. Because of honor, embarrassment, guilt, or convention, he keeps the whole thing in his head and shares it with no one. No one listens to his story and helps him make some sense of the matter or discover his true feelings. In fact, what he'd really like to do is forget the whole thing.

Time passes, and the experience recedes into a dark corner of his mind. It becomes almost invisible, but he doesn't forget. A man must make peace with the abortion. Judging from the men I talked to, it is an uneasy peace, not a resolution. Because the mystery is still inside a man's head, isolated, almost untouched, there's no way to tie up the loose ends. It's all confusion.

When men get confused they get resentful. "I think she may well have taken the money and gotten a bikini wax with it," says one man. It's not surprising that many men hunker down in callous cynicism. It's what's expected from them. The generally accepted view seems to be that, although they are primarily to blame for unwanted pregnancy ("I'm not sure why it was all my fault, but I damn sure knew it was," says another man), their main goal is to shirk responsibility, so they just don't care about the situation. But the fact is, men will endure the burden of guilt, if they can dodge the decision making, and they do care. Anger, cynicism, even sullen silence is usually a sign that men have been touched more deeply than they are likely to admit.

What *is* surprising is that when men did talk about this invisible event, they generally were not heartless or unthinking or disconnected emotionally. Instead, there was grief, self-recrimination, and a kind of sorrowful wondering, best expressed by the man who said, "It's so personal and mysterious, you can't help but think what might have been . . . I've got to think of the pain and the damage it did to her, because I know about the pain that it does to me."

In a strange way, this chapter is about men's attitudes toward fatherhood, about an elusive quality that might be called the fathering instinct. I don't imagine that term is found in many textbooks or anywhere else for that matter. Men are often imagined to be sperm-sowing machines, tin and fiberglass robotic erections, spurting out wild oats in every direction with little thought to where their seed lands or what happens to it. Women are supposed to have a corner on biological clocks, on longing for children, on the anguish of what might have been. It's just not so.

"Maybe abortion doesn't affect a man as deeply as it does a woman, because it's not our bodies," said a friend of mine. "Nonetheless, you are very much aware that it is something that was *yours,* too." I've known this guy since we were kids. He's one of three or four men in my life who are like brothers to me. A girlfriend of his had an abortion over twenty years ago, and he never told me anything about it, until I asked him, point-blank, for this book. Of a dozen men I specifically asked about abortion, only two claimed they hadn't been involved in an abortion. Five men had been involved in more than one abortion.

The voices speaking from the next several pages are not here because they are pro-life or pro-choice or anti-anything. This is not a political debate with all sides represented, four-minute time limits and formal rebuttals. It's not science or medicine or self-help. These are a few men puzzling over an enigmatic, yet all too real piece of their private lives that they've never talked about before, finally saying something out loud about a secret that they have kept too long.

I've only been in love one time. It was the first time I felt I loved somebody more than myself. Just a neighborhood girl I really cared for. We were going out. She would treat me like gold and I would treat her like a doormat— which was the way I thought you were supposed to treat a girl. I tried to dominate her, to own her. I tried to tell her how to live. It's what I saw my father do, and I really thought that's what love was at the time. The woman does what the man says and the woman is glad to do that.

All we did was have sex. I don't know why I was surprised when she got pregnant. Like a fool, I didn't take any precautions. She wasn't on birth control.

She wanted to have a child. But I didn't want one, because I knew I'd have to marry her. Otherwise, her family would have killed me. They were good Catholics in a small town. If I'd disgraced their daughter like that—believe me —they would have literally shot me.

Instead, I begged her to have an abortion. I said, "Listen, Sue Ellen, I'm in no financial position to take care of you and a child. I don't want to live in poverty. I want to give you the same things that my father gave my mother," etc. etc. I said, "Don't you see this would just ruin everything. I'd have to quit school and get some kind of a construction job and just be nothing." That kind of thing.

She didn't care. She wanted to have that kid. She said, "I can work, you can work, we can make it." She wanted to get married, too, that was the bottom line. Even though I was in love with her, that was too big a step for me. Absolutely not. Just as things were looking up for me, everything seemed to be collapsing.

We talked about it for a couple of weeks, and she finally put it totally on me. "Wagner, I'll do what you want me to do. It's your decision."

"Hey, let's do it," I said. At that time, I was looking out for Number One.

I drove her down there to have the abortion. The place was like a catacomb. The receptionist was a big, fat lady who wasn't nice or friendly like you'd expect at a doctor's office. Kind of surly, she just shoved papers at us. "Fill out this."

Then I waited outside. Generally, every woman seemed to have somebody waiting for them. A diverse crowd. Some in suits. I was dressed in beat-up pants, a bad shirt, and a baseball cap, just like today. Every one of us is sweating bullets. Just going nuts. There wasn't a sound except cigarette lighters flicking.

The funny part was, I saw another couple in there who were good friends of mine. We completely ignored each other.

She was in there about an hour. When she came out, she just had this overwhelming sadness, this quiet sadness.

We talked a little in the car on the way back. She cried a lot and she kept telling me that she loved me. I think she was saying that to rationalize to herself why she did it. The more she said it, the worse I felt. I said to myself, "Wagner, you're doing the right thing." But deep down where I live, I said, "No, you're just being a coward in this situation."

The worst part was, it was her birthday. I went to her house and they had a little get-together for her birthday, with a cake and her family. You talk about a weird situation, man. Me and her both were just completely drained emotionally, and they don't know *what's* going on. I forgot to get her a gift.

I got to admit, the way she did it, she really put it on me. Put the total decision on me. Here's her body getting my decision on it. That made it worse. I could have dealt with it better if she hadn't wanted to be in that position, if she had said, "No, I'm having the kid," or "You're right, I'm not having it." It's her body, but I had her brainwashed. I made all the decisions.

Once it was over, we never talked about it again. We kept our mouths shut. She did have some real prophetic words, though. She said, "Wagner, you're going to regret this all your life." I told her, "No, no." But inside me something would spark and cling to that. She was right. I'll never forget it. I'll never forgive myself.

"I'm pregnant."

"You couldn't be pregnant. You're on the pill." I hadn't been struck by lightning lately. Why this? It's the same odds. I was young. Nothing had ever happened to me. I hadn't been drafted to go to Vietnam. I'd had no doses of reality.

"Are you sure it's me?" was my immediate thing.

"I've also checked it out," she said, "and I'm gong to have an abortion."

I didn't even have the sense to do the proper thing, to take her out there, to pay for it. I finally did pay for half, but she had to ask me to.

Everything just dissolved after the abortion. Then, boy, there was about a month where she wouldn't talk to me and she wouldn't have sex with me.

I consulted my friends. They said, "I don't know what to tell you. Try to cheer her up. Buy her flowers or something like that." But it seemed that whatever I did was wrong. Finally, I became really resentful. I just assumed I paid for half of it, it's done, now let's get back to things. I didn't have any sense of the psychological ramifications. "Oh, you don't want to fuck tonight? Well, I understand that you're a little sore." But she was really spooked—like any woman would be—locking doors, not returning phone calls and stuff. She doesn't want to talk about it, didn't tell me anything . . . and I wasn't going to listen to it anyway. That was not the era of the caring man or I wasn't the caring man, in any case. I just wanted to get back into the groove.

I saw this as a temporary slowdown, almost in terms of dollars and cents. It would cost you a day at work and it was expensive—almost five hundred bucks. "I realize it took a big bite out of the old checkbook, babe. I'll buy the drinks tonight. You know, two hundred and fifty bucks is a couple weeks' salary. How much more aware can I be, baby?" It was out of my scope of comprehension. I just got this opinion that women got real mean when they had abortions. "Fuck her, if she wants to act like that. What the hell did I do?"

Boy, the next one really got it. Like the guy from New Jersey who gets in a collision. It's obviously his fault, but he gets out of the car and starts screaming. "Let me see your fucking insurance card! Look what you've fucking done to me! This is a vintage car!" I just went on the offensive.

The second time I was approached my response was, "Fuck you. I'm sterile. Go to somebody else. Don't ever come to me!"

Of course, all my friends are going, "Yeah, give it to her. Deny it. I know she's sleeping with other people."

Those were two in about a six-month period. Left cross, right cross. But that was it. Never again.

We were kind of long-distance romancing it, much more fervently on her part than on mine. I'd just gone on to the big city and thinking about my hometown was the last thing I wanted to do. So I'd go back to see Janet and we'd do what people that age do, which is have a lot of sex. And I enjoyed it a lot. But I was more interested in excitement than a good woman. Janet was one of the best women I've ever been with, second only to my wife.

A few years later, after we had broken up, I was back home visiting for some reason. I wasn't there to see her. I just happened to run into her while I was in town. We were sitting there talking and the story surfaced slowly. Her friends told me later that it had been really traumatic for her. Right about the time it happened, I'd been blowing her off big time, so I pretty well fucked her up good for quite a while.

When she told me, I was 24. I didn't know what to think, do or say. I was completely dumbfounded. It was after the fact. She'd already done the deed. I certainly didn't argue with her choice of terminating the pregnancy. In fact, I was very glad that she had and very grateful that she had. At the time, it sure seemed damn convenient.

I know that is a terrible thing to say. But when you're that age, the idea of getting somebody pregnant, particularly somebody that you're not even dating anymore, it just seems like there's nothing worse that could happen to you in your life. Looking back on it now, I realize that there are a lot worse things that can happen to you than a mistake.

The first one surprised us, because we considered ourselves to be liberated, modern people. We expected that the abortion would not be a big deal. We were pretty young, in our early twenties. We were both starting our careers. We had no money. We did not think that we could have a child at that time and continue with our lives. So we did it.

I remember I was very nervous. I remember I didn't want to stay. I remember that there were a lot of women in the waiting room who were very distressed. And that I ran. I dropped her off there, said, "I'll see you later," and I met her at home later in the day. I went on about my business. We didn't talk about it afterward.

The next year was pretty rough. We'd been married three or four years and had gotten through the worst part of the first few years of the marriage when you're fighting all the time because you haven't figured out how to merge your personalities or what issues are worth fighting about. The marriage was going pretty well, and then we had this very bad year. We weren't getting along.

About one year after the abortion, we went down to visit my parents, who were staying at some resort out of town. It was a long drive. It's always distressing to see my parents. It wasn't a happy occasion. Then on the way back we got lost on the highway. It was really dark, and we didn't know where the hell we were. We didn't know how to get back on the road. We kind of gave up and said, "We'll just drive for a while until we find something."

The road seemed to be endlessly dark and we started talking. We tried to figure out why we weren't getting along so well. It occurred to one of us that it was a year since the abortion. That was the first time we realized that we felt we had killed something that we had made together and that it would have been alive and might have been our child.

We talked and shared how disturbed about it we both had been. That cleared up the problems we'd been having for the last year. We hadn't known that we were angry and upset and hadn't been willing to face the facts.

Abortion is presented to you as something that is easy to do. It doesn't take very long. It doesn't cost very much money nowadays for a middle-class person. You say, "Well, it's okay."

But it wasn't okay. It left a scar, and that scar had to be treated tenderly and worked on in order for us to get on with our lives.

I don't think abortion is easy for anybody. The people who say it's easy either don't want to face the pain of it or haven't been through it, because it's really a tough experience.

Now, it's also one of the reasons we had our first child. The next time we thought she was pregnant, we were really distraught again, because we thought we weren't ready to have a child—still—and we were seriously considering another abortion.

I was with some old friends, and I did not want to let on what was happening. Obviously, I did, because I was mooning around. Finally, I was alone with this woman who said, "Rick, what is it?"

"Ah, it's terrible," I said. "Lisa's pregnant, and I don't know if we can go through with an abortion again."

"Lisa's pregnant?" she said. "That's *wonderful.*"

"What do you mean 'wonderful'?"

"You can have a baby. It's great."

"But we're not ready. My career isn't set."

"When's it ever going to be set? What are you waiting for?"

"You know, you're right," I said. I got up from her living room and I literally ran home. I said to Lisa, "It's great you're pregnant. We don't have to have an abortion. We'll have the baby." She wasn't sure, but I kind of convinced her.

As it turned out she wasn't pregnant. But we were so disappointed that she wasn't, we then set about making sure we could have a baby. We had our first child. We've had a second child since.

She smoked a lot of cigarettes. Didn't want to talk much. For some weeks after that, she was pretty emotionally bruised. It certainly cast a shadow over our relationship. Sexually it affected us. I don't recall making love at all between the time we first heard about this and when she got the abortion. I don't think we made love for several weeks after that. And when we did, it was pretty apparent that there was this presence between us—which was the aborted child.

There was also this resentment on her part that, no matter how supportive I was, I hadn't gone through it and I couldn't understand. I was a man and a good deal responsible and that was that.

I have wondered from time to time whether it didn't cast a permanent shadow on that aspect of our relationship. If so, it would be a very, very subtle one. I don't even think that it's there too often. But once in a while, I wonder if a troubled moment or an awkward communication physically traces to that time.

The first one was some kind of family planning/repro-
ductive services clinic, so there was this faintly Unitarian
air of moral earnestness about it—concerned people,
granny glasses, plants with names, cute plastic cubes on
people's desks filled with pictures of Chevy Royales. The
pittance which I was requested to contribute was one
hundred and fifty bucks. That may be misleading, because
I don't know if I was part of a pool or the sole philanthropic
benefactor.

The second time it was slightly over two hundred dollars
and we went to the Women's Rape Crisis, Abortion and
General Anti-Man Clinic, a division of the National Female
Women Sisters and Lesbo Death to All Men Society. I got
to sit in a waiting room and wait for a couple of hours,
which I suppose is what decency requires. But during this
period of time I was the object of much scornful eye-balling
by these crop-headed, broad-beamed disciplettes of Wom-
anism.

Maybe it was paranoia on my part. But they saw me
sitting there and knew I had not come for a Dalkon Shield.
I got a couple of poison toad stares, like "You and your
kind should be hunted down with submachine guns and
flame throwers, trailed back to your stinking caves and
flamed out before you can multiply." Basically your Iwo-
Jima-last-stages-of-mopping-up atmosphere:

"There's one. Get the interpreter up here on the double."

"Hello. I am a man, like yourself. Give in to the Female
Womanhood Sisters. You will not be harmed. You will
merely be neutered and reeducated. Many promising careers are open in interior design and hairdressing."

I felt like I should have had a caption, something small
and tasteful, a sign I could hold underneath my chin:
"*These* are responsible!"

On the final occasion, I don't know if she went to a better class of abortionist or what. That was a private physician and cost me three hundred.

I got the sense—and this may be wildly misplaced self-regard or something—but I got the impression it was some kind of gambit. "We'll take the big slob right up to the precipice of abortion and see how he performs in that instance." When I said with alacrity, "Sure I think you should have one. I think everybody should get one," and immediately assembled the funds—exact change, crisp new bills—this was mute evidence of insincerity on my part. Which is quite false, because I truly wanted her to have one. I really, really did.

I offered to go to the office with her and was rejected in some of the most scathing of terms, actually with a depth and breadth of zoological allusion that I have seldom since encountered. Although the denunciation took place after I'd handed over the money. I wrote the check, was soundly tongue-lashed, and things then proceeded with the coolness and formality of a Heidelberg Dueling Society Convocation. "Thank you. Thank you very much."

"Hey, don't mention it, sweetheart. Here's a couple hundred extra in case you got twins."

So I was not privileged to get into that sanctum. I think she may well have taken the money and gotten a bikini wax with it. There was no alteration in her form.

I t's unfortunate that the present political atmosphere is so polarized that you can't say, "I think I should have the right to have an abortion, but an abortion is a terrible thing." Because that's the truth of it. An abortion *is* a terrible thing. Even though you should have the right to have it, and even though it might be better for the lives of the people who are here in order to have it, it doesn't make it less painful.

My wife says that she doesn't have tremendous qualms about the act of abortion. It isn't a person yet. It isn't even a fetus. It's microscopic, you can't even see it. That's what she used both times to tell herself, "We can get through this. It's okay."

On the other hand, you see your wife's body changing. It changes so fast. Her breasts get larger immediately. Her nipples get brown. The areola gets wider. You see changes in her right away with the new hormones coursing through her. Everything's been triggered. So it's not invisible. It's not like you expect it to be. Something is there. You can see it. Your wife can feel it.

That's why abortion is so difficult. If there weren't physical evidence that something was going on, it might be easier to handle. You might be able to keep it in the realm of fantasy. But there *is* evidence that something is going on, something very real, something physical, something magical.

I can't remember what kind of birth control we were practicing. I think it was a diaphragm. I do not personally recommend them. Nasty. Women can never get them out.

"Honey, I can't get hold of this thing. Come see if you can get it for me."

"Damn thing's slippery. I'll just run down to the hardware store and get a pair of vise grips. I'm handy around the house."

So we weren't too dedicated to this whole diaphragm business. Obviously, we slipped up one too many times and Ginger got knocked up. The first I knew of it she said, "I went to the doctor. I'm pregnant. I've decided to get an abortion and I have an appointment on Tuesday."

I didn't argue with her. "Do you want me to go with you?" I said.

"Absolutely not. *Absolutely not!*"

The iron door slammed very loudly. I thought, "This tells how far my involvement with this woman goes. It's fine to sleep with her and take her out on dates, but when it comes to something like this, she doesn't trust me one bit with any part of the action." I didn't argue with that response either.

So she went and got her abortion. I felt completely helpless. It's not like she's got the flu. She's in bed, mad and hurting, sore in all kinds of places, and it's pretty much your fault. You knocked her up. I'm not sure why it was all my fault, but I damn sure knew it was.

We didn't have sex again for a month or two. This experience did something to our relationship which is hard to describe. She'd slammed the iron door. I'd seen it slam and stepped back. Although we stayed together for a year or so after that, neither one of us felt there was any future in it. It was merely convenient. Then after a while it wasn't convenient anymore. I helped push her out as much as she left. I made it very clear without saying so that I'd had it. She ran off with a gym teacher, and I was very happy that came to pass, because now I didn't have to make a decision. I wasn't very displeased at all, not too downhearted. I got messed up for a while after that, but I don't think she had a whole lot to do with it. There was just the natural transition of going from a crazy young man to an adult man.

The day was cold and gray. Drizzle and snow mixed. It made me feel so empty, I couldn't seem to catch my breath. We didn't have much to say on the way there. I just held her hand and kissed her when she went into wherever it is they take these women. Her lips were dry as paper.

Then I sat in a plastic chair and chain-smoked for two hours. Read a year-old copy of *Smithsonian,* cover to cover, twice. Looked for faces in the pattern of the floor tiles. Anything to keep from thinking.

When she finally came back down the corridor, she was so white, washed out. I could feel how weak she was as soon as I put my arm around her. I knew she was in pain by the way she hunched her shoulders.

It took forever to get a cab in that shitty weather. When I finally got one, it was a fleet cab—a rattletrap, no shocks, doors don't close all the way, the backseat sprung so bad we were sitting on the floorboards. She had been really good keeping it all together in the clinic and on the street, but once we got in the taxi, she began to sob real quietly, like so the driver wouldn't hear. Every pothole we fell into, she gasped and dug her fingernails into my hand. I cried, too, all the way home, holding her, no way to protect her. "A little late for that now, fuckhead," I thought to myself.

I got her into the apartment and into bed. Then I had to run out and buy her some of those giant sanitary pads with a belt for the bleeding. There seemed to be lots of blood the next couple of days. Once she was asleep, I climbed into the shower, mentally kicked myself around some more, cried some more. It was just stupidity. I wasn't a fucking kid. I knew where babies came from. Hell, I had the entire God damn sexual revolution behind me. It's her body and all, but we'd been together for a couple of months at this point and I hadn't even *asked* her what kind of birth control she was using. She wasn't using anything. She thought she couldn't get pregnant. I never have been able to figure out why not.

Even though I knew it was for the best, that doesn't mean I wasn't sorry it happened. I loved her. The night before, I asked her to marry me. She was the one who wasn't sure, she was the one who felt trapped by the pregnancy. She had to be able to choose.

The procedure, in a technical sense, is very much like the most common operation gynecologists do—that's a D&C. Since it is a very small extension of that, once you have made the commitment to do it the technical difference is not that much, nor do you *see* that much that is different.

But when you are involved in second-trimester abortions, it's more graphic. You are involved with the termination of something which could be called a life. That's where you have real problems in this profession. With second-trimester abortions, it is sometimes hard to get staff, and some doctors just refuse to do them, because there is the very real probability of recognizing something that is a human form. There's more of a human-looking person there, and that causes you to confront the issue.

Most of us go through a lot of emotional changes trying to formulate an opinion about abortion, even though we don't publicize it much. The profession doesn't allow for a lot of public soul-searching. I don't have any beef with the pro-life people who consider the act of abortion murder or me a murderer for committing that act. Essentially, it comes down to a question of priorities. I'm prepared to go a lot further than a lot of the pro-choice people and allow for the philosophical possibility that I may be destroying a life. But it is life in its rawest form which has no name, as opposed to somebody who has developed relationships, who has obligations, who has responsibilities and has other people depending on her.

During my internship in an inner-city hospital, I saw a lot of women die from illegal abortions. It was something to see young, healthy women die. I remember taking care of somebody who was called a septic incomplete—that is, suffering from the infectious complications of a back-alley abortion. She was a young mother with a couple of kids. In the process of taking care of her over a series of days, I got to know her two other children and her husband reasonably well. I would talk with them with some frequency about her progress.

I came down the day after she had died, and the kids ran up to me. "How's Mommy?" they asked me. "When is she coming back home?" I don't think I'll ever forget that.

Those practical aspects of the question formed my political philosophy. Given the fact that women will have abortions whether they are legal or not, as long as medical science has not found a way to absolutely prevent pregnancy across the board, then it is incumbent on society to make those abortions safe so that people don't die. Unlike any other medical circumstance that I am aware of, a simple stroke of a pen brought a dramatic change overnight. It wasn't like smallpox or polio in which people died less frequently over a period of time as medical wonders became disseminated. One day women were dying. The next day they stopped dying. It's that simple.

Emily and I were engaged, but not yet married, when she got pregnant. So there was a complexity to the pressure we were under. If we hadn't been engaged, there would have been no thought of having a child; and if we'd been married, we probably would have swallowed hard and had it. We were literally in between.

For a few days we really went back and forth on it. I found myself feeling pretty supportive of her desire to have a child if that was what she wanted to do, though it would clearly have upset a lot of our plans and expectations.

In retrospect, I suppose my willingness to be supportive of that choice reassured her enough not to have the child. She needed to know that it really was her choice, that I wasn't pushing her.

Some self-deception and some unwitting deception on the other person goes on. I don't know in my heart of hearts that if she had acted on my willingness to have a child that I would have been able to sustain that willingness. Maybe I sort of knew that my support was what she needed to make the decision not to have a child. I don't know.

I've had a hell of a time dealing with it, actually. To this day I still think about it. I'll go to bed and I'll think about it and say to myself, "Man, what a terrible thing to do. What a cop-out. You don't trade human life for material niceties." Which is what I was doing, because I was hoping for a better future, more goods I could buy. I don't have a good rationalization for it either. I'm not one of those people who believe that it's only potential life. I've come to believe more and more that the baby in the womb is just that—a human life. I wish I didn't. I wish I could make myself believe differently, but I can't. It would make it easier to deal with mentally. When you have the opposite view and you go through with the abortion anyway, well, that's worse than anything.

So, you see, I'm kind of stuck. She did it for me. I feel like I murdered somebody. I wish I could do it over again, if I could just go back in time and relive those years. If she'd had the child, even if we'd got married and everything, it wouldn't have been that bad. I've seen other people do it. Reality's such a bitch sometimes, you know?

Guilt manifests itself in a lot of ways, too. Now I want to go picket abortion clinics. You'll probably see me get arrested one day. The trespass thing. I'll be there one day on your TV screen.

We went together to a clinic in midtown. There was a strangeness walking into a high-rise office building to get an abortion, like you're going up to take a business meeting. The doorman asks you which floor and then he kind of looks at you. You wonder how many people he's looking at every day going up to the clinic. It must be dozens. You wonder how other people are dealing with the coldness and impersonality, the business aspects of the whole thing.

When we got up to the clinic, there was just a waiting room with maybe thirty people waiting. The thing that struck me was the extraordinary cross section of people there. There were 15-year-old black girls and 45-year-old Park Avenue women. We were right about in the middle of that. Most of the women seemed to have their husbands or boyfriends with them. I didn't feel strange being there, just sort of depressed, the way everyone else seemed to feel. None of us were looking at one another, not so much out of embarrassment, but out of a real sense of being in our own private torpor.

It took a long time. When she emerged, she was fragile, but more emotionally so than physically. I was unsure about what to feel toward her. It's hard to know what the Miss Manners advice would be in this situation. The only reasonable thing is to recognize the different conflicting feelings that are swirling in the couple who come out of a high-rise office building onto a crowded street after an abortion.

In a strange way, it was liberating. After the abortion, I realized that I had successfully broken every single commandment the nuns had ever harped on over the years— except one or two having to do with certain Mediterranean deviant sexual practices. I fully expected to go out to the mailbox one morning and find a tastefully engraved notice of excommunication, personally signed by the Pope and suitable for framing.

I did not feel any of the moral remorse we were urged to feel in parochial school, because I am firmly of the belief that life is not present in the corpus until you can break a decent fart. This is far more indicative of the human condition than any kind of brain wave activity.

After the abortion, we still weren't using contraceptives. We were using the rhythm method. I'm going, "What an idiot I am. I ought to just shoot myself in the head." It was like I had no control over my hormones. It was crazy.

I got her a kitten after her abortion, some sort of surrogate, I suppose. But when we split, I ended up with the cat. That cat had just a plethora of kitties. This was one fecund cat. Out of this abortion grew many little critters. It took me a little while to get around to having her spayed.

Ever since then, I've been cool in my relationships. I did learn. I never had another abortion. One girl told me she was knocked up just six or seven months ago and I said, "Hey, fine. I believe in life. Have the child, go get a blood test, and if it's mine, I'll pay the child support for the rest of my life."

"Bullshit," she told me. "You don't know what you're talking about. I'm going to have an abortion." In that situation, I don't feel so responsible.

It's ironic, but going through that divisive, romance-killing experience together is a big part of the reason we stayed together. We had suddenly grown up. It forced us to look at each other—really look. She realized that she could honestly trust me. I saw she was a whole person—not just "a girl"—strong and independent. We got married about a year later. She wanted it and I wanted it. If we hadn't gone through with the abortion, sooner or later one of us would have decided we'd been railroaded into it. Instead, we're still married, still in love. We have two beautiful children, a boy and a girl.

When one is faced with the question, "Well, what's it going to be? An abortion or a formalization of the relationship?", it's always a termination point, it's time for adieu. I'm afraid I pretty much have the sensible psychology of a father dog: "Let's get them pups on to Abilene, because there's many new and interesting scents on the wind." So one trots off with spittle hanging from one's dewlaps and one's tail carried in a jaunty manner.

I've always felt abortion was preferable to littering the landscape with kids you have no intention of minding. I don't really regret the abortion because, gee, there have been many times since when I had no facilities to feed, clothe, and otherwise care for a small genetic replica of myself.

Also if you know that there is a high probability that the relationship will not persist in the face of reproduction, then you run the risk of one day opening the door nineteen years down the road in your physical decrepitude and getting floored by a haymaker from some lummox who looks vaguely like you.

"That's for what you did to my mother."

"Uh, what was your name again?"

I used to know the date of the abortion. The anniversary would be a bad time for both of us, because we were in love at the time. I've forgotten it now.

Oddly enough, I don't have really strong feelings either way. I'm certainly not against abortion. I believe it is a woman's right. But it's not something I bother myself with. I had a vasectomy a few years back, so I don't have to deal with that anymore. I get little pamphlets and junk mail from both sides wanting money, especially now that the battle is on again, and I don't even open them too often.

I t's one of the few secrets I have from my wife. I'd say the reason it's a secret is about ten percent not wanting to go through the awkwardness of talking with her about another woman in my life, sex, and having babies. This is not a subject you need to share to strengthen or otherwise affect your marriage. I don't see how it could possibly do any good to talk to her about it.

The other ninety percent is that it's not any of her business. I owe it to the other woman—who had to go through so much more than I did—I owe it to her to keep my mouth shut. It may not be good, but it's wise and it's sure a lot easier.

W e've never talked about it since. Never. It was only mentioned once. Just before our first child was born, out of the blue she said, "If I hadn't had the abortion, that child would be five years old now." We both let it drop. I don't know what her reasons are for not saying anything. She's my wife and we've been together ten years now. Me, for the first few years, I didn't want to hurt her again by bringing it up. I really didn't feel like it was my place to drag buried memories back into the open. Even though it happened to both of us, she was the one who I felt had suffered all the physical pain, and for all I know there is a lot of psychological damage hidden behind the silence.

I've got mine. I knew if either of us went too far, we might open an emotional floodgate we'd spent a long time screwing tightly shut.

It wasn't until years later that it really began to prey on my heart and on my mind. It still does. I still feel a lot of remorse, not only because I treated a good woman badly, but now that I'm entering into what I *want* to be my time to have children and be a father, I start to think about the preciousness of what was lost. That makes me feel very sad. I feel in my heart that I should have done more of something, said something, been there . . . I don't know.

Now I know how incredibly hard it is to be a father and how much stress a relationship has to endure, even when you really love each other and have a child you prayed for and planned for and wanted from deep down inside yourself. I don't know what would have happened with a child I didn't want. I hate to admit it, but I probably would have voted with my feet. Faced up to my responsibilities with my backside. "I'm out of here."

I wonder if I would still be married to Evelyn. You have to wonder about what kind of damage it does to live the rest of your life knowing that you were at least part of it. It's not like she had her appendix out. It wasn't my decision. I was part of the cause, and I certainly didn't resist in any way. I can't help but think, "Am I guilty of being an accomplice in the taking of a life, or at least in not bringing it to fruition?" There's guilt, but more than anything, there's just sadness. I don't know what to do about it.

Did we talk about it? Yeah. Did we agonize over it? Yeah. Have I put it behind myself? Yeah. But I've been thinking about what happened a lot more recently, since the birth of my son. I just kind of wonder if we had been in a different situation and had the child what that child would have become. Although I wonder what would have been, I don't regret it. I'm a strong believer in abortion. But still there's always the mystery of what might have been.

Eight: **Dads**

Fatherhood is the big Time Machine for men. It connects men to the past and propels them into the future, but not in the idealized, easy way of science fiction. It is a machine made of human emotions, so it works strangely when it works at all. The past is muddied by bitterness or cast in the unreal golden light of nostalgia. Instead of immortality, the Time Machine throws a crude gauge of a man's own mortality before his eyes.

"My whole thing is trying to figure out what my dad was thinking about all those years, what he thought of me. Like trying to find out what your dad was *doing,*" says a 47-year-old musician and composer. Men spend much of their lives looking back over their shoulders at their fathers and wondering who those men really are and whether or not they will ever measure up to their father's expectations.

The problem is, men's fathers are not human beings. They are either paragons of manly virtue, or hellish scoundrels, or some godly combination of the two. They hide behind the screen of adulthood and machismo, or disappear into their work, and never reveal themselves in any honest fashion to their children. As a 59-year-old war correspondent and newspaper reporter said of his father, "He was at a remove. You just never could reach the man. Maybe I'm presenting him as being an isolated poor soul, but that's far from the truth. I think he was the larger victim, because I don't think he was aware that he couldn't love. At least, he couldn't express love. I'm sure he did love. He was just a hard man to get to know, and a kid shouldn't have to get to know his father. It should be open for him."

The picture of Dad only clears up as he begins to die. No one hides from death. The physical strength that buoyed the son deteriorates, the prescience that amazed him turns out to be a parlor trick. As a 38-year-old housing contractor explained watching his father die of an incurable illness, "Not only are you seeing your father die, but a lot of bubbles are popping, too. The misconception that you have that your father is smarter than you, stronger than you. I was stronger. Every one of these was just bursting. All of a sudden, there was this role reversal, and Jesus, there was no preparation for it. No matter how old you are, you go from being a kid with no responsibilities to being the one in charge, and in charge of your *father*." Then, just as a man is beginning to see his father as flesh and blood, not unlike himself, his father is gone, and he hasn't found out anything substantial.

I have two sons, Sean and Noah, 6 and 3 years old respectively. I enjoy fatherhood, but there is one thing that I've found very disturbing about it. They force me to live in the present, un-masked and without illusions about my own grandeur. All my purported wisdom and smug superiority turns to grape jelly in the face of, "Why, Daddy?" No matter how I react, I almost always end up feeling inadequate to the task of raising them. At least once a day they put me on an emotional roller-coaster ride from the heights of selfless love to the rushing adrenaline rage of frustration. One minute you just want to strangle them, the next you look at those beautiful sleeping faces and you are suf-fused with such a palpable attachment to them that you feel you're almost in pain. Like a lot of men, I prided myself on my composure and the fact that I had mastered my temper along with a lot of my other feelings. My mind and body hadn't undergone that kind of emotional out-of-control, those butterflies in the stomach, and the surge of synapses snapping since I was about 18. It is a humbling experience. But it's great to be here, in the present again.

Some men see fatherhood primarily as a step toward immortality. A 42-year-old man, expecting his first child in a few months, put it this way: "You recognize that you're going to die, and you want to feel that you've contributed something worthwhile. Maybe if you're Jonas Salk and you've invented the polio vaccine, maybe you've contributed something that's really important and fundamental, that makes the world a better place. Then you can die with a sense of satisfaction and accomplishment. Most people aren't going to achieve that. So the other thing is children. You die with a sense of satisfaction and completion in that you've created something that goes on and you've contributed to its growth. You've created a human being that you care about, that's valuable and important to you. That's essentially the two choices that you have: Nobel Prize or a child."

But the immortality of fatherhood has two sides. The child who carries your genes and dreams into the future is also a constant, unrelenting reminder of your own years streaking away into the oblivion of the past. A 50-year-old father of two teenagers said, "I'll never forget the time when John was about 14 and he fell off his skateboard and really hurt himself. He was crying, and I ran over to where he'd landed and picked him up. As I walked to the house, I was suddenly aware that his sneakers were banging around my legs almost down to my ankles. Something weird happened. My life flashed in front of my eyes sort of like they say it's supposed to just before you die. I saw the hair on my arms was turning gray and felt my shoulder twinge a little bit with what's probably the start of arthritis, and I envied my son."

I received two unexpected gifts when I interviewed my father for this book. First of all, he told me the story of his life in a plain, man-to-man way that I hadn't heard before. For instance, I'd always imagined his joining the Marines during World War II at the age of 17 as some kind of adventure story. In fact it was a desperate attempt to escape from a broken home where he had borne too much of the burden for supporting and holding together the family since at least the age of 12. "To be very honest and blunt about it, I had been exposed to all of this so young in life that I was discouraged with life. I signed up with ten thousand dollars' worth of life insurance and never intended on coming home except in a box," he told me. Then while waiting on board a troop ship to become part of the second wave in the deadly amphibious invasion of Iwo Jima, he got a letter from home saying his mother had remarried and everything would be fine there. The burden he was running from vanished. "When we got on the beach there and they told us to dig in, I couldn't dig deep enough or quick enough," he said. "There were fifty or sixty men in our machine-gun platoon, and we got back to Guam with eight." He showed himself to me in flesh and blood.

The second gift came after the interview was over and the tape recorder was turned off. We were just sort of winding down with a little small talk about my two sons, when my dad turned to me and said, "I don't know what you're doing or how you're doing it, but keep it up. It's working." That quiet confirmation from my father of me and my life, my manhood, meant the world to me. That's the handful of words so many men wait for all their lives, but never hear.

Dad was a big man. He was six-four, he came from a big family. It's hard for me to say much about what he was like before I was born. I know what he'd tell you about his life.

He said that he was in the fledgling Army Air Corps at Kelly Field, Texas, that he trained as a pilot. He had some pictures beside an airplane. Well, fuck, anybody can stand beside an airplane and have a picture made. Then you hear family stories about how his mother bought him out of the service after a few months. You could do it then by paying for the price of the uniforms that a man was issued. He didn't serve his full time, and he never flew. He told people he was a captain. He was an enlisted man.

He said he used to ride motorcycles in the carnival. They had these big wood planking and scaffolding bowls constructed at carnivals and fairs. The steep sides of the bowl sloped down to a flat basin in the middle of them. Grandstands were built around the upper opening. They would ride these motorcycles around and around the inside of that. He used to do that, he said. He did ride motorcycles, I know.

He was a baseball player. I was never in a position to see him play anything. I'm not saying that he wasn't.

He was just a mean, mean, son-of-a-bitch. He ran a pulp wood business. As a kid I would see him working the men on a crew, and I would wonder how in the hell can they take it. You'd see him with niggers with muscles like watermelons, and the old man was a big man, but he wasn't muscular like they were. He'd just berate the living hell out of them, hit them.

These men would get their pay on Friday and get drunk as shit. The money's all gone by Saturday night, and they're in fights. When we went to pick up the laborers on Monday morning, this man was laying on his front porch, and the sun was just beginning to come up. He didn't move when Daddy blew the horn, you know. So he got out and called him and walked over there.

"Come over here and help me," Daddy said. So we get out and go over there, and this guy is laying on the porch and he's out. His intestines are out also. His stomach had been slashed, and they're stuck to this porch floor. The average person would panic, wouldn't they? No medical background at all. He beats on the door and gets his woman up. Hell, she's in bed in the house asleep. Her husband's out here with his guts lying on the porch. He gets some water and rags, and he soaks those guts up. The guy's still alive. He sticks them back in.

He had to go further, too. While he's doing all this, my daddy has got this woman threading up a needle. He sews him up with a needle and thread and takes him to the hospital. The guy lives. So you see him do things like that on the one hand. On the other hand, he'd be so God damn mean to them. Using ax handles on them, that sort of thing.

What was he like? He was a product of his times. I've seen him be the ultimate in fairness toward some of those men, but that's not to say that he was a champion of civil rights. Maybe it was a matter of discipline, but he always had us address the men as "Mister" and say "sir" to them. That was a little out of the ordinary for honkies back then.

From the standpoint of teaching me anything of value, I guess he pounded into your head that you're going to be honest. It wouldn't have done to be anything but honest.

I learned a certain disregard for personal safety, so I could do things that were usually mortally dangerous, certainly stupid. That grew out of the association with him, because of what he said.

He'd tell little half lies. Not that he didn't teach us not to lie by example. By example, hell, it was by fist. He would say things like that stuff about him being a captain in the Air Force. I don't believe to this day that he was. He would say he was related to Zane Grey, because he happened to read a lot of Zane Grey westerns. No relation to Zane Grey. I'm the family historian. I researched all the genealogy. I know damn well we're not related, never were. How could you be at one time and not at another?

His ego was badly in need of bolstering. A kid doesn't know that. Besides that, it casts you in adversarial roles. He was unfair and harsh, and that's a grossly unwholesome way to come up, parent to child.

My dad could go anywhere and do anything, because he was loved by, admired by or feared by everybody from the FBI to organized crime. The reason he was feared by people was that he was so God damn honest. His word was his bond. He'd never think of cheating. Cheating was for lawyers, politicians and everybody with titles after their names, priests, you name it. If you handed him $500,000 and said, "Danny, keep it. I'll be back," it would be there. But then he'd figure a way to talk you out of half of it.

He had this romance about him. That always put you in a different category, because the people who you're supposed to admire were the people who were taking graft, kick-backs and whatnot. The people you were supposed to admire the least had a certain amount of honor and piety about them. Dad never fit into either category. He was a hustler who never got a legitimate job until he was about 35, and then he drove a delivery truck. But if you were hungry, or if you were down and out, and you asked him for something, he'd give it to you. I remember him saying to me as a kid, "Sal, never lend money to anybody." Then two minutes later somebody walked up to the car and said, "Danny, can you lend me some money." He peeled off a couple hundred dollars and gave it to him.

He had the biggest heart, and he was real straightforward. My old man told everybody what he thought, from Jack Kennedy to the cop on the beat. He'd met everybody, and he was doing shit for everybody. If you messed with his family, I can't prove it, but I have a feeling that there is a good chance that you'd die.

One of his non-salaried jobs was as a bartender. This guy came in, put a gun to his head at a bar he was working at and was going to walk him downstairs and kill him. Rob the place and kill the old man. The guy never made it down the stairs. I know that my father died of old age, so something happened. I don't know exactly what, but that gave me a sense of, "If something is important, don't let the assholes take it away from you." Of course, that worked back in the '50s. I don't know how well it works today, unless you're a lawyer or an inside trader on Wall Street.

My old man was one of those guys who was sharp and underprivileged at a time when there was absolutely no chance. Plus he got into his alcoholism at a very early age. He was one of those Thunder Road guys, driving Model T's loaded down with Mason jars full of white lightning over dirt roads, being chased by revenuers, when he was in his early teens. Plus he was drinking the shit at a regular pace at that time, too. His dad died when he went into a cave to check on a still where the fire had gone out. There was gas in the place. When he lit a match it blew him up. Industrial accident, not covered by any kind of workers' comp at the time.

By the time I was growing up and getting my start, the

old man was pretty much a burnt-out case. He was the town drunk. For the older kids, it'd been a little bit better, because the old man had gone through a nine-year spell of being sober, but being very unhappy the whole time.

He worked in the factories then. Both hips got broken when an I-beam fell on him, so he was considered disabled after that. He collected disability, which was a good way not to have to go work anyplace. He walked fine, as far as I could tell. Even when he was pretty shit-faced, he could still motor around.

He was half-breed Indian. The other half was Irish. So he didn't make it a point to go drink quietly someplace. He would drink and then he would go get obnoxious—as I have been known to do—and get up in people's faces. Or he'd go right to the middle of town and want to go into one of the few nice bars in town all smelly from drinking muscatel three or four days running. And then he'd want to get nasty with people in there. A swell guy.

Anyway, to me he was my old man. I didn't know from anything. I didn't know how other people lived. I thought this was probably the norm. I figured other people's parents got along the way mine did, with lots of arguments. I thought everybody's dad got shit-faced and obnoxious at inappropriate times. This is the way life is, isn't it? That's probably why I've grown up being more tolerant of other people. "Jeez, everybody's got to go through this, everybody's like this."

The old man wasn't just totally out of it, he was pretty sharp, and I always liked hanging around with him. I always learned stuff. I think of him fondly, even though there were lots of bad times.

He'd let me stay up late and watch movies with him, and even ask, "Why are they doing that?" He would explain to me.

They're bringing back all these old black-and-white movies from the '30s and '40s to TV. I'll see a movie and I'll flash on stuff in it. Eventually I'll realize I watched this with the old man. That's probably why I like slang and blond babes in tap pants and teddies. He always tuned in the old movies from before the Hayes Commission. It was pretty wild shit. They didn't have nudity, but they didn't make any bones about what they were trying to pass for tits and ass on screen in those days. I developed my taste for this without knowing it, late at night in a half-sleep with the old man explaining life to me the way it really was.

Of course, the old man died when I was 12. Even though it's terrible to say it, that got rid of a whole lot of burden off everybody. You didn't have to overcome the old man anymore. You only had to overcome where you were at all the time, plus these people who were going to have an attitude.

His name was Pearl, because they were expecting a girl and somebody had written that name into the Bible there at his space on the family tree. They'd written it in ink. When he was born, he had a stem. What could they do? He had to go through life being a half-breed Indian named Pearl. So he was kicking ass the whole time behind that. I got his Irish-Indian blood and my old man's attitude.

I got a kind of respect for the old man, despite all the reasons maybe not to. So I've always had a chip on my shoulder for all these small town shitheads, who think they're better than everybody else, who always looked down their nose at me. I've always had a hard time with charity, because when I was a kid my old man didn't like charity. He would take his disability checks, but he would never go with his hand out. Eventually I grew up and learned what was really going on. I visited other homes and saw that things were somewhat different than the situation I was in. There wasn't anything I could do to change it, but I never felt lesser than those people.

In my neighborhood, you were either a worker or a crook. It was the same with the Irish and the Jews. My father was a great guy, and he broke his ass working ten, twelve hours a day to give us everything. He's still alive today, and whatever he does is for his sons. I had a good relationship with him, but he had that kind of Italian dictator style. He wasn't brutal. He was a loving father, but he didn't influence me to go in any direction.

I looked at my father, who was a house painter, working his ass off for whatever it was—two hundred a week—then I see some guy driving a brand-new Cadillac, hanging out in the same bar every day. Whatever he did, it didn't take much energy. You knew he was a gangster, but, shit, he had a lot of money and he just sat there. Why would I want to paint houses like my father when I could make money like this guy?

My father didn't like that. He saw this as an injustice and a contradiction of his beliefs.

I started working for those guys when I was a teenager. I had a ring worth more than my father's entire net worth, including the old car he used to drive. But that's all right. I still sat down to dinner with them once or twice a week to make them happy. With what I used to spend to go out to dinner by myself or with a friend, my father could have lived for a week. I don't remember pound for pound what the money situation was then, but I knew I spent more in a couple of days than my father would make in a week, breaking his ass for ten or twelve hours a day. He just pretended it wasn't there and my mother would do the same.

It's the same thing that happens when one of these wise-guys gets hit. The reporters interview the family and the neighbors, and everybody loved this guy. He was great, he's a saint, a wonderful man.

We both know that's bullshit. We both know what he is, but you lie to yourself. You lie, because you love this person, or you're related to this person, or you're afraid of this person. But you bullshit yourself first, and then you bullshit anybody who asks. It's a method of survival.

My father paid for all my tuition at the college prep parochial school he sent me to. Paid for all my textbooks, because that's something he wanted to do. I bought all my own clothes, because I wasn't going to go down and get some twenty-dollar suit at the discount stores.

"We're going now." I knew we were going to the hospital. I went over to my little sister's crib. I took my hands, put them inside the crib, and held them behind the bars, so my elbows were inside.

"I'm not going," I said. They tried to talk me into it, but they couldn't. They ended up literally prying me off and carrying me to the car.

Then my mom promised me she wouldn't leave me. We walked into the hospital. At one point, they had me on a table, and they wheeled me into this elevator. The door closed without her. Then they had me counting backwards from a hundred. I was out by the time I got to ninety-four.

The next thing I knew, I woke up in the middle of the night. When I look back at it, I realize it was one of those rooms where you have eight other beds, all kids and teenagers. There were two 14-year-olds who had busted their legs in a car accident. When I started crying, they gave me comic books to shut me up.

Then a guy who I thought was old—he was maybe 30—he came in his bathrobe and hung out with me. He was a patient who heard me crying, got up and walked over to where I was. To this day I can still see his face. He got me through that night. My parents were there first thing the next morning at seven o'clock.

I wasn't really aware of this at the time, but I realized later that because of this incident, I really was no longer willing to trust my folks too fully. To me, it was a life-or-death situation, and my mom walked out on me. Not to mention my dad. In my memory, he didn't even come in out of the car, although I'm sure he did.

It's funny. In my family growing up, it was just taboo to consider that my father could be wrong about something. I grew up being tremendously critical of my mother and hardly at all critical of my father. It was so taboo, it didn't even creep into my thinking. For example, there at the hospital. My mother walked me all the way to the elevator. My dad, I don't remember where he left me. Yet, in my own mind, it was my mom who I decided I couldn't trust.

When I was about 10 years old, my old man bought a brand-new 1955 Ford Fairlane, two-tone blue. We'd had it about six months. It had been through the winter and in this climate you got all the salt on the roads for the snow, so it had a couple of dings and little rust spots on the side panels. One day, I decided I was going to do my dad a big favor. I was going to wash his car. So I asked my mom for some soap and a bucket. I went out to wash the car and found all the little rust spots on it. I went in and got a Brillo pad. I went around to every single one of those rust spots and I rubbed them off with that Brillo pad.

He comes home and I had rubbed all the paint off. It was about four shades lighter where I had scrubbed it. There were all these quarter-sized circles on his car about two feet off the ground all the way around the car. This is why I think my old man is a great fucking guy: I'd be dead today, if he wasn't. Why he didn't kill me I'll never know. He had the patience of Job, he must have had. I wasted his first new car. He didn't buy another new car for ten years. I guess he thought that I at least showed some initiative, so he didn't come down on me.

When you're a dumb, fat kid, it's tough. When you get on the scale in gym class, you were like the laughingstock. The other kids stepped on it and hit sixty pounds. But when the fat boy steps on it, they went wild. The guys are just slapping each other on the back, falling over laughing at your weight.

My dad was a merchant marine. He was never home. When he was, it was flat-top time. He was grabbing me by the golden locks and dragging me to the bathroom, cutting my hair off. Then he'd talk to me. But first, the hair.

My mom was kind of weird, calling me a big fat zero,

mentally retarded idiot and that I was going to grow up and be a hood and get sent away. I was being watched at school, they were taking notes on me. I figured I might as well be what they were accusing me of. Not a mentally retarded fruit, because I knew I had *something* going for me. I did start feeling that nobody loves me. In the pecking order at school, I was pounded on and didn't fight back. Get knocked down and smile. They laugh at you and kick you when you're down.

My father got off the ship and noticed that. He decided to send me to boxing lessons. The gym had this hideous smell of alcohol and old leather and sweat. It just knotted my stomach to get near it. The problem was my weight again. It matched me up against people four or five years older than me. They'd beat me up, knock the wind out of me, give me black eyes. There was no sympathy there. I was being used as a punching bag rather than really learning anything. I was a live bag out there in the ring.

My dad would come home off the ship, and everything would be broken, the washing machine and the car, bikes. He'd yell at me for not fixing them. God, here I am 7, 8, 9 years old. How am I supposed to know how a TV works really? So that's when I kind of lost myself.

My dad would show up off the ship, and it was, "You asshole, see that fat fucker over there? That's what you're going to look like if you don't shape up."

"Yeah, yeah, yeah."

Then he would ship out, he hugged my sisters and kissed them. What would be wrong if he just hugged me? Said that he loved me? Instead, he'd get all macho, "See you around, asshole."

At about sixth grade, things radically changed. That's about the time that my parents split up. I can't quite express it. I want to say it was such a shattering or depressing or difficult experience. But that's not quite right, because in some ways it was a great relief.

My mother told me that my father had left. I cried about that. But my actual feelings toward him were pretty unreachable. I just didn't know what they were. It was clear to me I didn't want this to happen, and I clearly felt abandoned. But in fact, I'd been abandoned all my life. He was never home and never demonstrably interested in the children.

Between alimony, child support and child visitation rights, my mother's driving force was that my father was basically evil. Because he was evil, that gave her a lot to work against. My father's perspective was, "Your mother's a real bitch. She's out to kill me. She's out to really screw me over. Life's not fair to me, anyway, and now she's really trying to get me." They hated each other for a really long time, and I got all the benefits of that.

My older brother and sister managed to get out of both homes shortly after the divorce, but I was there for the long run. My younger sisters were somewhat insulated. Just as the first child takes the brunt of the parents' experimenting on how to be a parent, I took the brunt of how my parents experimented on being divorced.

Being my mother's confidant was too much for me. An example: We were having a court appearance for child visitation rights. At this point, they'd been divorced a few years. I'm 14 or 15. The judge asks the children to come up and give their opinion about what they would like, as if they should have some sort of say. It was just like total betrayal to her for me to say anything like, "I would like to see my father." In order to be my mother's good son, I had to totally reject my father. Sitting there with him and my mother in the courtroom, I'm sort of stuck. What do I say? I feel in some ways I need to have access to this person who's my father, especially since he is supposedly fighting to see me. Maybe that means that he wants to give me something that is worthwhile—I'm still pretty needy. Yet, if I say anything along that line, my mother will overhear it and be devastated. I got in that bind a lot with my mother and father.

I did say that I would like to be able to choose. I didn't say I wanted to go see my dad. That was my way of hedging.

About the time I hit puberty, I thought I was going nuts. I'd hear voices, or thought I heard voices speak to me in my head. It was like a word was being said that I didn't quite catch. Words, just words, reverberating in my head. It was probably just some sort of growing pain, but I thought I was going crazy. I didn't tell anyone this. I *couldn't* tell anyone this, but I was scared shitless, in a state of terror for about four or five months.

I remember sitting in social science or citizenship classes, where it was impossible to concentrate. My mind would just whirl off on a tangent and I would remember that I was crazy. A bolt of terror would go through me, sitting there in a fucking icy fear, quaking in pain. Walking home at night from a high school dance, alone, I would howl with the pain and loneliness.

My mother was in the hospital, and I didn't talk to my

father at all. I remember going into his bedroom one night and telling him that I thought I was crazy. All he said was, "Don't worry about it. You're not," rolled over and went to sleep.

For me to do something like that points out to me from this distance of time how frightened I was. It didn't reassure me at all. I was disappointed in him. I wanted him to console me or tell me *something,* but it wasn't within his power to do that. That's all. At the time, I probably hated him for it.

Then it stopped as inexplicably as it began. My nerves quieted down. Insanity settled in and everything was fine. I'm real good at shutting out pain with booze and drugs and everything else now, but that was the most fearful time of my life.

I had acquaintances whose fathers disowned them. I knew better. My parents wouldn't do that, they just wouldn't, but there was still a lot of anxiety on my part. God, yes. But I'd fallen completely and overwhelmingly in love for the very first time, and I just had to tell them. I just had to. I couldn't keep it to myself.

I went home for Christmas vacation. It was the first one I'd been home for in quite some time. I took the red-eye, which meant that I got into town at eight in the morning. They have a breakfast nook in their kitchen at home and I sat down. We were just talking and stuff and I said, "Well, I have something to tell you and I can either wait until the end of the visit or I can tell you now. I'd rather tell you now." I went through this whole thing where I had been exploring my feelings and my sexual identity and really had come to the conclusion that I was kidding myself in trying to date women. I'd started to date men and realized that I was gay.

It got real quiet, and no one said anything for a little while. I remember my dad looking out the window. It was a snowy day, bright and snowy. He said, "You know, we have a lot of other things in the world that are a lot worse than what you've just told me. I don't want to lose sight of that. I won't lie to you. It's really hard to take this. I won't lie. But you could have been a junkie, or a lot of other things, so I'm not going to worry about this. There's a hell of a lot of other things for us to worry about as people."

I thought to myself, "God, that's my dad!" He floored me.

It was about 2 A.M. when I called the doctor. I lied and told him the contractions were only three minutes apart, so he'd tell us to go to the hospital. So they got Joan suited out in standard-issue backless hospital fashion, all hooked up to a fetal monitor. The doctor checks her out, probably realizes that I was lying because she isn't dilated very much, and he goes off to take a nap somewhere. I put all our stuff away and start doing the breathing they taught us in natural childbirth classes.

About four or five hours of this, there's no more of this, "Oh, I think I'm about to have another contraction." Joannie and I are both about soaked down with sweat, she's digging her fingernails about an inch deep in the back of my hands, and it's, "Oh, No! Here comes another one. They're coming too fast! They're coming too fast!

AHHHHHHHH!" And I'm doing what I called the *hoo-ha* breathing. "Hoo! Ha! Hoo! Ha! Hoo! Ha!" I had to remind myself to blink.

We decided that's enough of this natural bullshit. We need some drugs. Give us Demerol, and give it to us now. The doctor comes in to check her out. His whole hand and part of his arm seemed to disappear into her vagina, and she screamed. I thought I was going to have to punch him out right there.

The obstetrician is from Rumania, so he has this kind of sweet, lyrical version of a Bela Lugosi Dracula accent. "She is dilated. We are ready to have the baby. She does not need drugs. The pain will change soon. Let's go." He was right.

We had to go about ten yards from where we were to the birthing room on the other side of the hall. The nurse standing there says, "You want me to get a wheelchair for her, Doctor?"

"No, she can walk." And she did.

I tried to tell her she would be okay, while they cranked and pulled on the bed in the room until it had been transformed into a kind of comfy, cushioned torture chair. They put her up there with her feet in the stirrups so that her knees were up by her head.

"Bear down. Push! Push! Push! Push! Push! Push!" I don't know if I ever saw a human being work so hard. It was startling. The top of the baby's head would just begin to show. The contraction would stop and the baby's head would withdraw back inside.

Finally, Joan was getting very tired and they decided the baby shouldn't be in stress in the birth canal much longer, so the doctor sent out into the hall for two interns, two young strapping guys. When she pushed during a contraction, these two guys would throw their forearms across her abdomen and press down so the baby couldn't come back up inside. Within another couple of minutes he was out. I didn't actually see him come out, because I had my eyes locked on my beautiful wife. But I heard him. It sounded like when you have a great day fishing and there are two or three big fresh fish flopping around the deck of the boat all at once. Flappity-flappity-flappity, those wet arms and legs flipping around free. They laid him up on Joan's bare belly, and he squinted up at us with one eye like a shrunken pirate.

"Come, Frank, look!" the doctor said to me. "She delivers the *placenta,* isn't it beautiful?" The way he said *placenta* came out like the name of some exotic Spanish wine. He put scissors in my hand and said, "Here is the umbilical cord. Be a man. Cut, cut, cut." I wondered if it would be like cutting spaghetti or a garden hose. It was just about right in between the two.

Then I put my arm around Joan and they left us with our new baby for about forty-five minutes. It was wonderful. I was so happy, the tears were running down my cheeks. Look, I'm crying again now just thinking about it and it's been six years.

When my daughter was born, that was a big change. There was some real tangible evidence that redefined life. The responsibility was really hard for me to accept for a long time. It's still hard for me to accept: A little person who lives or dies based on what I do. You've got this little baby now. You made her. She's completely helpless without us. I had all the worries and dreams, like forgetting her somewhere.

I'd be home with her. She'd be napping and I would

think, "Oh, yeah, I better go to the store and get something or other." I'd start heading for the door and I'd think, "Oh, wait a minute. I can't just do that anymore."

Or I'd be at work, and suddenly I'd remember her and go, "Oh, shit, where's Laurie? Oh, God, did I leave her at home?" I'd have to think real hard. "Oh, yeah. Oh, yeah. I really did take her over to my mom's. I didn't leave her in the truck. She's not out in the parking lot."

When I was 42 years old. I woke up and realized that I didn't have a history. I'd had a series of unrelated events. Each relationship would last for a couple of months, or at the most a year, and I would be off with someone else, doing something else. This was a ridiculous way to lead a life. I had nothing significant to show for it.

I certainly can't take any great satisfaction out of writing a couple of episodes of a TV sitcom about some talking animal. Some of the stuff I wrote is quite clever, and it pleases me, but it has no meaning or value beyond the paycheck, except that it makes people laugh. It's a nice thing to have contributed laughter, but you can't base your life on that.

I felt incomplete. I felt like I was a child. I'd been a child all my life. In my forties, I was still childlike. I don't believe that you can truly become an adult until you have a child. People who are 60 or 70 years old and still childless are still essentially children. They are not complete.

My prospects of having any kids didn't look too promising. Then out of the blue, I met Carol, who is very classy, anchored and centered in herself. She's not prone to hysteria like I am. She's calm and comfortable with who she is. Despite the fact that she has three kids, we wound up getting married. Frankly, if I had known what the problems would be with the two older kids, I would not have done it. If I had this played out for me in a movie theater I would have said, "No way. That's absolutely impossible."

But as far as I was concerned, all the problems with the kids and everything were secondary to this core issue with me, which was aside from everything else I was getting from the relationship, I was looking to become a parent. This was certainly one of the reasons I could accept the difficulties and the compromise.

If it was something she did not feel comfortable with, then we should just go our separate ways. It wasn't the only element, but it was a key element.

It wasn't like I was looking for a brood mare. If I were looking for that, I'd had lots of opportunities with women who were not neurotic, but who were also not interesting or exciting or as compatible. I didn't want to go out looking for another woman while I had this woman here that I really cared about and felt I could live with. She's a really good match. I don't know if I'd ever find another one like that. You don't really think about it in that pragmatic context. There's a lot of emotions. But all that is there.

So, three and a half years later, nothing has happened. Carol is having a hard time getting pregnant. We're going to some big-time fertility specialist for a year and nothing happened.

Carol's girlfriend and her husband came over to dinner one night. The girlfriend just out of the blue said, "Well, Carol isn't going to have any children." Short and arrogant. Normally, I wouldn't have said anything. But it was too deep an issue and too important an issue for me to allow that to go unchallenged. If you don't challenge some things, it's almost like buying into them.

So really nicely, low-key, I said, "You know, it's my intention that we're going to have children." This started one of those arguments where everybody is smiling, but it's real intense. I finally had to say, "If she doesn't have children, if she can't get pregnant, then I'm going to end the relationship."

I had my wedding band on, and right around that point the ring turned oval. Here, look at it. I keep it on my key chain.

The ring was on my finger and was perfectly fine. Suddenly it squeezed my finger. You know how sometimes you adjust it or turn it. I went to adjust it and it won't adjust. In fact, it won't turn. It hurt. I said. "Look at this. My ring is turning." I had to grab some soap and water to pry this ring off. It wasn't easy to get off. I tossed it down on the kitchen table, and it stopped the argument. Nobody said anything after that. Carol got pregnant a couple of days later.

Consciously, she did believe that she wanted to have the kid, but there just were a lot of other factors: "How long is this relationship going to last? Look at the tension between him and the kids." Those other factors ultimately decided her on some subconscious level to hold off.

That wasn't my agenda. The longer this situation stayed the same, the more frustrating it became for me. From my point of view, now we're finally on track. So it's not even like I can hop up and down about it. It's a relief, but it won't be a real sense of relief until nine months from now.

I went through a shower. In the good old days, when I had my kids, you didn't have to go to showers. Women had to do that. But I went to a shower on the West Side. I love the West Side, because those people aggrandize every social change as if it was their invention. The new class, the new neighborhood. Most of those people on the West Side of Manhattan don't have a pot to pee in, most of them are unemployed filmmakers, but they are a walking, talking sociological experiment.

The shower was for a woman who was 40. The husband is 48. Most of the people there had little children, and knew each other from Lamaze classes.

Here are these guys—sharp guys—talking about which kid backpack fits better to cart the kid around. They didn't get down to Evenflo nipples, but if somebody had had a bottle they would have got to it. Of course, I had to go out on the terrace to smoke a cigarette, as if they were going to carry the smoke home with them and the baby would have secondary smoke inhalation when they breathe on it.

I went home from this thing going, "Not me. Look at these assholes. I don't need that. They're an incredible inconvenience. Did you ever hear a baby cry? What a horrible sound." It was all a memory for me. I never like any kid one year younger than my own, and my kids were all grown now.

About six months later, the woman who I am in love with got pregnant. Now, if there is a God, He's a very mean God. So I slit my wrists and took a tepid bath. But I didn't die. I had to live through this one. My kids thought it was curious, but wonderful. They said, "Daddy, you were a good father to us."

Somebody said to me, "You going into the operating room with Sophie? You going to Lamaze class and help her push?"

"No!"

It wasn't my choice about having the baby or not having the baby. I still read in the papers about some guy told a woman he wouldn't love her anymore if she didn't have an abortion. It never occurred to me that you could get away with something like that, let alone that you'd want to. I didn't have any influence or control over Sophie's life to do that. I wasn't part of that conversation. It was my choice what to do about me, in the sense that I wasn't sure I wanted to make all these changes. I said, "Okay. I'll be there. I'll put up the money. I'll see the kid on weekends. Whatever."

I had a chance to have a few days off, so she and I went and laid down on the beach in Puerto Rico. I said to myself, "Jesus Christ, the only thing I've ever done really well, that I'm really pleased with is being a father. What the fuck am I so upset about? It's not inconvenience, because God knows I create my own inconvenience at every turn and every chance I get. Life is inconvenient. That *is* life. As a matter of fact, if you're in love with somebody, and you do what they need to get done, it's not inconvenience. If it's a sacrifice, then it's not really affection, and you're in the wrong place."

So I'm lying there on the beach, and I say to Sophie, "Why can't we move in together and really do this?" I obviously had not been as forthcoming prior to that, because she said she was going to invite me over to dinner after we got back from Puerto Rico and tell me to go fuck myself. So I wound up the night saying, "Please." I'm the big loser in this one. "Please let me be nice and come through here, okay?"

I had needed time to think. Once I made the decision, it wasn't a big one at all. I can't imagine now having a question about it. It's interesting how the cards are dealt to you.

Sophie, now we're married, is one of the most natural mothers of all time. She looks at me and just thinks about the baby and starts smiling. The baby is terrific, and I'm acting like one of those people at the shower who were making me break out in pimples, the way those guys talked.

Now for the first time, "Oh, shit! Am I looking older? Do I look ridiculous with my daughter?" Nobody says, "You look nice with your granddaughter," *yet*. Sophie said she heard somebody say it, but I think she's just zinging me. The fact is, I'll be 65 when she's fifteen. When my other kids were 15, they were all 15 about the same time, I was 36. That's a different world.

The day we brought the baby home it went through the switch-over from its fetal circulatory system to the one that you and I enjoy. My heart is pumping blood through its many chambers. When his heart made that transition, there was no place for the blood to go. The chamber that pumps the blood to the aorta and the body hadn't formed. Once it started, the heart was pumping the blood to his lungs, and all the fucking blood in his body got pumped to his lungs. There was nothing anywhere.

He was making a sound breathing sort of like you do if you get kicked in the solar plexus and lose your breath. We couldn't tell what it was. What the fuck's he going to tell you? Called the doctor, and they said bring him in. He looked like shit. Waxy looking.

As God and fate would have it, we were only five minutes from the Children's Hospital. I'm literally going through red lights. We go into the emergency room. I let them out of the car, and I go park. I walked back in, and there are doctors and nurses flying full speed throughout the whole area. I don't see my wife. I get up to the end of the corridor and there she is.

"It's our baby," she said. Social worker takes us and walks us over to a private room. And says, "It looks bad."

The doctor walks in. "We don't think we can save it. We don't know what it is."

We start to get into the world of suspended animation and disbelief. You don't breathe. A cardiologist comes in. Explains about the heart problem. By one in the morning, the baby is stabilized. We found out a day or two later that the baby had arrested twice in this process, and they had brought him back.

Then we start the vigil. There is no telling whether or not there was brain damage. Until you can tell that, there was no deciding whether or not he should have the operation.

The little fart comes out of it. When he was born he came out crying, but he was built like a little ox—broad shoulders, barrel-chested, little baby biceps, nifty head. A neat-looking phenomenon.

Here's this little guy, and he's got tubes in his nose and tubes in his mouth and tubes sticking up his groin and in his arms and legs. There are bandages all over him, because they couldn't stop him bleeding. He looks like he's been through a knife fight. We had him baptized and given last rights that night at the same time. Little fucker never had a chance, but he pulled through it.

Three or four days after he was stabilized we knew that he was going to be okay. There's no brain damage. Then the doctors tell us, "Now, what we have to do is give him a heart operation." They make him like a rotary engine with only two chambers. Eventually, at age 3 or 4, they'll go back and rework it again.

"Do the operation," we tell them. Then they explained to us that the operation itself has become somewhat routine.

What they can't guarantee is coming off the heart-lung machine, whether it'll work. So we had to go through that shit again.

He did it. The kid did it.

The problem is, when I say he's doing well, as I talk to you now, I don't know that he's still alive from moment to moment. I guess that's what every parent goes through when they're not in the presence of their child, but this one is especially so, because of his tenuous position.

At this point in my life, the challenge that I see is figuring out how to finally be more honest with the emotional domain, how to—and this is a very female desire—accomplish that intimacy that I've always craved and have not been able to have, somewhat out of fear, somewhat out of the fact that it's not a male thing to want.

I feel fortunate to be in another marriage with a child. I really didn't want to have any children, but eventually I got negotiated into it. That was my first real experience of working out a fundamental disagreement in a different way than "all or none" fashion. Traditionally, if I disagree with you, I either get my own way completely or give up and let you go ahead and do it just the way you wanted. Then I'll sit over there and be resentful. "Fuck you, I'm not going to have nothing to do with you. That's it.

By this time, with this person, I was able to sit down over a period of time and slug it out. I could say, "Okay, I now want to do this also, and these are the ways I want to do it." We have come to a true compromise. Such a thing *is* possible.

Having a child forces all this stuff out on the table even more so than before: How do you achieve and how do you express love for another person? With a child it's a little bit more straightforward and easier to do that. But by virtue of doing it with my child, I'm looking at how I do it with my wife also.

What I'm finding out is that you can be angry and then you can get over it. With a child, it's not possible to carry a grudge. You've got to deal with what's happening with your kid right now. He's two and a half, and when he gets pissed off, it's right now. Two minutes later, he's happy. If I get pissed off and I stay pissed off at him all day, it ruins the whole day. Plus it's very hard to do. I've tried. "You're a real shit, kid." It just doesn't work. He forced me to be a little more present with my anger. Get pissed at him, realize that I can get pissed and yell at him, and it can be all over. I feel better and can go on.

That's much different than how I've dealt with adults. I always held it back and held it back. Don't get angry, because you shouldn't blow up at people. There's that hidden possibility you could get too carried away.

Since I'm able to get away with it with my kid, I'm working at doing more of that with my adult relationships. That doesn't mean I'm yelling and screaming at people, but I'm trying to be more honest with my wife, let her know a little more quickly when I'm bothered by things. I realized how destructive the holding back is, how quickly I can move into a resentful mode. Once I move into that mode of operation, nothing goes well. I just get more pissed and more resentful. Life just goes to shit. I don't want to give anything to anybody, I just want to get out the door. It's good to know life can be different.

When I was young, I did a tremendous amount of camping. After my kids were born, I haven't hardly been camping at all, because little kids and camps don't work out so well. Only in the past year have we started doing it again. For fourteen years, I've had someone less than 3 years old. Now I don't, because my youngest is 5.

We went out to a state park, trailers and tents. It was after the season was over, so it was pretty uncrowded. To get into the place, I've got to do the signing in. I've got to sign a card about who's staying at the campsite and what their relationships are. I'm writing: "Nathaniel—Father, son, son, daughter, daughter." And I realize like it's the first time, *I'm the father.*

I'm old hat at setting up tents and making camp. So I'm getting the camp put together and sending the kids out for kindling and firewood. They've never done this, and they've never seen me set a wood fire from scratch. So they're amazed, because I'm a real natural kind of guy, but they've never really seen this side of me before.

"Wow, Dad! All right!" Then we're sitting around the fire, and I can feel this newfound respect they've got for Dad.

At one point, everyone else has gone off to bed. My son, Carl, and I are sitting there alone. He walks over next to me, and he just puts his arm around me, and he's just hugging me. He hugged me for a good half a minute. He said, "I love you so much."

I was blown away. He's a tough one, and it's such a wonderful feeling.

Men make better mothers than women. Men can just do it as an intellectual pursuit or a logical process. They can rear children and they don't have to deal with their own emotions, biology and hormones while they're doing it. I could take anybody's kids—but it's even more important to take your own kids—I can have them all day long, and do a full day's work. Kids have a great time, don't get killed by predators or starvation, don't drown in their own shit or anything like that. At the end of the day, I've done eight hours of carpentry work, and I've had a pretty good time. The kids have gone out and become more autonomous by living their own lives and dealing with the world themselves in a semi-safe environment—I've never killed a kid, I swear to God. I've never caused a kid to have a major injury or go into the hospital. I've never caused a real giant psychological trauma. And yet, I've spent weeks and weeks, months and months, years and years all by myself, taking care of kids.

It just worked out that way. My wife has worked in an office where she didn't feel like she could do it or had some restraint. I have a more autonomous job.

A lot of it is my own personality. I know this isn't real with other guys. If men had to do this all day long the way women generally do it, at home with no escape, they'd find themselves acting like women.

Men can be better mothers if they do it and remain men. I maintained my "manly lifestyle." I did my work. I was a construction worker on houses. I didn't get bogged down in some kind of maternal child care routine. It's not that big a deal. What women don't understand about children —and men don't either—is that children are little independent creatures all by themselves. They don't have to have a mother with them all the time. They will make a mother feel like she has to be with them all the time. They will make a father feel he has to be with them all the time, or that he has to make the mother feel that way. They're programmed initially to make parents feel like there's a 100 percent necessity going on here. Women are hormonally and biologically more susceptible to this than men, so there's a better chance of a man breaking this "horrible cycle" and letting the children become independent. Men's main function with children is teaching them to break away, but we wait a damn long time to do it.

I was lucky enough in a divorce to have my wife remarry, so that the children decided to stay in the house with me without having to pick between the two of us. Being suddenly totally immersed in family enabled me to be very reflective and self-conscious about my own function.

I knew pretty early on, after I owed the loan company a lot of money, that I was not going to be a United States Senator. I would have liked to have been, but between incompetence, laziness, and lack of money, it wasn't going to happen.

I was a little bit nasty, prior to becoming the most singularly responsible for the family. A little bit nasty and somewhat aggressive in terms of ambition, even though I recognized that I was going to have to cheat to get where society assumed I would get.

Now that I was more responsible than nine out of ten fathers, my primary function was to take care of those I am affectionate toward, these four teenagers, all one year apart. I found the short-term experience of making things happen for them was quite satisfactory, better than most other things. It can be pretty exciting without being in an auditorium or a stadium. It doesn't have to be accompanied by applause or good reviews. There was no isolation. We were all very loudly practicing life and how it happens in the second half of the twentieth century.

I found that there was a reality factor on ambition. A reduction in society's pressure about who I am and where I have to get produced an interesting calm, a relaxation, not a leveling. It wasn't wimpy or saccharine. It was a stabilizing influence on my life.

I look at my father and his absolute inability to deal with emotions, and what little I know of his father, my grandfather, who I never knew, who was an alcoholic and brutalized his wife and some of the kids. I look at the unconscious carrying forward of this behavior, generation upon generation. That is never understood, never talked about. When you live the behavior, you're not necessarily in touch with it. Where does the crack open in something like this?

What happens is you reincarnate. You fight fire with fire. You become what your father was, because that was effective in dealing with him. You don't know really what's going on, but you wind up like him. You're a different person with different abilities, but where does the crack open up?

Life's a pretty tough thing to live. We don't come into this world prepared for it. We grab whatever tools are available from those people with whom we grow up. Learning different behavior is something that is not only an act of great self-awareness and consciousness, but it's not easy. Most people don't have the time. They're caught up in too many jams emotionally and too many neurotic tics. They learned to cope twenty years ago, but things have changed, and they're still doing the same thing they did then. Now it's inappropriate, but nobody can tell them. Even if people are telling them, it doesn't sink in.

Just having kids puts everybody into a twenty-year state of stress, regardless of anything else. You're trying to climb the ladder. There's finances to worry about. There's not that much time for reflection. You're battling for survival, and after it's all over you can reflect on the experience you've just had, but essentially what you've done is, you've chiseled the unexamined behavior into stone in your children. By the time you wake up, they're busy chiseling away at the next generation.

I am constantly saddened by the inability to have a different relationship with my father. It would be very nice to be able to talk with him about *anything* really. But it's not to be. As long as he's relaxed, he can be just a normal human being. But now and then, the old head rears up that he's still your father, and he starts laying this shit on you, and it's like he owns you. He's still your father no matter what you are, and if you don't put up with it, then there's something wrong with you. He just won't listen. You cannot talk about these things, because it's too threatening to behavior that he's lived with all his life, since when he was young. For him to explore at this stage why he does things, it's just not going to happen. It's not possible.

My brother calls up. Says, "Dad's gone."

"What?!" I go. I'm half asleep. It's four in the morning.

"Dad's gone."

"Wait. Wait. Wait. What d'you mean?"

"He's gone."

"He's dead?"

"No, no, he's *gone*. You better get up here. I can't take it anymore."

"What the fuck is going on?"

"He split," he says. "We don't know where he is. I think he's in some trailer park about five miles south of here."

"What are you talking about?" My wife is just waking up and she asks me who it is. "It's my brother. Dad's gone. But it's not what you think."

"You better get up here," my brother says. "I've had it. I've dealt with it too long. I can't take it anymore. Get up here."

So I get in the car and drive two hundred miles to find out what the hell is going on. As I'm walking in the door, my mom says, "Willy, I called the cops on him."

"Wait," I said. "Slow down. Mom, where's Dad?"

"He's . . . he's . . . with *her*."

"Ma, who is he with?"

"He's with that girl that he met in the bar."

So this whole story comes out. They were doing this electrical job in a nearby town. After work the guys were hanging around this bar, and all the wives of the guys who lived in the area started going down to the bar. So it got to be a thing after work every day where everybody's hanging out for a couple of hours, having a couple of drinks, and then going home. It turned out that old Dad got a wild hair up his ass and fell in love with a girl with about three teeth in her mouth and two kids who lived in a trailer park. Now he's moved in with her. Left my mother.

My mother called the state troopers on him. Said he was missing. They go down to the trailer park, try to get him out.

"No," he says. "I'm staying here. I love her."

They went back to my mother and said, "I'm sorry, ma'am, but there's nothing we can do about it."

That's when my brother called me. I said, "Okay, let me try to straighten this out." I told my brother to call him up and tell him to meet me down at this bar.

We drive down there and go in the bar. Here's my old man. I've never spoken a word about anything meaningful to the fucking guy in my whole life. We've gone through things: He's threatened to drop-kick me up the stairs and pound me into the ground like a stake a few times, because I've done something wrong, and we all know about the story where I wiped all the paint off his new car with a Brillo pad, so he knows I'm an asshole. Now he's acting like a total jerk.

I'm sitting down across the table from my old man. What am I supposed to do? I'm supposed to talk this guy into going back to this woman that *I* don't even like that much? I mean, what the fuck are you going to do? And I'm cursing my brother out. I'd like to kill him, you know? This is the same day that I got called up in the morning. Now it's twelve hours later, four o'clock in the afternoon. So I get a couple of beers and I'm sitting down in the bar and I say, "So, Dad, you know, what are you doing?"

"Oh, gee, Willy. I feel so bad. I feel so bad."

"Jesus, Dad, you really fucked up this time, man. What are you *doing?*"

"I can't help it, Willy. I love her. I love her, you know?"

"Oh, God, Dad, arrrgh!" But I got ahold of myself and I

said, "Look, if you want to leave your wife, there are more gracious and graceful ways to do it." I said, "You can't just walk out on her. You got married in 1945. She's been depending on you for all these years."

So I had to get this real serious rap down. It was just insane. My old man is sitting across the table from me, acting like a 16-year-old farm boy. He had reverted. Afterward, when I thought about it, it was so perfect that it filled me with so much emotion. I didn't react until days afterward, and I wrote this song that lasts about seven minutes. If you could stop and think about where those people were coming from in 1945, what happened to them and where they thought they were going. They didn't think they were going anywhere. I don't think they had any ideas.

My father had run away from home again like he had at 16 to join the army. But he wasn't like me. I have it easy with words. I have been exposed to intellectual ideas and literary concepts and had read Faulkner and Tolstoy and you name it, all this fucking bullshit. I had all kinds of things to think about to give it some point of reference. He was just a guy who followed his gonads the same way he followed them when he was 16 years old. He hadn't progressed intellectually one whit. Emotionally, I don't think he'd progressed one whit. I'm not even sure who he was and what he was at that moment. But here I was, his son, and I was helping him with something he should have helped me with.

I was thinking to myself, "Boy. Okay. What now?" So I said, "Dad, it's no good. You got to go back. You got to go back, because you been with that woman all these years. I don't care if you don't like her. I don't care if you don't love her. But the honorable and manly thing to do is to go back. You've made a mistake." I had to say things I'd never even thought about, because it never happened to me before. I said, "I don't care what you want to do, I don't care what you want. I'm your son and it's really weird for me to be talking to you about this kind of thing, but the bottom line is, you made your bed and you got to lie in it. If you had these thoughts and feelings a long time ago, then you should have spoken about them. If they just occurred to you, then you have to be man enough to put them off for a while until you straighten out what's going on. If you want to leave a woman, this isn't the way you do it."

What was in the back of my mind, but I didn't say it, was "You don't run off to a trailer park with a half-drunk woman who doesn't have half her teeth and two kids." I did say, "If you're going to go, go gracefully. Explain it to her, that you don't want to be with her anymore. Set up a relationship that exists with that. If you want to go, go someplace interesting. If you want something, you could do better than this, Dad." All of a sudden, I was the father and he was the child.

"I've known women," I said, "that you would've died for, you know? But it's what's appropriate. I'm not with them now, I'm with my wife, because I love her. If I decide to change something, I owe it to her to try to explain it to her."

But that had never entered his mind. He hadn't been led through life. He'd bolted from one thing to another and not thought about it. He had gotten married after the war and not thought about it.

He ended up going back. She took him back and made his life hell for ten years. Still does. I felt sorry for him afterwards, because he didn't do what I said he should do. He didn't explain it to her. They didn't talk. They didn't work it out, and they didn't split up. Now, because they've gotten on in years, they've reached a new understanding with one another that allows them to go on with what they're doing. Now, because they're older, they recognize that all that shared time means something to them, so they cleave together. It's too late to do anything else. They've come to an understanding and they're happy.

For Christ's sake, I went down to see them this winter in Florida where they have a part-time retirement home in a trailer park and I said, "Well, Dad, you been trying to move to a trailer park for twenty years, and you finally made it."

My dad was 44 when he had his first heart attack. When he had bypass surgery, I got a call on a pay phone. I was scared and it was awful. It was a weird thing to go to a hospital and see your dad just ash white and really scared for his life. I saw him in a completely new light—as a vulnerable human being. I saw my dad cry for the first time.

I get home about twice a year these days. We go out fishing and hiking and it's just great. I'm at a point in my life where my dad is a friend now rather than my father. We're good friends. It used to be my mother, but now it's my dad who writes to me all the time and who calls on the phone.

Now his dad—my grandfather—just had a heart attack Sunday. Dad could barely talk to me on the phone. I've had to face this with him already—he's had a total of three major heart attacks and two bypass surgeries. He's 56 but I don't see him living much longer. But that's okay with me, because he's lived his life to the fullest. He couldn't squeeze another ounce out of life than he already has. I've come to terms with him dying twelve years ago. But he's never had to do that with his dad. To see him going through that is unnerving, reassuring, heartbreaking. I càll him two times a day now. I don't give him any advice, just make sure he's okay. He still pulls the macho stuff on me like, "You don't have to call me. Don't waste your money."

"I'll determine whether I'm wasting my money or not, Dad. It's my money. Don't worry about it."

I see him growing as a human being. Or maybe he's not growing. Maybe he's just revealing himself as one, and letting me see it. I'm growing up, too.

After my mother died, I decided, "Okay, my dad's sick. I'll just make a life with him." Then he turned brutally sick within months. There's a point where you begin to figure out that he's losing his grip, physically and mentally. The big thing that clued me in was that my dad was giving up. But when you see someone who you love more than anything in life say, "No, I don't care. I'd just as soon die," it's too much. There were times when I'd grab my father and say, "You can't fucking do this to me. By doing this, you're saying that you don't care about me."

Then I'd get home and think, "Of course, he'd say that. He just lost his wife. It isn't anything personal to me." He was just saying, "You're all right. You're going to make it. I think I'll check out." But, boy, you take it so personally, because you interpret it that he doesn't give a fuck about you. Death is personal.

Then, to boot, if you've ever seen a person die of cancer, it's the scariest thing. They become skeletons in front of your eyes. They're getting smaller and smaller. God, I was there every fucking day.

Then there was this turning point, when I finally figured out that my dad was going to die. I said to my girlfriend, "He's going to die, and he's going to die real fast. You watch him." I knew so much about cancer that it was like I knew too much. I had a clairvoyancy that I didn't want to have. All of a sudden, my life was dominated by this death.

Then that ended, and it was a relief as any slow agonizing death is. Now I'm back here.

I went back East and met with my father. That sounds sort of formal, but I stayed at his place a couple of evenings. Before I'd arrived there, I'd recognized that he had gotten old. His wife—my step-mother—had divorced him, and he was now living by himself. He basically had no money. In his settlement with his wife, she got the house and gave him a certain amount of money for it and he was living off that. Because I was starting my career in the entertainment business, I wasn't really in a position to give him anything. Like, I knew he needed a new television set, and I regret the fact that I didn't buy him one, because I could have done it. I didn't do it because I didn't know how long my money would last.

He was no longer able to drive, because he kept crashing the car, so he couldn't get insurance on it. He had difficulty walking. So when it was wintertime and there was ice on the ground, he wouldn't venture far from the house. It was kind of sad, because this was the guy who was really smart as a whip, just a clever guy. When I got into trouble, I could go to him for advice and get good advice. His mind was quick, and he would see the angles right away.

But at a certain point, even before I went back, I knew that help wasn't there anymore. He'd slowed down. He'd had a couple heart attacks. I'd have to walk him through the process. The relationship was changing. I was the father and he was the child.

He was pleased. He was pleased with me as the person I'd become. He was pleased with my success. It was clear that he was living his life through me. He didn't have anything, but he was taking great joy in what I was doing.

I know he wanted to move out here to California. He had this idea he could live with me. That was not an option that I could accept. He still reacted to me like I was a child in a lot of ways. Even when I spent a couple of days with him, there were moments of anger. So I regret that I didn't get him the TV, and I regret that I wasn't big enough to have him live in my house for another nine months or a year that he had.

For my father, what I turned out to be was all wrong. When I was growing up, I didn't want to be like him. In some ways, I look a bit like him, but not much. The older I get, the more I look like him. But I turned out to be just like him. I have the same ways, my manner, my style. My alcoholism is certainly his. His faults and strengths are mine.

A perfect example: my father was retired military reserve. He never forgot it. He was one of those people who rolled his socks and kept them in perfect order. His drawers looked like he was still in the army. He would sit in front of the refrigerator on a Saturday, if he was ever not working,

and organize the contents according to size—not usefulness, but size—with military precision. He'd get up in my
mother's cabinets and do the same thing. He'd roar, "How
can anybody be such a slob!"

Everything had to be done that way. I would be out mow-
ing the lawn, clipping the hedges or trimming the gardens.
He'd come out and watch me for a while. Invariably, whatever tool I was using, he'd grab it out of my hand and say,
"I'll do that." Which was mortifying.

One time when I was teaching school, we had the kids
working out in the yard. There was this boy who was very
taciturn, needy. We'd asked him to go and do his share
with a shovel, digging in the garden. He was just stabbing
at it. That made me livid. I went over and I said, "Give me
that! *I'll do it!"* I stopped dead in my tracks, because I was
my father at that moment. It got in me.

My father had six heart attacks in two years. He smoked
and didn't stop drinking until after the fifth one. I was sober
for about four months and I decided that I needed to make
peace with him, if he was going to die. We had a very
unresolved relationship. I was gay, an alcoholic, and in the
theater, and he didn't want any of this. We didn't have a
really unfriendly relationship, but it wasn't there, the resolution wasn't there.

So, I wrote out this long history of "Things I Need to Talk
to My Father About"—this moment and that moment, leaving medical school, being gay, all this stuff that I wanted
to get resolved.

I drove up to my parents' house with a friend. We talked
through what I planned to do. At some point, she asked
the question, "Do you really think this is a good idea? Isn't
this mostly for you? Maybe he's not ready for all that." I
agreed, and I decided that I wouldn't do that.

While I was there, a moment came when no one was in

the house except my father and me. There's a small bed-room that is connected to my parents' room through a walk-in closet. He had put a big dresser of his in that room.

He called me. He had pulled up a chair to the dresser. He was quite ill. It was only a month before he died. He asked me if I would go through his dresser with him.

In the dresser were photographs of his parents and him when he was a child. In my pocket, I have a silver medal that he won when he was 11 years old for the one-hundred-pound standing broad jump in the Public School Athletic League. He gave it to me. As we went through those things, almost all the issues I had written out, except things that didn't need to be dealt with, they all came out in a natural way, as we looked at the relics of his life.

For me, the symbol of the resolution was when he picked up the ring that he had received for twenty years of outstanding salesmanship, and he said, "If I gave you my ring, would you wear it?"

"Hey, come on," I said. "You're not giving away the leg-acy yet."

"I want to know," he said. "If I give it to you, will you wear it?"

"Absolutely. I would be thrilled."

"It's yours."

That made everything right. Years of discomfort and dis-appointment on my part and his part, just got right. Every-thing went right after that.

They called me the day he went back in the hospital. By chance all my brothers were in town from all across the country. My sister and her husband who travel the world were in town. The grandkids were all there. I was three hundred miles away. My sister called me and said, "Dad said that this is it."

"I'm coming," I said. "Tell him to wait until I get there."

When I arrived everyone was there in the room. My mother said, "We have to decide about extraordinary measures, and I don't want to do it. You and I will decide." We decided no, just like that, while we were walking to the room.

He was all tubed up, ostensibly unconscious. I started shouting at him, "I'm here! I love you!" I grabbed his hand. He squeezed my hand and wrinkled his brow and died. Everyone was standing there, and it was a wonderful experience.

I'll tell you that no matter how hard the relationship was with my father, I only now remember the resolution. I have wonderful feelings about him. I never think of him except in terms of those last few weeks, when we had the opportunity to heal each other and everything was forgiven.

Because my mother is a teetotaler, my father would drink before he came home, and then he'd bring home two cans of beer back with him. There was no alcohol in the house, but he'd have his two beers every night. They got taller over the years. Two Schaefer beers in a paper bag, every night, no matter how much he'd had before he came home. Two cold ones.

At his funeral, you have the final moment when the family is alone and they close the casket. My brother had two Schaefer beers in a paper bag in a cooler in his car, and we went out there, got the bag, and we put them into the casket. My mother, all of us agreed it was the right thing to do. And they were cold ones.

I was really frightened when my father died. The guy was 67 years old, and he didn't look as though he was terribly sick. I didn't expect him to die.

Since I am the oldest son, the oldest child in the family, I took care of the things that I needed to take care of. I was in charge of the funeral arrangements, making sure my mother was taken care of, supporting my brothers and sisters.

The day that he was to be buried, I really broke down. I felt a tremendous loss for my father, but also it was a tremendous fear for myself.

I remembered standing with my father at my grandfather's wake. I was a little kid at the time—9 or 10. My father seemed very young and very vibrant. He turned to me and said, "You know, the Wheel keeps turning. Grandpa's fallen off. Now I'm on top of the Wheel."

At the time, I looked at him and really couldn't get what he was talking about. But I realized what he was saying the day I buried him.

The Wheel keeps turning. He fell off and now I'm on top of the Wheel. There's no stopping it.